INTRODUCTION TO
Structured Microsoft BASIC

Thomas W. Doyle

and

Jeremy I. Clark

Raytheon Company

D. C. HEATH AND COMPANY

Lexington, Massachusetts Toronto

To Nila, for all of her patience and support
   T. W. D.

In the memory of my grandfather, B. F. Clark
   J. I. C

Photo Credits

Figures 1.2, 1.3, 1.7, and 1.8(d) courtesy of International Business Machines Corp.
Figure 1.4 courtesy of Intel.
Figure 1.5 courtesy of Memorex.
Figure 1.6 courtesy of Seagate Technologies.
Figures 1.10(b) and 1.11 courtesy of Hewlett Packard.

IBM PC and PC-DOS are registered trademarks of International Business Machines Corporation.
MS-DOS and GWBASIC are registered trademarks of Microsoft Corporation.

Published simultaneously in Canada.

Printed in the United States of America.

International Standard Book Number: 0-669-19944-3

10 9 8 7 6 5 4 3 2 1

Preface

BASIC is an easy-to-use programming language that comes with the operating system of most IBM PCs and compatibles. It is powerful enough to provide solutions to problems in business and everyday life. With an understanding of the problem to be solved, a good plan of attack, and familiarity with the BASIC programming language, the student can create solutions to many common problems.

The Purpose of this Guide

This software guide can be used in any introductory course that teaches computer programming concepts and style using the BASIC programming language. It is designed to teach the primary concepts of computer programming using a hands-on, step-by-step approach. The structured, top-down design approach used in this book helps encourage good habits for computer use and improved problem-solving skills. Each chapter ends with True or False and Fill-In questions, Short Answer Exercises, and Programming Problems that test students' recall of major points and give them experience in writing BASIC programs using the structured programming techniques presented. Upon completion of this guide, students will be amply prepared to write BASIC programs to solve everyday problems.

PC-DOS and MS-DOS 3.30

Almost identical, these twins are the *de facto* standard operating system used on the IBM family of personal computers and compatible machines. Because everyone who uses one of these computers must deal with the operating system to some extent, DOS tops the list of important software to become familiar with. DOS 3.30 was used for the examples in this guide, but the same commands can also be used with versions of DOS 2.00 and higher, including DOS 4.00.

BASIC Dialects

There are several dialects of BASIC. The most popular are Microsoft's GWBASIC and QuickBASIC; Borland International's Turbo BASIC, True BASIC (a powerful, structured version of BASIC from its originators, Kemeny and Kurtz); and BASIC and BASICA, IBM's two versions. GWBASIC, one of the more popular dialects of BASIC, includes graphics capabilities.

BASIC has certain characteristics that are present in every version. The Microsoft and IBM versions are upwardly compatible (that is, BASIC and BASICA programs will run in GWBASIC, and GWBASIC programs will run in QuickBASIC). **All of the programs in this book were tested and run on an IBM personal computer using BASICA under PC-DOS and GWBASIC under MS-DOS.**

The Guide

This software guide presents a step-by-step approach to programming concepts and how these concepts are implemented using the BASIC programming language. It covers the following general topics:

- An introduction to microcomputers
- An introduction to the DOS operating system
- Individual descriptions of different programming concepts and how to use them

Each chapter demonstrates a particular aspect of programming and how BASIC commands are used in relation to it. Each BASIC command that is introduced in the text is accompanied by a box that describes its purpose and syntax, as well as giving examples and any special notes about how to use it. Integrated examples using the BASIC commands are developed in each chapter to demonstrate programming concepts. We provide hints on programming techniques and style, as well as guidelines for documenting and debugging programs.

This guide can also serve as a reference manual. The BASIC commands are described in boxes that are separate from the main text so that a complete description and several examples of the command are easy to find and in one location.

Examples

Many examples are used to demonstrate programming concepts and to show how these concepts can be used to solve common problems in business and in everyday situations. Good programming style and practices are emphasized throughout the text so students not only learn how to use BASIC to solve problems, but how to write structured BASIC programs that are easily maintained as well.

Program Disk and Answers to Programming Exercises

A diskette containing all of the example programs and a copy of the answers to the programming exercises are available from the publisher.

Acknowledgments

We would like to take this opportunity to thank the many people involved in making this book a reality. We are especially thankful and indebted to Peter Gordon of D. C. Heath for giving us the chance to write this book. Thanks go to Kitty Sheehan and Kathleen Savage for all of their time spent on the project, as well as to Anne Starr, Irene Cinelli, and Cia Boynton. Special thanks also go to Ernest Colantonio for allowing us to adapt from his work and to Mike Michaelson of Palomar College for his consultation. We would also like to thank Paul Ohme of Northeast Louisiana University, Paul W. Ross of Millersville University, and Claiborne W. Sharp, Jr. and Carol Hall of Louisiana State University. Finally, thanks go to Vikram Kachoria for his cooperation and assistance throughout the creation of this book.

T. W. D.

J. I. C.

Contents

Chapter 3   Introduction to BASIC   65

Chapter 4   Introducing Microsoft's BASIC   85

Chapter 10   Functions   231

1

The Microcomputer

Learning Objectives

After reading this chapter, you should know the following:

- What is meant by the term *microcomputer*
- The basic operations performed by all computers
- The four major hardware components of a typical microcomputer system
- The major components inside a microcomputer's system unit
- The three major types of microcomputer displays
- How the various special-purpose keys on a microcomputer keyboard are used
- The four most popular types of microcomputer printers
- The three major categories of microcomputer software
- How to turn on a microcomputer
- How to operate a microcomputer printer
- How to care for floppy disks

Introduction

We begin this first chapter by introducing IBM and IBM-compatible microcomputers, their hardware components, and popular types of software. (By *IBM-compatible* we mean any computer that works like a comparable IBM model and can run the same software.) Then we discuss a few helpful hints for working with microcomputers.

What Is a Microcomputer?

Its very name tells us that a **microcomputer** is a small computer, and a **computer** is an electronic device that performs calculations and processes data. Most people think of a microcomputer as being small enough to fit on top of a desk. Although some powerful models can serve several users simultaneously, most microcomputers are used by only one person at a time. For this reason, microcomputers are also often called **personal computers**.

Another characteristic of microcomputers is that their "brain" or **central processing unit (CPU)** consists of a single electronic device known as a **micro-**

1

processor. This device, a marvel of miniature engineering, controls the micro-computer, performs its calculations, and processes data. A microprocessor is just one type of **integrated circuit chip**, which is a thin slice of semiconductor mate-rial, such as pure silicon crystal, impregnated with carefully selected impurities. These chips are commonly used in computers and many other modern electronic devices.

One way to define microcomputers is by what they do. They can be used to help accomplish many different tasks. At the lowest level, however, a microcom-puter performs the same basic operations as all computers. This can be summed up as *input*, *processing*, and *output* (see Figure 1.1).

Figure 1.1   What a Computer Does

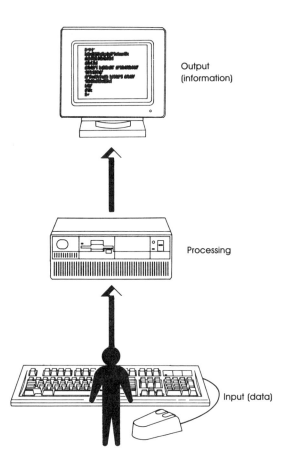

Output (information)

Processing

Input (data)

First, a **program** is needed to tell the computer what to do. This is a set of in-structions that controls a computer's operation. The program lets you enter raw **data**, which can consist of numbers, text, pictures, and even sounds. These data entered into the computer are called **input**. The program instructs the computer to process the data by doing calculations, comparisons, and other manipulations. The final result is processed data or **information**, hopefully a more organized and useful form of the original input. This information produced by the computer is called **output**. Keep in mind that there is no magic here—a program is needed to tell the computer what to do and the output information is only as valid as the original input data.

Although microcomputers perform the same basic operations as larger computers, they differ in speed and capacity. Larger computers can generally process data faster than microcomputers. They can also internally store more data at a time than microcomputers. These factors make larger computers better for performing lots of extremely complex and time-consuming computations. Microcomputers are also less adept than larger computers at handling several different users or tasks at the same time. On the other hand, microcomputers are superbly adapted to help with many work-a-day tasks like typing papers, figuring taxes, maintaining mailing lists, sending messages, drawing charts, managing finances, and even playing games.

Finally, microcomputers generally fall within a given price range. This range varies from little as $100 to as much as $15,000. Today the average price of a typical microcomputer used in business is around $1500. This is, however, a good deal less than the cost of much more powerful computers, which may run into many thousands or millions of dollars. Although microcomputers are by no means cheap, their prices have been generally dropping even as their capabilities have increased. For example, in late 1983 the list price of a basic IBM Personal Computer XT was $5675. The list price of its successor, a similarly equipped IBM Personal System/2 Model 30, was only $2545 when first released in mid-1987. Even though the newer Model 30 costs less than half as much as the old XT, it still has more than twice the speed and storage capacity, along with many other improvements.

Hardware

The **hardware** of a computer system is the electronic and mechanical equipment that make it work. Like a stereo system, microcomputer hardware generally consists of several distinct components connected by cables. Although there are several possible arrangements and many different models, Figure 1.2 shows a typical microcomputer system, the IBM Personal System/2 Model 50, which has four major parts: a system unit, display, keyboard, and printer. You will also notice, in this figure, a power switch, a floppy disk drive, and a mouse, all of which will be discussed later.

System Unit

From the outside, the system unit looks like a shallow box about the size of a portable typewriter. Figure 1.3 shows what the system unit of an IBM Personal System/2 Model 50 looks like on the inside. This central component houses important elements such as the computer's motherboard, microprocessor, memory, disk drives, and power supply.

Figure 1.2   A Microcomputer System

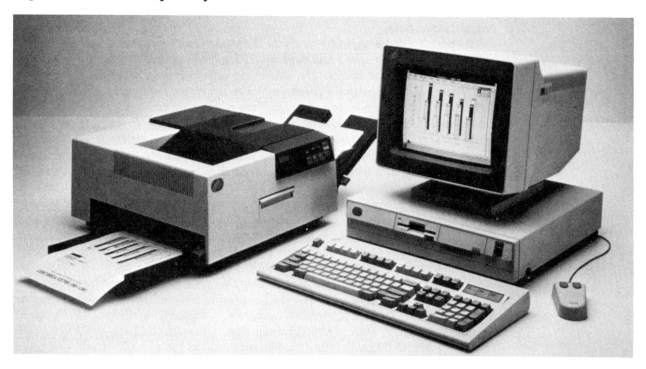

Figure 1.3   Inside the System Unit

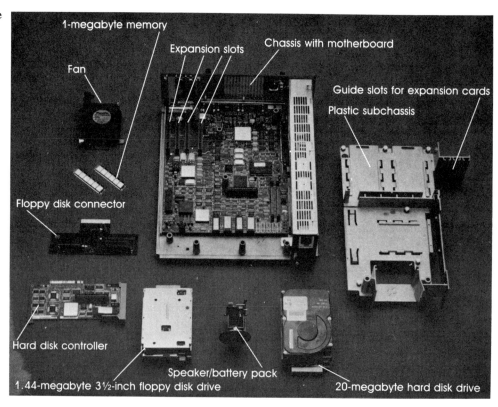

Motherboard

The main circuit board of a computer is called the **motherboard** or **system board** (see Figure 1.4). Among other components, the motherboard holds the computer's CPU, some memory, and much of its control circuitry. In addition, the motherboard contains the **bus**, a set of wires and connectors that link the CPU to memory and other computer components.

In most microcomputers, the bus is accessible through a series of **expansion slots**. Each expansion slot is an internal connector that allows you to plug an

Figure 1.4
A Motherboard
or System Board

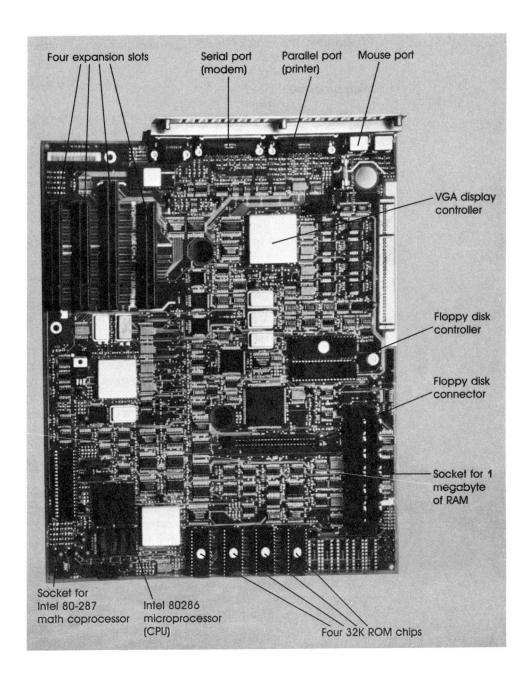

ditional circuit board into the motherboard. The IBM Personal System/2 Model 50, for example, has four expansion slots, which can be seen in Figure 1.4. Some computers come with eight or more expansion slots. A circuit board that plugs into an expansion slot is called an **expansion board, card,** or **adapter**. Such circuit boards make it possible to connect a wide variety of extra equipment to a computer, thus *expanding* its capability.

The motherboard or expansion boards also contain device controllers. A **device controller** is a set of chips or a circuit board that operates a piece of computer equipment such as a disk drive, display, keyboard, mouse, or printer. Recently, there has been a trend toward building device controllers onto microcomputer motherboards. The IBM Personal System/2 Model 50 shown in Figure 1.4, for example, has most of its device controllers on the motherboard.

Microprocessor

As we said, the microprocessor is a microcomputer's central processing unit (CPU). It consists of a single integrated circuit chip that is usually soldered or plugged into a socket on the motherboard (see Figure 1.4). IBM and IBM-compatible microcomputers use microprocessors from the Intel 8088 family, which includes the 8088, 8086, 80286, and 80386 chips. The 8088 is used in older IBM and IBM-compatibles such as the original IBM Personal Computer and PC/XT. The slightly more efficient 8086 chip is used in IBM's newer low-end models, such as the IBM Personal System/2 Models 30 and 50 X. The more powerful 80286 chip is used in mid-range microcomputers, such as the original IBM Personal Computer AT and the newer IBM Personal System/2 Models 50 and 60. Finally, the very powerful and fast 80386 chip is used in high-end models, such as the IBM Personal System/2 Models 70 and 80.

Memory

Memory is a computer's internal storage, used to hold programs and data. Also called **primary storage**, memory is measured in bytes. A **byte** is the amount of storage needed to hold a single character, such as the letter A. Since computers can store many thousands or millions of bytes, the terms **kilobyte (K)** and **megabyte (M)** are often used. One kilobyte or 1K is equal to 1024 bytes. One megabyte or 1M is equal to 1,048,576 bytes. In general, microcomputer memory is made up of two types of integrated circuit chips: RAM and ROM.

RAM, which stands for **Random Access Memory**, is temporary storage. Programs and data can be stored there while they are being used and then overwritten by other programs and data later. When the computer is turned off, RAM loses its contents. Most microcomputers can now have at least 640K of RAM on their motherboards. Many can have much more installed on expansion boards. For example, the IBM Personal System/2 Model 80 can be equipped with up to 16 megabytes of RAM.

ROM, which stands for **Read Only Memory**, is permanent storage. The contents of ROM chips, which are encoded at the factory, remain intact when the computer is turned off. The programs and data permanently stored in ROM can be read and used, but never erased, changed, or augmented. Many microcomputers use ROM to store programs and data that are used frequently but need never be changed, such as portions of the operating system. Most microcomputers contain at least one ROM chip as part of their primary storage. The IBM Personal System/2 Model 50, for example, uses four 32K ROM chips on the motherboard to store essential programs and data (see Figure 1.4).

Disk Drives

A **disk drive** is a piece of equipment that can read and write programs and data on magnetic disks. A **magnetic disk** is a semi-permanent storage medium that can be erased and rewritten many times. Most microcomputers can now be equipped with two basic kinds of disk drives: floppy disk drives and hard disk drives.

A **floppy disk drive** works with **floppy disks** (also called **diskettes**), which are inexpensive, flexible magnetic disks encased in plastic (see Figure 1.5). Floppy disks can be inserted and removed from their disk drives. The IBM Personal System/2 Model 50, for example, accepts a 3½-inch diskette, which can hold up to 1.44 megabytes of programs and data. Although most newer microcomputers now come with 3½-inch disk drives, many microcomputers still use 5¼-inch floppy disk drives. A typical 5¼-inch floppy disk holds 360K, but there are some drives that use 5¼-inch disks that hold 1.2 megabytes.

Figure 1.5   Floppy Disks

A **hard disk drive** uses one or more magnetic metal platters to hold programs and data (see Figure 1.6). Most hard disk drives have their magnetic disks permanently sealed inside. These disks are rigid, much faster, and have much greater capacity than floppy disks. Hard disk drives come in sizes ranging from 10 megabytes to several hundred megabytes. The most popular sizes are now 20, 30, and 40 megabytes. The IBM Personal System/2 Model 50, for example, comes standard with a 20 megabyte internal hard disk. On a microcomputer with a hard disk, programs are usually run from the hard disk. The floppy disk drive is generally relegated to copying software to or from the hard disk and making backup copies of important programs and data.

Figure 1.6   Hard Disk Drive

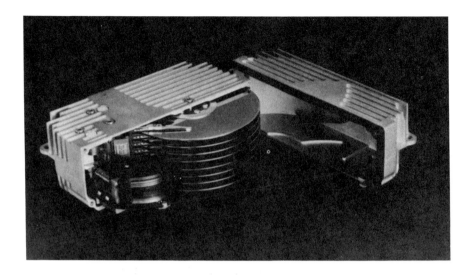

Display

A display, also called a **monitor**, is similar in many ways to an ordinary television screen. The display is used to present text and **graphics**, which are simply any kind of pictures, drawings, charts, or plots. The vast majority of computer monitors create text and graphics on the screen with tiny dots called **pixels** (short for picture elements). The number and size of these pixels determine a monitor's sharpness or **resolution**. There are three basic types of displays:

- **Monochrome Text** These monitors can only display letters, numbers, punctuation, and a limited set of other symbols in just one color, usually green on black, amber on black, white on black, or black on white.
- **Monochrome Graphics** In addition to text, these monitors can also display graphics on the screen. Only one color can be presented, but different shades of that color may be used.
- **Color Graphics** These monitors can display text and graphics in more than one color.

The capabilities of a particular display system are dependent on both the monitor itself and its device controller. The device controller for the display system is called a **display adapter**. For IBM and IBM-compatible microcomputers, there are several different display adapters that can be used. Some of these follow.

- **Monochrome Display Adapter (MDA)** This is the controller used with early low-end IBM microcomputers. It can only display text on a monochrome screen, but it generates very crisp, easy to read characters.
- **Color Graphics Adapter (CGA)** This is IBM's first microcomputer color graphics adapter. It can do color graphics, but the quality is rather poor. In other words, its low resolution makes text and graphics look rather fuzzy. Furthermore, the CGA is limited to a maximum of only 16 different colors, of which only only four can be on the screen at the same time.

- **Hercules Graphics Adapter** This adapter, made by Hercules Computer Technology, acts as a monochrome display adapter, but adds monochrome graphics capability.
- **Enhanced Graphics Adapter (EGA)** This color graphics adapter from IBM can do everything the CGA can do, yet is much better than the CGA. The resolution is significantly higher and the maximum number of different colors on the screen is 16 out of 64 possible choices.
- **Multi-Color Graphics Array (MCGA)** This is the display adapter built onto the motherboards of the IBM Personal System/2 Models 25 and 30. It can be used with either a monochrome graphics or color graphics monitor. It's maximum resolution is better than the EGA and can display a maximum of 256 different colors on the screen at once out of 262,144 possible choices.
- **Video Graphics Array (VGA)** This is the display adapter built onto the motherboards of the IBM Personal System/2 Models 50, 60, 70, and 80. It can also be purchased as a separate expansion board for other types of IBM and IBM-compatible computers. Slightly more advanced than the MCGA, the VGA can also do everything the EGA can do.

Keyboard

The keyboard is the primary device for entering text and telling the computer what to do. It is similar, in many respects, to a typewriter keyboard. Many microcomputers also have an auxiliary input device known as a **mouse**. This little box, which is glided across the table top, allows the user to manipulate objects on the display screen and select actions to be performed by pressing one or more buttons.

For IBM and IBM-compatible microcomputers, there are three basic keyboard designs. These are the original IBM Personal Computer keyboard, the original IBM Personal Computer AT keyboard, and the new IBM Enhanced Keyboard. Figure 1.7 shows all three of these keyboards. Besides the usual letters and punctuation marks that you're likely to find on any typewriter, a computer keyboard has other important keys:

- **Enter (or Return)** Analogous to the carriage return on a typewriter, this key is used to signal the end of an entry. Basically, it tells the computer to go ahead and process what was just typed.
- **Backspace** Like the Backspace key on a typewriter, this key is used to go back and type over a previously typed character.
- **Shift** Located at either side of the keyboard, one of the Shift keys is held down while pressing another key to produce a capital letter or the symbol shown on the top part of the key.
- **Caps Lock** This key is like the Caps Lock key on a typewriter, except that it works for only letter keys. When the caps lock key is pressed, capital letters will appear when you press letter keys. When Caps Lock is pressed again, small letters will appear when their keys are pressed.
- **Tab** Like the Tab key on a typewriter, this key is used to advance to the next tab stop.
- **Escape** The Escape key (abbreviated **Esc**) is often used to cancel a previously typed entry or to prematurely end a program.

**Figure 1.7   (top) Original IBM
PC Keyboard, (center) "AT-
Style" Keyboard, and (bottom)
IBM Enhanced Keyboard**

- **Break**   This key is very much like the Escape key and is used by some programs in a similar fashion.
- **Control**   Somewhat like a Shift key, the Control key (abbreviated **Ctrl**) is
  pressed in conjunction with other keys. It's used to control a program's actions by sending certain codes to the computer.
- **Alternate**   Very similar to the Control key, the Alternate key (abbreviated
  Alt) is also pressed in conjunction with other keys. It's used to give an alternate meaning to the keys pressed along with it.

- **Insert** This key (abbreviated **Ins**) is often used to insert a new entry between existing entries.
- **Delete** This key (abbreviated **Del**) is often used to erase an entry or a single character.
- **Function Keys** These are keys that are pressed to activate frequently used operations within a program. They are used differently by different programs. IBM-compatible keyboards have either 10 function keys along the left side or 12 function keys across the top. The function keys are labeled with an F followed by a number, like this: F1, F2, F3, etc.
- **Cursor Movement Keys** Most programs use these keys to let you move the **cursor** (a little blinking underscore or box) around the screen. In a word processing program, for example, the cursor marks the place where text is inserted, deleted, or otherwise manipulated. The cursor movement keys include Up Arrow, Down Arrow, Left Arrow, Right Arrow, Home, End, Page Up, and Page Down.
- **Numeric Keypad** This is an array of keys at the right side of a keyboard that resembles the layout of a calculator's keys. It includes the ten digits and other symbols that facilitate the entry of numbers and formulas. On the IBM PC and AT keyboards, the numeric keypad is superimposed on the cursor movement keys.
- **Num Lock** This key is used to switch the function of the numeric keypad. In one state, the numeric keypad acts as number keys. In the other state, the numeric keypad acts as cursor movement keys. You press the Num Lock key to switch between these two states.
- **Print Screen** If you have a printer, this key is pressed to send a copy of the current screen to your printer. On some keyboards, it is abbreviated **PrtSc**.
- **Pause** This key is used to temporarily suspend the operation of the current program.
- **Scroll Lock** This key is not used by very many programs and it has no standard function. Some programs use it to switch the Cursor Movement keys into a state in which they can move (or scroll) the whole screen up, down, left, or right.

Printer

A **printer** is a device used to produce permanent copies of text and possibly graphics on paper. Although a printer is not absolutely necessary to run most programs, it is an extremely useful addition to a microcomputer system. This is because computers are commonly used to produce letters, reports, books, tables, figures, charts, graphs, diagrams, maps, and pictures. Paper output, or *hard copy* as it's also called, is a convenient medium for distributing and communicating this work to others. The four kinds of printers most frequently used with microcomputers are dot-matrix printers, daisy-wheel printers, ink-jet printers, and laser printers.

Dot-Matrix Printers

A **dot-matrix printer** is an output device that uses tiny dots to create text and graphics on paper (see Figure 1.8). Just as graphics monitors use pixels to construct characters and pictures on a screen, dot-matrix printers similarly use dots of ink on pages of paper. Inside the dot-matrix printer a *printhead* is moved across the paper from left to right, and sometimes also from right to left (see Figure 1.8). This printhead may contain anywhere from 7 to 27 pins arranged in a vertical column. While most dot-matrix printers use 9 pins, more expensive printers with 18 or 24 pins are also fairly common. As the printhead moves horizontally, it constructs a character by repeatedly striking these pins against an inked ribbon and the paper. Electrical signals cause the appropriate pins to be thrust out at the proper moment to form the successive columns of dots that make up a character's image. Each column of the character is struck in turn against the ribbon and paper until the complete image has been formed. Dot-matrix printers are sometimes described as being impact printers because of the way the pins hit the ribbon and paper. This printing mechanism is most frequently used for text, but dot-matrix printers can usually produce graphics, too.

Dot-matrix printers are by far the most popular type of microcomputer printer. They are reasonably priced, fairly quick, and pretty reliable. The speed of a dot-matrix printer depends upon what print mode it is using. The fastest mode is called **draft mode**, in which characters are formed by just a single pass of the print head. Some expensive dot-matrix printers are able to achieve speeds of 400 characters per second in draft mode. Many dot-matrix printers also have a **near letter-quality (NLQ) mode**. In this mode, the printhead makes two or more passes over each character, slightly shifting its position each time. This tends to fill in the gaps between the dots and makes text appear more like it was produced by an electric typewriter. Using NLQ mode may slow some printers down to only 15 characters per second. Generating graphics with a dot-matrix printer can also be time consuming. Depending upon how dark the images are, it may take several minutes per page to produce graphics on a dot-matrix printer.

Daisy-Wheel Printers

A **daisy-wheel printer** uses a circular printing mechanism called a **daisy wheel**. Solid, raised characters are embossed on the ends of little "arms" arranged in a circle like the spokes of a wheel or the petals of a daisy. As this daisy wheel spins, a tiny, stationary hammer strikes the back of the proper character when it passes (see Figure 1.9). This impact drives the character pattern, which is embossed in reverse, against an inked ribbon and the paper. Daisy-wheel printers are true **letter-quality** printers because they produce well-defined text just like electric typewriters. Their prices are comparable with that of dot-matrix printers. Unlike dot-matrix printers, however, daisy-wheel printers cannot produce graphics. They are also noisier and slower than dot-matrix printers. The typical daisy-wheel printer can only print about 10 characters per second, and even the most expensive models generally cannot do better than 100 characters per second. Daisy-wheel printers are still fairly popular with microcomputer owners, but they are gradually being supplanted by 24-pin dot-matrix printers and laser printers.

Figure 1.8   (a) The Printhead
of a Dot-Matrix Printer, (b)
The Process of Printing a Dot-
Matrix Character, (c) The
pattern of dots within the
matrix that form the
character, and (d) An IBM
Proprinter XL24, a dot-matrix
printer

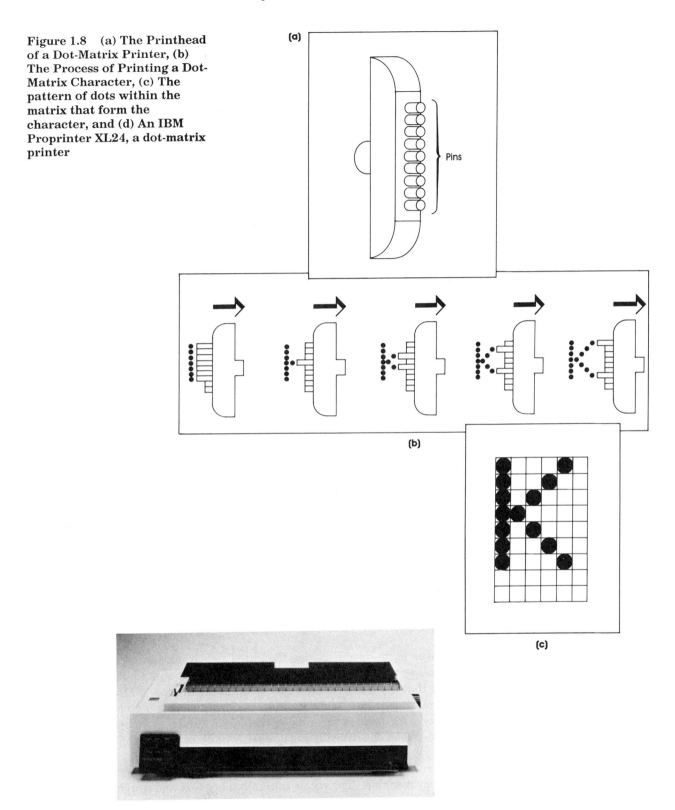

Figure 1.9   The Daisy-Wheel Printing Mechanism and a Daisy Wheel

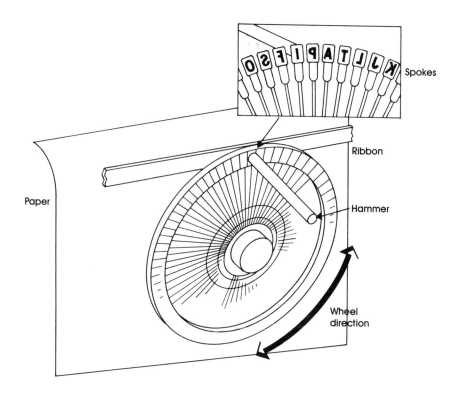

Ink-Jet Printers

An **ink-jet printer** has a mechanism that squirts tiny, electrically charged droplets of ink out of a nozzle and onto the paper (see Figure 1.10). (No pins or hammers strike the paper, so ink-jet printers are classified as nonimpact printers.) Ink-jet printers are fast, quiet, and can produce high-quality print, but they are slightly more expensive than dot-matrix printers. Some ink-jet printers have a tendency to clog their nozzle with ink and smear characters on paper. Many ink-jet printers, however, have the capability to print in color, a capability most other types of printers lack.

Laser Printers

A **laser printer** is an output device that uses tightly focused beams of light to transfer images to paper (see Figure 1.11). A tiny laser emits pulsating pinpoint bursts of light that are reflected off a special spinning mirror. This mirror reflects light onto a rotating drum. Light striking the drum causes it to become charged with electricity. An inklike toner is attracted to the drum in these electrically charged spots. When the drum is rolled over a piece of paper, the toner is transferred to the paper and an image is permanently fixed through a combination of heat and pressure. This image transfer process is similar to that found in a plain-paper photocopy machine. The result is high-quality text and graphics that almost look as if they were typeset. (Like ink-jet printers, laser printers are classified as nonimpact printers.)

Figure 1.10 (above) Ink Jet Printing, and (below) The Hewlett-Packard PaintJet Color-Graphics Printer

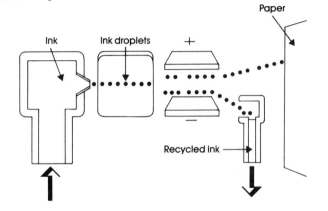

Figure 1.11 The Hewlett-Packard LaserJet Series II Laser Printer

Laser printers represent the most advanced printing technology. Although the images they produce are made up of dots, these dots are much smaller and more densely packed than the dots created with a dot-matrix printer. The typical microcomputer laser printer is capable of printing at a resolution of 300 dots per inch, both horizontally and vertically. This means 90,000 dots per square inch. Besides printing high-quality images, laser printers are also fast and quiet. The average speed of most laser printers is 8 pages per minute. This is equivalent to about 400 characters per second. Because laser printers don't use impact methods like dot-matrix and daisy-wheel printers, they are very quiet by comparison. The major disadvantage to laser printers is their cost. Prices generally start at around $1000. Despite the cost, more and more laser printers are being used with microcomputers every year. They are especially popular in office situations where the printer can be shared among several users.

Software

By itself, computer hardware is useless. Programs are needed to operate the hardware. As we mentioned earlier, a program is simply a sequence of instructions that tells a computer what to do. **Software** is a general term that refers to any single program or group of programs. In contrast to hardware, which is constructed from physical materials like metal and plastic, software is built from knowledge, planning, and testing. A person who creates programs is called a **programmer**. Programmers use their knowledge of how a computer works to plan sets of instructions that accomplish useful tasks. These instructions are entered into the computer and repeatedly tested and modified until they achieve the desired results. As we said earlier, programs and data are generally kept on magnetic disks, where they can be accessed and used over and over again. Note that the disks themselves aren't the software, they're just the medium on which software is stored.

As an analogy, think of a stereo system. The amplifier, compact disc player, and speakers are the hardware. The amplifier is like the central processing unit and memory, the compact disc player is like a disk drive, and the speakers are like the display, except they present audio instead of video output. The music, which is stored on compact discs, is like software, which is stored on floppy disks. Just as you can amass a huge music collection by buying more compact discs, you can build a bigger software library by purchasing additional programs on floppy disks. The stereo system is of little use without the compact discs and the compact discs are useless without the stereo system. Similarly, a computer system is useless without software and software is useless without a computer system on which to run it.

Just as there are different types of hardware, there are also different types of software. Basically, there are three major categories: *system software*, *programming languages*, and *application software*.

System Software

System software handles the many details of managing a computer system. A computer's **operating system** makes up most of its system software. This is the set of programs that controls a computer's hardware and manages the use of software. One small part of the operating system, for example, is a program that identifies which key you've pressed, determines the character that corresponds to that key, and forms that character on the display screen. Another example is a program that lets you erase the contents of a magnetic disk. Some system software is built into a computer's ROM chips, while other system software comes on magnetic disk and must be purchased separately.

Programming Languages

Computer programs are developed with programming languages. A **programming language** is simply a set of symbols and rules to direct the operations of a computer. There are many different programming languages in common use, each designed to develop certain types of programs. A few of the most popular programming languages are BASIC, Pascal, C, FORTRAN, COBOL, and Ada. Although it can be helpful to learn a programming language for some very specific applications, most people who use computers don't actually program them. They just use programs, such as operating systems and application software, that have been developed by professional programmers.

Application Software

Application software is the software that applies the computer to useful tasks such as helping you create documents, figure your taxes, maintain mailing lists, and draw charts. Also called **application packages** or simply **applications**, these programs are the real reason most people buy and use microcomputers. The three most widely used applications follow:

- **Word Processing** A **word processing package** is software that helps you prepare documents by letting you enter, store, modify, format, copy, and print text.
- **Spreadsheet** A **spreadsheet package** is software that lets you manipulate tables of numbers, text, and formulas. It is an extremely flexible tool that can be used to handle typical accounting chores, monitor investments, balance a checkbook, and work out a budget.
- **Data Base Management** A **data base** is an organized collection of one or more files of related data. A **file** is a mass of individual data items kept together on a disk. A **data base management package** is software that lets you create, add to, delete from, update, rearrange, select from, print out, and otherwise administer data files such as mailing lists and inventories.

Besides these "big three" application packages, there are many other types of popular software, including the following:

- **Communications** Using an auxiliary device called a **modem**, a computer can transmit and receive programs and data over ordinary telephone lines. Communications software makes it possible for a computer to use a modem to call other computers and access on-line information services.

- **Graphics** Graphics packages let you use a computer to create all kinds of pictures including graphs, charts, maps, paintings, drawings, diagrams, blueprints, simulated slide shows, and animated presentations.
- **Desktop Publishing** Combining the results of word processing and graphics, desktop publishing or page layout software lets you use a computer and laser printer to produce near typeset-quality documents.
- **Accounting** Accounting software lets you use a computer to record, analyze, and report business transactions.
- **Integrated Software** Integrated software combines word processing, spreadsheet, data base management, communications, and graphics applications in a single package.
- **Windowing Environment** Working closely with the operating system, a windowing environment allows you to divide your screen into a number of different boxes, or *windows*, and run a separate program in each one.
- **DOS Shell** A DOS shell is a program that enhances PC-DOS or MS-DOS, the operating system used with IBM and IBM-compatible microcomputers. Basically, it is an easy-to-use front-end to DOS that helps you execute commands and manage disk files.
- **Utilities** There are a host of small, specific programs called utilities that add handy features and functions to a particular operating system or application package. These include disk and file utilities, printer utilities, keyboard utilities, and desk accessories such as calculators, calendars, and address books.
- **On-Line References** Software to help you check your spelling, find a synonym, or look up a word's definition are all examples of on-line references.
- **Statistics and Math** Many programs exist for performing statistical analyses and helping solve mathematical equations.
- **Project Management** A project management package is software that helps you formally plan and control complex undertakings, such as the construction of a building, the development of a new product, or the installation of a large computer system.
- **Personal Finance and Taxes** Many programs exist for helping you manage your money and prepare your federal and state income tax returns.
- **Education** There is a wide range of programs for teaching skills and concepts, from learning the alphabet to designing physics experiments.
- **Entertainment** An amazing variety of microcomputer software exists for playing games, simulating cars and planes, and playing music.
- **Hypertext** A hypertext package is software that lets you store and retrieve all kinds of information in a nonsequential manner. In other words, you can randomly jump from topic to related topic, accessing any kind of information the computer can store, including text, graphics, audio, and video.
- **Expert System** An expert system is a computer program that contains a collection of facts and a list of rules for making inferences about those facts. Such software can use these facts and rules in a particular field to advise, analyze, categorize, diagnose, explain, identify, interpret, and teach.

Helpful Hints for Using a Microcomputer

Now that we've covered the general topics, let's go over a few specific details that can help prepare you for using a microcomputer.

Turning on the Computer

Sometimes, just turning on the computer can be an adventure. It seems that some manufacturers are fond of "hiding" the power switch. This has the practical purpose of making it difficult to turn off the computer by accident while in the middle of some critical task. Not being able to find the power switch, however, can make you feel lost before you even begin.

On the new IBM Personal System/2 computers, the power switch is a big red toggle right up front on the system unit. No problem here. On other computers, if the switch isn't immediately obvious up front, then it is probably on the right side of the system unit toward the rear. This is the case in IBM PCs, XTs, and ATs. Some models from other companies have the power switch mounted somewhere on the back side of the system unit or monitor.

Speaking of monitors, many color graphics displays have a separate power switch that must also be turned on, otherwise you will be looking at a permanently blank screen. The on/off switch is usually the top knob of three on the front of the monitor and is turned on by rotating it to the right. The other two knobs are the contrast and brightness controls, just like the ones on many television sets. If these three controls aren't right up front, they may be present as slightly protruding little disks located just under the bottom front edge of the monitor. Another possibility is the ever-popular back side of the monitor.

Operating the Printer

Like the system unit and monitor, the printer also has a power switch that must be turned on. This power switch is frequently positioned at the rear of the left or right side. In addition, there are at least three other buttons on most printers. Usually stationed on the top or front of the printer, these three buttons may be labeled On Line, Line Feed, and Form Feed. The **On Line** button is very important and is usually paired with an indicator light. When the On Line light is on, the printer is connected to and controlled by the computer, so that printing can occur. Make sure the On Line button is pressed so that the On Line light is on before attempting to print. The **Line Feed** and **Form Feed** buttons let you advance the paper in the printer, usually only when the printer is off line.

Caring for Floppy Disks

Although floppy disks are quite durable and can take quite a bit of punishment, there are a few guidelines you should follow in their handling.

1. Don't touch the exposed surfaces on 5¼-inch disks. Don't open the little metal door on 3½-inch disks.
2. Don't bend or fold 5¼-inch floppies.
3. Don't expose disks to extreme heat.
4. Keep 5¼-inch disks in their sleeves when not in use.
5. Don't write on 5¼-inch disks with pencils or hard-point pens.
6. Keep your disks dry.
7. Don't expose disks to strong magnetic fields (keep them away from magnets and powerful motors).

8. Always try to keep at least one backup copy of all important disks.
9. Carefully insert and remove disks from disk drives. Wait until the drive's red access light is off before changing disks.

Summary

In this chapter of the *Software Guide*, you've learned what a microcomputer is, what it does, and what kinds of software are available. In addition, you've learned a few tips for turning on a microcomputer, operating a printer, and caring for floppy disks. This material sets the stage for the next chapter, in which you will complete lessons to teach you how to use DOS, the operating system for IBM and IBM-compatible microcomputers.

Exercises

Multiple Choice

Choose the best selection to complete each statement.

1. A microcomputer is a computer in which the central processing unit consists of
   (a) a RAM chip.
   (b) a ROM chip.
   (c) a microprocessor chip.
   (d) a device controller chip.

2. A set of instructions that controls a computer's operation is
   (a) a program.
   (b) data.
   (c) input.
   (d) output.

3. The main circuit board of a computer is called the
   (a) expansion board.
   (b) device controller.
   (c) bus.
   (d) motherboard or system board.

4. IBM and IBM-compatible microcomputers use microprocessors from the
   (a) Motorola 68000 family.
   (b) Intel 8088 family.
   (c) Zilog Z80 family.
   (d) GTE G65SC816 family.

5. A byte is the amount of storage needed to hold a
   (a) single character.
   (b) single page.
   (c) single line.
   (d) single file.

6. Which of the following does NOT describe random access memory (RAM)?
   (a) It is temporary storage.
   (b) It loses its contents when the power is turned off.
   (c) It is permanently encoded at the factory.
   (d) It can be read and written over and over again.

7. The two most popular floppy disk sizes are
   (a) 3½-inch and 8-inch.
   (b) 5¼-inch and 8-inch.
   (c) 3½-inch and 5¼-inch.
   (d) 3-inch and 12-inch.

8. Which of the following types of display systems can present text and pictures on the screen, but in only a single color?
   (a) monochrome text display
   (b) monochrome graphics display
   (c) color graphics display
   (d) monochrome display adapter

9. Which of the following microcomputer keyboard keys is used to tell the computer to go ahead and process what was just typed?
   (a) Enter or Return key
   (b) Escape key
   (c) Control key
   (d) Function key

10. The most advanced and expensive type of printer in the following group is the
   (a) dot-matrix printer.
   (b) daisy-wheel printer.
   (c) ink-jet printer.
   (d) laser printer.

11. A set of programs that controls a computer's hardware and manages the use of software is called
   (a) an operating system.
   (b) a programming language.
   (c) an application package.
   (d) a data base management package.

12. Which of the following types of software lets you manipulate tables of numbers, text, and formulas?
   (a) word processing package
   (b) spreadsheet package
   (c) data base management package
   (d) operating system

13. Which of the following types of software lets you use a modem to transmit and receive programs and data over ordinary telephone lines?
   (a) communications package
   (b) graphics package
   (c) desktop publishing package
   (d) windowing package

14. Which of the following types of software lets you use a computer to record, analyze, and report business transactions?
   (a) graphics package
   (b) accounting package
   (c) DOS shell
   (d) utilities

15. Small, specific programs that add handy features and functions to a particular operating system or application package are called
   (a) on-line references.
   (b) hypertext programs.
   (c) spreadsheets.
   (d) utilities.

16. Which of the following types of software would be the best choice for maintaining a mailing list?
   (a) word processing package
   (b) spreadsheet package
   (c) data base management package
   (d) accounting package

17. Which of the following types of programs would you use to help plan and control the construction of a new office building?
   (a) word processing package
   (b) spreadsheet package
   (c) integrated software package
   (d) project management package

18. Which of the following types of software lets you store and retrieve all kinds of information in a nonsequential manner and then randomly jump from topic to related topic?
   (a) word processing package
   (b) spreadsheet package
   (c) hypertext package
   (d) expert system

_____   19. Which printer button determines whether the printer is connected to and
                        controlled by the computer?

        (a) Power   (c) Line Feed

        (b) On Line   (d) Form Feed

_____   20. Which of the following should you NOT do to a floppy disk?

        (a) Keep it in its sleeve when not in   (c) Keep it near a magnet when not in
use.   use.

        (b) Keep it away from extreme heat.   (d) Keep it dry.

Fill-In

1. An _____ microcomputer works like a comparable IBM model and can run the same
   software.

2. At the lowest level, the basic operations of all computers can be summed up as input, _____,
   and output.

3. The _____ of a computer system is the electronic and mechanical equipment that
   make it work.

4. A microcomputer's motherboard contains the _____, which is a set of wires and
   connectors that link the CPU to memory and other computer components.

5. _____ is temporary storage for programs and data, which can be used and then
   overwritten by other programs and data. _____, on the other hand, is permanent
   storage encoded at the factory with frequently used programs and data that need never be changed.

6. Most microcomputers can be equipped with two basic types of disk drives: floppy disk drives and
   _____.

7. The number and size of a monitor's _____ determine its sharpness, or resolution.

8. The _____ is the display adapter that comes built onto the motherboards of high-end
   IBM Personal System/2 microcomputers.

9. Many microcomputers have an auxiliary input device known as a _____, which is a
   little box with one or more buttons that is glided across the table top.

10. On an IBM keyboard, the _____ Movement keys include Up Arrow, Down Arrow,
    Left Arrow, Right Arrow, Home, End, Page Up and Page Down.

11. _____ printers are by far the most popular type of microcomputer printer.

12. _____ is a general term that refers to any single program or group of programs.

13. BASIC, Pascal, C, FORTRAN, COBOL, and Ada are all examples of popular programming
    _____.

14. _____ software is the software that applies the computer to useful tasks such as helping you create documents, prepare a budget, or maintain a mailing list.

15. _____ packages let you use a computer to create all kinds of graphs, charts, maps, paintings, drawings, diagrams, slide shows, and presentations.

16. Combining the results of word processing and graphics software, _____ software lets you use a computer and laser printer to produce near typeset quality documents.

17. _____ software combines word processing, spreadsheet, data base management, communications, and graphics applications in a single package.

18. A _____ environment allows you to divide your screen into a number of different boxes and run a separate program in each one.

19. A _____ management package is software that helps you formally plan and control complex undertakings.

20. An _____ system is a computer program that contains a collection of facts and a list of rules for making inferences about those facts.

2

The DOS Operating System

Learning Objectives

After reading this chapter, you should know how to do the following:

- Explain what a disk operating system is
- Explain why there are different versions of DOS
- Boot DOS with the computer turned off
- Boot DOS with the computer turned on
- Obtain a directory listing of a disk's files
- Explain the structure of a DOS file name
- Use the special DOS keys
- Change the default disk drive
- Obtain a disk and memory status report
- Clear the display screen

- Format a diskette
- Format a system diskette
- Copy files
- Copy entire diskettes
- Change file names
- Erase files
- Display a text file on the screen
- Send a text file to the printer
- Run an application program
- Create and use DOS subdirectories
- Use DOS batch files

Introduction

An operating system is a set of programs that helps you use the hardware and software resources of a general-purpose computer. It's what you use to tell the computer to perform common tasks such as running application packages, managing disk storage, and controlling peripheral devices such as display screens and printers. In one sense, an operating system is like a toolbox that contains all kinds of utility programs to perform many of the little jobs that most users need. These utilities are like tools; some are used everyday by almost everyone, while others are more exotic and may only be used occasionally, even by experts.

A **disk operating system** (or **DOS**) is kept on a floppy or hard disk. When the computer system is turned on, some components of the operating system are loaded from disk into primary memory and remain there until the computer is shut off. These components, called **resident routines** or **internal commands**, are kept in memory because they are the most essential or the most frequently used parts of the operating system. The other components of a DOS are kept on disk and are temporarily loaded into memory only when they are needed or specifically requested. As a result, these latter commands are often called **transient routines** or **external commands**.

An important characteristic of a disk operating system is the abundance of utilities to deal with files that are stored on disks. A file, you'll recall, is just a collection of related data that is kept on a disk. Since most programs, text, and numerical data are kept in disk files, almost everything you do with computers involves working with files. Every computer user, therefore, must deal with an operating system to some extent. This chapter will teach you how to use the most popular disk operating system for IBM and IBM-compatible microcomputers.

MS-DOS and PC-DOS

The two most popular operating systems for IBM and IBM-compatible microcomputers are MS-DOS and PC-DOS. Both versions were written by Microsoft Corporation; however, PC-DOS was written for IBM. Although there are some minor differences between MS-DOS and PC-DOS, from the average user's viewpoint they are virtually identical. The major distinction is that PC-DOS is generally used with IBM computers, and MS-DOS is used with many IBM-compatible computers made by companies such as Compaq, AT&T, Tandy, Zenith and others. From now on, everything we say about MS-DOS will also be true for PC-DOS, and we'll just refer to both of them generically as DOS.

DOS Versions

Because computer technology changes so rapidly, an operating system like DOS is not a static entity. Operating systems must be constantly updated to accommodate new computer models and new capabilities for existing models. So far, there have been several official releases, or versions, of DOS. Although bugs have been worked out and improvements made over previous versions, the driving force behind each new release of DOS has been a new hardware capability, usually related to floppy or hard disk drives.

It's important to know which version of DOS you are using, because some hardware and software can only be used with more recent versions. Fortunately, each new version of DOS is **upwardly compatible** with former versions—that is, almost everything that worked with previous versions should work with the new version. So, you probably don't have to change the way you did things before unless you want to take advantage of the added capabilities of the new version. In fact, you usually don't have to buy the latest version of DOS each time a new release is issued. As long as the version you have works with your hardware and software, you can continue using it.

DOS versions are denoted by numbers such as 1.00, 2.10, and 3.30. The number to the left of the decimal point reflects a major classification; the numbers to the right represent more minor differences. The higher the number, the more recent the version. Throughout this guide, we'll be using DOS 3.30 for all of our examples.

General Features of DOS

DOS provides many capabilities, both simple and complex. We'll be discussing some of its most-used simple features, such as the following.

- **Booting Up with the Power Off**   DOS can automatically load itself into memory when you turn the power on.
- **Booting Up with the Power On**   DOS can be reloaded and reset without having to turn the power off and then on again.
- **Keeping Track of the Date and Time**   Once you initially tell DOS the date and time, it will keep track of them until you turn the computer off or reboot.
- **Listing File Directories**   You can instruct DOS to produce a directory of some or all of the files on a particular disk.
- **Using Special Keys**   By pressing certain keys on the keyboard, you can tell DOS to cancel an input line, pause screen scrolling, cancel a command, print the screen, or echo input and output to the printer.
- **Changing the Default Drive**   DOS lets you specify the disk drive it will assume when a drive designation isn't explicitly given.
- **Checking Disk and Memory Status**   DOS can produce a report of useful information about a disk and primary memory.
- **Clearing the Screen**   DOS lets you erase your display screen.
- **Formatting a Diskette**   DOS lets you prepare a new diskette so that program and data files can be stored on it. It can also install itself on a new diskette if you tell it to do so.
- **Copying Files**   DOS permits you to copy files onto the same disk or from one disk to another.
- **Copying Diskettes**   DOS allows you to copy an entire diskette with a single command.
- **Changing File Names**   DOS lets you choose new names for existing files.
- **Erasing Files**   DOS allows you to delete unneeded files from a disk.
- **Displaying Text Files**   You can have DOS display text files on your screen.
- **Printing Text Files**   You can have DOS send text files to your printer.
- **Running Programs**   You can tell DOS to run application programs such as Lotus 1-2-3.
- **Using Subdirectories**   You can create, use, and remove subdirectories, which are like separate little disks on a large disk.
- **Using Batch Files**   You can create and execute collections of DOS commands stored in special text files called batch files.

Getting Started

Although DOS is a rich and powerful microcomputer operating system, you can quite easily learn its most commonly used features. For the most part, these features are invoked by issuing commands to DOS. A command is simply a word or mnemonic (memory aid) abbreviation entered at the keyboard that tells DOS to run a particular program. Once DOS has been initially loaded into memory, it's constantly on the lookout for these commands. In the following lessons you'll learn most of the DOS commands you're likely to need. You'll also be introduced to general concepts about the keyboard, display, disks, and disk drives that you'll be using in this and later parts. Wherever it's useful, figures will actually show you what you should see on your computer screen at a given point. These screen views will help you as you go through each lesson's steps.

DOS 3.30 comes on two floppy disks; one is labeled DOS Startup and the other is entitled DOS Operating. Previous versions of DOS also came on two disks, but these were labeled DOS and DOS Supplemental Programs. If you are using one of these earlier versions of DOS, you just need the DOS disk. If you are using a computer with a hard disk or one connected to a local area network, DOS may already be installed on it, but you can still use the DOS floppy disk or disks for the following lessons.

As you go through the lessons, you will be given instructions on what to type. In this text we'll use **bold** print to indicate what you're supposed to type. It doesn't matter whether you use uppercase or lowercase. DOS ignores case when processing commands.

Booting DOS

The first thing that you must do is turn on your computer and load DOS into primary memory. This process is often called *booting DOS*, *loading DOS*, or simply *starting DOS*.

Insert the DOS Disk

With the computer shut off, grasp the DOS 3.30 Startup disk (or DOS disk for previous versions) by the label and remove it from the sleeve (be careful not to touch the exposed parts around the oval slot and circular hole if it is a 5¼-inch disk). Hold the disk with the label side up and the oval slot pointing toward the computer. If your computer uses 3½-inch disks, hold the disk with the label up and the metal door pointed toward the computer. Insert the disk into the A drive and close the disk drive door. If your computer has two disk drives, side by side, the A drive is the one on the left. If it has two half-height drives arranged vertically, the A drive is the one on the top. If there is only one floppy drive, then it is the A drive.

Turn the Computer On

If you have a color display, turn it on by twisting the top knob on the front panel to the right. If you have a monochrome display, you don't need to turn it on because its power cord is plugged into the computer. Turn on the computer by flipping up the big red switch, which is located right up front on the system unit of most new IBM or IBM-compatible computers, or at the rear of the right side of the system unit on older models. You should hear the cooling fan begin to whir.

Watch the Display and Wait

Once the power is turned on, the computer goes through some self-tests to ensure that it is working properly. One of these tests checks out all of the primary memory installed. This could take a few seconds or several minutes depending upon how much memory the computer has. So, if nothing appears to be happening for a couple of minutes, don't be alarmed. After the power-on self-tests are complete, the computer will access drive A to see if the DOS disk is there. You should see the little red access light go on and hear the disk drive whir and click. Assuming the computer is in working order, the disk drive door is properly closed, and there is nothing wrong with the DOS disk, the DOS command processor and internal commands will be loaded into main memory and a message such as the following will appear on your display screen:

```
Current date is Tue  1-01-1980
Enter new date (mm-dd-yy): _
```

Enter the Date and Time

Type today's date in the form of mm-dd-yy or mm/dd/yy. In other words, type in the month number, a dash or slash, the day of the month, another dash or slash, and the last two digits of the year. Now press the **Enter** key. After you have entered the date, a message like this will appear:

```
Current time is  0:00:36.90
Enter new time: _
```

Type the hour, a colon, and the minute, then press the **Enter** key. If it's afternoon, add twelve to the hour as in the military fashion. For example, if it's 2 P.M., enter **14:00**. You can enter the second and the hundredths of seconds if you happen to carry a stopwatch and feel so inclined. However, just the hour and minute are sufficient. After you do this, your screen should look something like the screen in Figure 2.1. The A> on the last line is called the **DOS prompt**. It indicates that disk drive A is your default drive and that the DOS command processor is patiently waiting for you to enter a command. The **default drive** is the disk drive that DOS assumes you want to use unless you specify otherwise.

Note: Many computers now have a battery-maintained clock/calendar that makes entering the date and time unnecessary. If the current date and time presented by DOS are correct, all you have to do is press the Enter key each time in response.

Rebooting DOS

Occasionally, something goes wrong in a program and the computer may seem to be "stuck." Or, after working with a program you may have to "reinitialize" the computer, or bring it back to the way it was when you first turned it on. You could, of course, just shut the computer off and boot it up. There's another way, however, to reboot the computer without shutting it off.

Press Ctrl-Alt-Del

DOS has a special combination of keypresses that will reboot the computer without having to shut it off first. All you have to do is press the keys marked **Ctrl**, **Alt**, and **Del**, and hold them down at the same time for a moment.

Figure 2.1   Booting Up DOS

```
Current date is Wed  1-01-1980
Enter new date (mm-dd-yy): 7-13-89
Current time is  0:00:36.26
Enter new time: 7:51


The IBM Personal Computer DOS
Version 3.30 (C)Copyright International Business Machines Corp 1981, 1987
              (C)Copyright Microsoft Corp 1981, 1986

A>_
```

Watch the Display and Wait

In most cases, the screen will go blank, the computer will beep, and the disk drive will spin and blink its red access light just like it did when you first turned it on. If all this doesn't happen, a serious program error has probably overwritten a crucial part of DOS in memory and you will have to shut the computer off and boot it up as described earlier. If all is well, DOS will again ask you to supply the date and time.

Enter the Date and Time

After you enter the date and time as you did originally, DOS will once again display its copyright message and the system prompt, as shown in Figure 2.1.

Listing a Disk File Directory

As we mentioned before, programs, data, and text are kept on disks in files. Every file has a name, size, creation date, and creation time associated with it. DOS can display this information for you if you use the directory command.

Enter the Directory Command

At the DOS prompt, type in the letters **dir** and press the **Enter** key. As with all DOS commands, it doesn't matter if you use uppercase or lowercase letters. DIR is is the abbreviation for the DOS directory command that will list the directory of the default disk on your display screen. Remember that the default disk is the one in the disk drive that DOS assumes you are currently working on, and its letter is indicated by the DOS prompt. Right now, your default disk drive should be A, so the DIR command will list the file names, sizes, and creation dates and times for all the files on the floppy disk in drive A. Figure 2.2 shows what the screen looks like when it stops scrolling.

Figure 2.2   Listing a Directory

```
COMMAND   COM    25307   3-17-87   12:00p
ANSI      SYS     1678   3-17-87   12:00p
COUNTRY   SYS    11285   3-17-87   12:00p
DISPLAY   SYS    11290   3-17-87   12:00p
DRIVER    SYS     1196   3-17-87   12:00p
FASTOPEN  EXE     3919   3-17-87   12:00p
FDISK     COM    48216   3-18-87   12:00p
FORMAT    COM    11616   3-18-87   12:00p
KEYB      COM     9056   3-17-87   12:00p
KEYBOARD  SYS    19766   3-17-87   12:00p
MODE      COM    15487   3-17-87   12:00p
NLSFUNC   EXE     3060   3-17-87   12:00p
PRINTER   SYS    13590   3-17-87   12:00p
REPLACE   EXE    11775   3-17-87   12:00p
SELECT    COM     4163   3-17-87   12:00p
SYS       COM     4766   3-17-87   12:00p
VDISK     SYS     3455   3-17-87   12:00p
XCOPY     EXE    11247   3-17-87   12:00p
EGA       CPI    49065   3-18-87   12:00p
LCD       CPI    10752   3-17-87   12:00p
4201      CPI    17089   3-18-87   12:00p
5202      CPI      459   3-17-87   12:00p
        22 File(s)      9216 bytes free

A>_
```

This is the directory of the PC-DOS 3.30 DOS Startup floppy disk. (If you are using a different version of DOS, the directory will be somewhat different.) Listed are the names, sizes, and creation dates and times of all the files on the DOS Startup disk. Notice that each file's name has two parts: a **primary file name**, which can be up to eight characters long, and a three-letter **extension**. We'll have more to say about this file name format later in this lesson. The number to the immediate right of each file's name is its size in bytes. A byte, you'll recall, is the amount of storage needed to hold a single character. Finally, listed with each file is the date and time it was created or last changed. So, for example, the file FORMAT.COM is made up of 11,616 bytes and was created at 12:00 P.M. on March 18, 1987.

At the very bottom of the listing, DOS informs you that there are 22 files in the directory and 9,216 bytes of empty room left on the disk. As you can imagine, it's pretty important to be able to see what's on a disk and how much room is left. For this reason, DIR is one of most frequently used DOS commands.

Incidentally, most of the files that you see in this directory listing with an extension of COM or EXE are external commands or transient routines of DOS. These are programs that reside on the DOS disk until you specifically call them up. In contrast, the DIR command is an internal command or resident routine. It too is a component program of DOS, but because it's used so frequently it's loaded into memory when DOS is booted and it's kept there. This means that DIR is not stored by itself in a separate file on the DOS disk; once you've booted up, you don't need the DOS disk in drive A to use the directory command.

Examine Another Disk's Directory

The DIR command can also be used to list the directory of a disk in a drive other than the current default drive. You can do this by specifying the disk drive designation after typing dir. For example, to list the directory of a disk in drive B, you could enter this command:

dir b:

The **b:** is the designation for the B disk drive. If you have a computer with two floppy drives, remove the DOS disk from drive A, insert it into drive B, close the door, and enter **dir b:**. You should see the same directory listing you saw in Figure 2.2. After you're done looking at the directory of drive B, make sure to put the DOS disk back into drive A.

If your computer has a hard disk drive and no second floppy drive, try entering **dir c:**. You should see some kind of directory listing, though it will probably be different from the one in Figure 2.2. This difference exists because many additional files are most likely stored on your hard disk. Note that the hard disk is usually referred to as the C drive regardless of whether a B floppy drive is installed.

Look for a Specific File

Frequently, you'd like to be able to check if a particular file is on a disk without having to look at the entire directory. The DIR command can do this for you if you give it the name of the file you're looking for. All you have to do is enter the name of the file after typing dir. Then DOS either lists an abbreviated directory with only that file in it or tells you the file is not there. For example, enter this command:

dir a:format.com

Figure 2.3 shows what you should see on your screen.

DOS File Names

This is a good time to digress a bit and discuss DOS file names in more detail. First of all, notice that each file in the directory you listed has a unique name. No two files in the same directory can have the same name because DOS wouldn't be able to tell them apart. Two files on different disks, however, can have the same name. As we mentioned before, a file's full name can consist of two parts: a primary filename and an optional extension. The first part, or **file name** as IBM calls it, can be from one to eight characters long. It can include any of the characters you see on the keyboard except for the following, which are considered invalid in file names:

. " / \ [ ] : | < > + = ; ,

Figure 2.3   Looking for a
Specific File

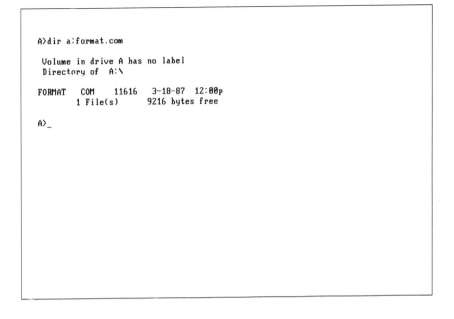

```
A>dir a:format.com

 Volume in drive A has no label
 Directory of  A:\

FORMAT    COM    11616   3-18-87  12:00p
           1 File(s)        9216 bytes free

A>_
```

The second part, an optional short name, is called an **extension**. It is separated from the primary filename by a period and has from one to three characters in it. These characters also can be any of the keyboard characters except those invalid ones we just listed. If a file's name does have an extension, you must use both parts when telling DOS to do something with that file. Extensions are most often used to further classify files. For example, here are some of the more common file name extensions along with the types of files they usually designate.

.COM	DOS external command files and other programs
.EXE	Executable program files
.SYS	DOS system configuration and device driver files
.BAT	DOS batch files
.BAS	BASIC language source code files
.PAS	Pascal language source code files
.FOR	FORTRAN language source code files
.ASM	Assembly language source code files
.TXT	Ordinary text files
.ASC	ASCII files
.DOC	Document files for some word processing programs
.WKS	Lotus 1-2-3 Release 1A worksheet files
.WK1	Lotus 1-2-3 Release 2 and 2.01 worksheet files
.DBF	dBASE III PLUS data base files

Finally, a file name can be prefaced with the designation of the disk drive that it's on. For example, A:FORMAT.COM is the specification for the file containing the FORMAT command on the DOS disk in drive A. Note that the colon must be used to separate the disk drive letter from the filename.

Look for a Specific Group of Files

Not only can the DIR command find a single file on a disk, it can also be used to list a group of files if their names have some characters in common. This is possible through the use of the DOS global filename characters, * and ?. These characters can be included in a filename or extension to give you greater flexibility in designating DOS files. The * character can be used in a file specification to symbolize any character or group of characters. For example, *.SYS means "any file with an extension of SYS." The ? character is used to symbolize any single character. For example, MO?E.COM means "any file that has an extension of COM and a four-letter filename beginning with MO and ending with an E." Both global file name characters can be used together in the same specification, too. For example, ????.* means "any file with at most four characters in its first part." Try these examples yourself:

> **dir *.sys**
> **dir mo?e.com**
> **dir ????.***

Figure 2.4 shows what you should see on your screen after entering the command **dir *.sys.**

Figure 2.4	Looking for a Group of Files

```
A>dir *.sys

  Volume in drive A has no label
  Directory of  A:\

ANSI     SYS    1678   3-17-87  12:00p
COUNTRY  SYS   11285   3-17-87  12:00p
DISPLAY  SYS   11290   3-17-87  12:00p
DRIVER   SYS    1196   3-17-87  12:00p
KEYBOARD SYS   19766   3-17-87  12:00p
PRINTER  SYS   13590   3-17-87  12:00p
VDISK    SYS    3455   3-17-87  12:00p
          7 File(s)     9216 bytes free

A>_
```

Using Special DOS Keys

Like most software, DOS assigns special meanings to certain keys and combinations of keypresses. You've already learned some of these. For example, you know that you must press the Enter key after typing in a command. This tells DOS to go ahead and process that command. The Backspace key can be used to correct typing errors on a line before the Enter key has been pressed. Finally, you learned that pressing the Control (Ctrl), Alternate (Alt), and Delete (Del) keys all at the same time will reboot DOS without having to shut off and then turn the power back on. Let's explore some of the other keys DOS uses.

Press the Escape Key to Cancel a Line

As you've probably already discovered, it's pretty easy to make typing mistakes when using a keyboard. If the command you're typing is short, and you haven't pressed the Enter key yet, the easiest way to fix a mistake is to backspace over it and retype it. If the command is long, or if you really messed up, you can cancel the entire line you just typed and start all over again. To do this, just press the Escape (Esc) key. For example, type the following line at the DOS prompt (but don't press the Enter key):

This line is really messed up!

Let's say what you really meant to type in was **dir**, and you realized your mistake before you pressed the Enter key. Just press **Escape** to cancel this line. When you do this, DOS will display a \ (backslash) after the exclamation point to signal that this line has been canceled and it will skip down to the next line so you can start over again. Enter **dir** and you'll see the familiar DOS directory again.

Press Ctrl-Num Lock to Pause Screen Scrolling

As you watch the DOS directory scroll by on the screen, notice that the first part of it disappears off the top. Sometimes, information scrolls by before you get a chance to read it all. It would be nice if you could temporarily stop the screen so that you wouldn't have to take speed reading lessons to use the computer. Fortunately, DOS can accomplish this pause for you if you hold down the Control key and press the Num Lock key. On the newer IBM Enhanced style keyboards, you have to press the Pause key instead of Ctrl-Num Lock. In either case, this action will immediately pause any screen that is scrolling by. To resume scrolling, just press any key (except a Shift, Lock, Ctrl, or Alt key). Enter **dir** and press **Ctrl-Num Lock** or the **Pause** key. Figure 2.5 shows what can happen. You can pause and resume scrolling as many times as you wish.

Press Ctrl-Break to Cancel a Command

Let's say that you've entered **dir** by mistake and you don't want to wait for the whole directory to scroll by on the screen. Or perhaps you've seen enough and you just want to stop it. You can cancel a DOS command by pressing the Control and Break keys at the same time. This action stops a command from finishing its job normally. In many cases, Ctrl-Break will also terminate programs other than just DOS commands.

**Figure 2.5   Pausing Screen
Scrolling**

```
A>dir

Volume in drive A has no label
Directory of  A:\

COMMAND  COM   25387   3-17-87   12:00p
ANSI     SYS    1678   3-17-87   12:00p
COUNTRY  SYS   11285   3-17-87   12:00p
DISPLAY  SYS   11290   3-17-87   12:00p
DRIVER   SYS    1196   3-17-87   12:00p
FASTOPEN EXE    3919   3-17-87   12:00p
FDISK    COM   48216   3-18-87   12:00p
FORMAT   COM   11616   3-18-87   12:00p
KEYB     COM    9056   3-17-87   12:00p
KEYBOARD SYS   19766   3-17-87   12:00p
MODE     COM   15487   3-17-87   12:00p
NLSFUNC  EXE    3060   3-17-87   12:00p
PRINTER  SYS   13590   3-17-87   12:00p
REPLACE  EXE   11775   3-17-87   12:00p
SELECT   COM    4163   3-17-87   12:00p
SYS      COM    4766   3-17-87   12:00p
VDI
```

Enter **dir** and press **Ctrl-Break** to terminate the directory command before it would normally finish. Figure 2.6 shows how this might appear on your screen. The ^C signifies a Ctrl-C character which has canceled the command.

On IBM PC and AT style keyboards, the Break key is right next to the Num Lock key and it's also labeled Scroll Lock. On the newer IBM Enhanced style keyboards, the Break key is the same as the Pause key. On all types of keyboards, you

**Figure 2.6   Canceling a
Command**

```
A>dir

Volume in drive A has no label
Directory of  A:\

COMMAND  COM   25387   3-17-87   12:00p
ANSI     SYS    1678   3-17-87   12:00p
COUNTRY  SYS   11285   3-17-87   12:00p
DISPLAY  SYS   11290   3-17-87   12:00p
DRIVER   SYS    1196   3-17-87   12:00p
FASTOPEN EXE    3919   3-17-87   12:00p
FDISK    COM   48216   3-18-87   12:00p
FORMAT   COM   ^C

A>_
```

can also cancel a command by holding down the Control key and typing a C. Note that Ctrl-Break (or Ctrl-C) is different from the Escape key. Escape will cancel a line typed in at the DOS prompt before the Enter key has been pressed. Ctrl-Break cancels a command after the Enter key has been pressed and the command is already executing.

Press Shift-PrtSc to Print the Screen

Frequently there's a sequence of commands or some information on the screen that you'd like to save. If you have a printer connected to your computer, DOS can produce a hard copy of everything that's currently on the display screen. On IBM PC and AT style keyboards, you press one of the shift keys along with the key marked PrtSc (Print Screen). On the newer IBM Enhanced style keyboards, you simply press the key labeled Print Screen. If you don't have a printer, you'll just have to take our word for it; if you have a printer, make sure it's turned on and press **Shift-PrtSc** or press the **Print Screen** key. You should get a copy of what's on your screen right now.

Press Ctrl-PrtSc to Echo to the Printer

Notice that the printout you got from the previous step contains only one screen of text. This output would be less than desirable if you wanted a hard copy of the entire DOS directory because the whole directory doesn't fit on a single screen at once. Pressing Ctrl-PrtSc (or Ctrl-Print Screen on the Enhanced style keyboards), however, will cause whatever you type and the computer's responses to be displayed both on the screen and sent to the printer. This echoing will continue until you press Ctrl-PrtSc again. So you could, for example, get a hard copy of your entire computer session.

To get a hard copy of the DOS disk directory, press **Ctrl-PrtSc** and then enter **dir**. You should see the directory information being displayed on the screen a bit slower, as it is also being sent to the printer. When it's done and you get the DOS prompt again, press **Ctrl-PrtSc** to turn off printer echoing.

Changing the Default Disk Drive

So far, you've been doing all your work on the A disk drive. The DOS prompt has been A>, which indicates that drive A is your current default disk drive. Thus, whenever you enter a command that doesn't explicitly specify a particular disk drive, the A drive is assumed. For example, when you enter **dir**, you get a directory of the disk in the default drive, which is currently drive A. If your computer has more than one disk drive, and most IBMs and IBM-compatibles do, you may sometime want to change your default drive from A to B, or to C if you have a hard disk. DOS makes it easy to take advantage of this feature, which is also called *switching drives*.

Enter the Designation of the New Default Drive

If you have a computer with two floppy drives, you can change your default drive from A to B by typing **b:** and pressing the **Enter** key. If you have a computer with a hard disk, you can change your default drive from A to the hard disk by typing **c:** and pressing the **Enter** key. As soon as you do this, DOS responds with a new prompt, which indicates the new default drive. So, if you have two floppy drives and you enter **b:**, DOS responds with B> as the new prompt. If you have a hard disk and you enter **c:**, DOS responds with C> as the new prompt.

Use the New Default Drive

If you have two floppy drives, remove the DOS disk from drive A and put it into the B drive and close the door. Now enter a DIR command, such as **dir *.sys.** The directory listing you get now will be of the new default drive, B or C (see Figure 2.7). Although this might not seem terribly exciting at the moment, being able to change the default drive easily enables you to make full use of all of your installed disk drives. As you become more proficient with DOS and application packages, you'll find yourself switching default disk drives often. For example, on systems with two floppy drives, you may leave the DOS disk in drive A and a disk containing a particular application program in drive B. Then, after booting up, you would switch to drive B to run your application program.

Figure 2.7   Changing the Default Disk Drive

```
A>b:

B>dir *.sys

    Volume in drive B has no label
    Directory of  B:\

ANSI     SYS     1678    3-17-87   12:00p
COUNTRY  SYS    11285    3-17-87   12:00p
DISPLAY  SYS    11290    3-17-87   12:00p
DRIVER   SYS     1196    3-17-87   12:00p
KEYBOARD SYS    19766    3-17-87   12:00p
PRINTER  SYS    13590    3-17-87   12:00p
VDISK    SYS     3455    3-17-87   12:00p
        7 File(s)        9216 bytes free

B>a:

A>_
```

Switch Back to Disk Drive A

Enter **a:** to change the default directory back to the A drive. If you put the DOS disk in drive B, remove it and put it back into the A drive.

Checking Disk and Memory Status

You've already learned how to use the DIR command to examine the contents of a disk's directory. In addition to this, DOS provides a command that can display a status report about a disk and the memory installed in your computer. This report contains some interesting and useful information. With DOS 3.30, this command is on the DOS Operating disk. If you're using DOS 3.30, take the DOS Startup disk out of drive A and replace it with the DOS Operating disk. If you're using a previous version of DOS, you don't need to change disks.

Enter CHKDSK

With the appropriate disk in drive A, type **chkdsk** and press the **Enter** key. This will invoke the DOS check disk command and produces a report on your screen that looks something like Figure 2.8. If you're not using DOS version 3.30 or if your computer has more or less than 512 kilobytes (512K) of primary memory, the numbers in your report will be different.

Figure 2.8   The CHKDSK Report

```
A>chkdsk

    362496 bytes total disk space
     53248 bytes in 3 hidden files
    300032 bytes in 22 user files
      9216 bytes available on disk

    524288 bytes total memory
    399984 bytes free

A>_
```

Examine the Status Report

This status report tells you several useful things. It tells you that the total capacity of the disk currently in the default drive is 362,496 bytes (equivalent to about 100 pages of text). Admittedly, the "53,248 bytes in 3 hidden files" statement doesn't make much sense. You can simply ignore it in this case. The hidden files mentioned in the report are parts of DOS that are kept on the disk, but do not appear in the disk directory. These files contain important DOS programs that are kept hidden from you so that you don't rename, change, or delete them. The CHKDSK report then tells you that there are 22 ordinary user files on the disk and that they occupy 300,032 bytes of space. That leaves 9,216 bytes of empty space still on the disk. Finally, CHKDSK tells you that 524,288 bytes (or 512K) of primary memory are installed in this computer and that 399,984 bytes of these are free for use by application programs. The difference between these latter two figures, 124,304 bytes, is the amount of primary memory taken up by the parts of DOS that remain resident—the command processor and the internal commands.

Clearing the Screen

By now, you've probably accumulated quite a collection of commands and directory listings on your screen. Although this does no harm, it can be a bit distracting. Or, perhaps you want to type a sequence of commands and then do a print screen, and you would like to start off with a clean slate. Don't worry, it's easy to tell DOS to erase the screen.

Enter CLS

To clear the screen, simply type **cls** and press the **Enter** key. DOS will then erase everything from the screen and start you off again with the system prompt on the first line in the upper left corner.

Formatting a Diskette

Before a new floppy disk can be used to store programs and data files, it must undergo an initial preparation known as formatting. This preparation is not done at the factory, so you must do it with your own computer for each brand new diskette you're going to use. Although you usually format a new diskette only once, you can format a previously formatted disk in order to clear it off completely. Formatting a floppy diskette consists of the following procedures.

- Checking the diskette for bad spots
- Wiping out any information that might be on the diskette
- Building a directory that will hold information about the files that will be on the diskette
- Marking off the empty space into equal-sized chunks called **sectors**
- Copying DOS onto the diskette if specified to do so

The DOS FORMAT command can automatically do all this for you.

Get a Floppy Disk to Format

For this lesson you'll need a new floppy disk or a previously used disk that can be completely erased. If you are going to format a diskette that's not new, double-check to make sure it doesn't have any programs or data files on it that you want to keep. Formatting a disk erases everything that's on it.

If it is a used 5¼-inch diskette, also make sure that it doesn't have a write-protect tab on it. If you hold the diskette right side up with your thumb on the label, you should be able to see a little square notch cut into it on the left edge. If this notch is not covered up, then it's not write-protected and it's all right to use. If the diskette has a gummed tab covering the notch, then remove the tab. If the diskette has no notch, then it's permanently write-protected and you'll have to use another diskette.

Put the DOS Startup Disk in A and the New Disk in B

On a computer with two floppy disk drives, make sure the DOS Startup disk is in drive A. Put the disk you want to format into drive B and close both doors. If your computer has only one floppy disk drive, just make sure the DOS Startup disk is in it. The FORMAT command will tell you when to put the new diskette in.

Enter the FORMAT Command

On a computer with two floppy disk drives, type **format b:** and press the **Enter** key. On a computer with just one floppy drive, type **format a:** and press the **Enter** key. The FORMAT command will then tell you to insert the new diskette into drive B (for two-floppy systems) or drive A (for single-floppy systems). Insert the disk as indicated, and press the **Enter** key.

Wait for FORMAT to Finish

The formatting procedure will take a minute or so, during which you should see the disk drive access light go on. When the procedure is done, the FORMAT command will tell you how much room is on the disk and if it contained any bad sectors. The command will then ask you if you want to format another diskette and you can enter **n** for no. You'll then get the DOS prompt back again. When you're done, your screen should look something Figure 2.9.

Figure 2.9 shows you that there are 362,496 bytes of total disk space and all of that space is available for files. In other words, no bad areas were detected. If there were any bad sectors found on the disk, less space would be available. DOS would mark these sectors as unusable and prevent them from being used to store files.

Formatting a System Diskette

The diskette you've just formatted can now be used to store programs and data files. It cannot, however, be used to boot the computer because it does not have DOS installed on it. If you want to format a diskette so that DOS is installed, the procedure is slightly different.

Figure 2.9   Formatting a
Diskette

```
A>format b:
Insert new diskette for drive B:
and strike ENTER when ready

Format complete

    362496 bytes total disk space
    362496 bytes available on disk

Format another (Y/N)?n
A>_
```

Use the /S Parameter

Many DOS commands can be given options that specify a slightly different way of performing their tasks. The FORMAT command, for example, can be instructed to install the operating system on the disk it's preparing. To do this, simply type /s after the drive designator of the disk to format. The /s tells FORMAT to put the DOS internal commands and the command processor on the disk being formatted. You can try this out by reformatting the disk you just formatted. This time, however, enter this command:

format b:/s

Examine the Disk's Directory

Now the FORMAT command will tell you that the system was transferred and that 78,848 bytes were used by the operating system. Only 283,648 bytes are left available on the disk. Enter **dir b:**. Your screen should look like Figure 2.10. Notice that only the file COMMAND.COM is on the new system disk. It does not contain any of the external command files that are on the DOS disk. So, although you could boot up with this new disk, and you could execute internal commands such as DIR, you could not use any external commands such as CHKDSK or FORMAT unless you somehow copied their command files onto it.

Copying Files

Once a diskette has been formatted, it can be used to store program and data files. But how do you get files onto the new diskette? One way is by using the DOS COPY command. The COPY command can be used to duplicate one or more files on the same or on different diskettes. As a very versatile command, COPY can be used in several different ways.

**Figure 2.10   Formatting a
System Diskette**

```
A>format b:/s
Insert new diskette for drive B:
and strike ENTER when ready

Format complete
System transferred

    362496 bytes total disk space
     78848 bytes used by system
    283648 bytes available on disk

Format another (Y/N)?n
A>dir b:

 Volume in drive B has no label
 Directory of   B:\

COMMAND  COM    25307   3-17-87  12:00p
        1 File(s)    283648 bytes free

A>_
```

Copy a Single File (the Long Way)

Let's use the COPY command to copy a single file from the DOS Startup disk onto your newly formatted disk. For starters, we'll do it the longhand way and then we'll show you the shortcut. To copy the file FORMAT.COM from the DOS Startup disk onto your new disk, first make sure the DOS Startup disk is in drive A and the new disk is in drive B. Then enter this command:

copy a:format.com b:format.com

The first file name is the *source*, or what you're copying from—the file FORMAT.COM on the disk in drive A. The second file name is the *target*, or what you're copying to—a file named FORMAT.COM on the disk in drive B. After you do this, DOS will tell you that one file was copied. If you enter **dir b:** you should see the file FORMAT.COM in the directory of the disk in drive B. Figure 2.11 shows what you should see on your screen.

Copy a Single File (the Short Way)

In most cases, if you omit certain information, DOS will assume the default values. For example, if you don't supply a disk drive designation in front of a filename, DOS will assume that you mean the default drive. Similarly, if you don't specify a name for the target file, the COPY command will assume that it is to use the same name as the source. This assumption will work as long as the source and the target files are on different disks. So, another way to copy FORMAT.COM would be to enter this command:

copy format.com b:

Figure 2.11   Copying a File

```
A>copy a:format.com b:format.com
        1 File(s) copied

A>dir b:

 Volume in drive B has no label
 Directory of  B:\

COMMAND  COM    25307   3-17-87  12:00p
FORMAT   COM    11616   3-18-87  12:00p
        2 File(s)    271360 bytes free

A>_
```

This command means copy the file FORMAT.COM on the disk in the default drive
to the disk in drive B and give it the same name. Try this shorter command. Realize, however, that you will be copying the FORMAT.COM on drive A to the
FORMAT.COM that already exists on drive B from our first copy operation. If you
choose a name that already exists as the target, DOS will happily copy over it, de-
stroying whatever was in that file before. Since we're copying the exact same file,
there's no problem here. As a rule, however, you should be very careful about the
name you choose for a target file. If it already exists on the disk you're copying to,
the original version will be overwritten.

Copy a Group of Files

By using the global file name characters * and ?, you can copy several files all at
once with a single COPY command. For example, with the DOS Startup disk in
drive A and your newly formatted disk in drive B, enter this command:

copy *.* b:

This will copy every single file on the disk in the default drive to the disk in drive
B. Figure 2.12 shows what your screen should look like when this command is
completed.

Copy a File to the Same Disk

All the examples we've covered so far have copied files from one disk to another.
Also, the target file names have all been the same as the source file names. This
arrangement, however, needn't always be so. The COPY command can be used to
duplicate a file on the same disk. The only catch is that you have to choose a different name for the target. Remember that no two files in the same directory can
have the same name.

**Figure 2.12   Copying a Group
of Files**

```
COMMAND.COM
ANSI.SYS
COUNTRY.SYS
DISPLAY.SYS
DRIVER.SYS
FASTOPEN.EXE
FDISK.COM
FORMAT.COM
KEYB.COM
KEYBOARD.SYS
MODE.COM
NLSFUNC.EXE
PRINTER.SYS
REPLACE.EXE
SELECT.COM
SYS.COM
VDISK.SYS
XCOPY.EXE
EGA.CPI
LCD.CPI
4201.CPI
5202.CPI
        22 File(s) copied

A>_
```

One common reason for duplicating a file on the same disk with a different name is for backup purposes. Let's say that you are going to change an existing file. If that file is especially important, you might want to keep a copy of the original version before you change it. One of the great advantages of using computers is the ease with which they can copy files. So, before you change your file, make a copy of it and give the copy a different name. As an example, with your DOS disk in drive A and your newly formatted disk in drive B, enter this command:

copy b:format.com b:format.bak

This will create a copy of the FORMAT.COM file on the disk in drive B and it will be named FORMAT.BAK (BAK for backup). Now you can go ahead and make your modifications, safe in the knowledge that you've retained a copy of the original file.

Copying an Entire Diskette

DOS has a more specific copy command that lets you copy an entire diskette all at once. What's more, this command automatically formats the target diskette if it's new. When you need an exact copy of an entire diskette, the DISKCOPY command can do the trick. DISKCOPY only works, however, if the source and target are the same type of disk. For instance, you cannot use the DISKCOPY command to duplicate the contents of a 5¼-inch diskette on a 3½-inch diskette. To see how the DISKCOPY command does work, let's make an exact copy of our DOS Startup diskette on the new diskette we've been working with.

Put the DOS Operating Disk in Drive A

With DOS 3.30, DISKCOPY is an external command stored on the DOS Operating disk. So, the first step is to put the DOS Operating disk into drive A.

Issue the DISKCOPY Command

If your computer has two identical floppy disk drives, enter this command:

diskcopy a: b:

If your computer has only one floppy drive or two drives that are of different types, such as a 5¼-inch drive and a 3½-inch drive, enter this command instead:

diskcopy a: a:

Follow the Directions

The DISKCOPY command will tell you which drive to put your source and target diskettes into and when to do so. Remember: the DOS Startup diskette is the source, and the new diskette is the target. If your machine has only one floppy drive, you may have to swap the source and target diskettes in drive A several times. When it's done, DISKCOPY will ask you if you want to copy another diskette and you can enter **n** for no. If you have two floppy drives, Figure 2.13 shows what you should see on your screen when DISKCOPY is done.

DISKCOPY is a very useful command for making backup copies of especially important diskettes. In fact, the documentation that comes with many software packages suggests that you use the DISKCOPY command to duplicate all of your

Figure 2.13   Copying an Entire Diskette

```
A>diskcopy a: b:

Insert SOURCE diskette in drive A:

Insert TARGET diskette in drive B:

Press any key when ready . . .

Copying 40 tracks
9 Sectors/Track, 2 Side(s)


Copy another diskette (Y/N)?n


A>_
```

original diskettes as soon as you get them. Furthermore, they say that you should put the originals away for safekeeping and only use your copies. Then, if you should accidentally erase something or if a diskette you use daily should become damaged or wear out, you would still have your original diskettes from which to make additional copies. These are good suggestions, and DISKCOPY will work fine as long as your software is not copy-protected.

Changing File Names

When a file is originally created, the name it's given isn't set in stone; DOS lets you change file names very easily. Perhaps you've thought up a more appropriate name, or you want to abbreviate a long name. Another reason to change a file name is that you want to copy a file onto a disk that already has a file of the same name. If you don't change the name of the file already on the disk, copying a new file of the same name onto the disk will destroy the original file's contents. The DOS RENAME command allows you to change the names of one or more files.

Rename a Single File

Changing a single file's name is quite easy. Just type rename (or its abbreviation, ren), followed by the file name you want to change, and then the new name that file is to have. For example, put the copy of the DOS Startup disk you made earlier in drive A and enter this command:

rename format.com format.bak

Now enter this command to see what you've done:

dir format.*

Your screen should look like Figure 2.14. The directory shows that you've successfully changed the name of FORMAT.COM to FORMAT.BAK. This procedure would be very useful if you wanted to copy a new version of the FORMAT.COM file to your disk, yet still keep a copy of the original version. Since the backup version is safely stored as FORMAT.BAK, you could now copy a new FORMAT.COM onto your disk.

Before you go on, change FORMAT.BAK back to FORMAT.COM so that the DOS Startup disk copy is like it was before. This time, however, try using the abbreviated form of the RENAME command:

ren format.bak format.com

Rename Several Files at Once

By using the global file name characters * and ?, you can rename several files at once. For example, with a single command you could rename each file on your DOS Startup disk copy with an extension of EXE, and give it an extension of BAK. Try entering this command:

ren *.exe *.bak

Figure 2.14   Renaming a File

```
A>rename format.com format.bak

A>dir format.*

 Volume in drive A has no label
 Directory of   A:\

FORMAT   BAK    11616    3-18-87  12:00p
         1 File(s)      9216 bytes free

A>_
```

Now enter this directory command to see what you've done:

dir *.bak

Your screen should look like Figure 2.15. There are now no files on your disk with
EXE extensions. They all have BAK extensions instead. Before you go on, change
them all back to the way they were with this command:

ren *.bak *.exe

Figure 2.15   Renaming a
Group of Files

```
A>ren *.exe *.bak

A>dir *.bak

 Volume in drive A has no label
 Directory of   A:\

FASTOPEN BAK     3919    3-17-87  12:00p
NLSFUNC  BAK     3060    3-17-87  12:00p
REPLACE  BAK    11775    3-17-87  12:00p
XCOPY    BAK    11247    3-17-87  12:00p
         4 File(s)      9216 bytes free

A>_
```

Erasing Files

Just as you accumulate old memos, notes, letters, and other scraps of this or that on your desk, disks can also become cluttered with unneeded files. Occasionally, it's necessary to clean up a bit and discard those items that you know you no longer need. Once you throw something away, however, it may be difficult or even impossible to get it back again. Be careful, therefore, to discard only files you're sure you can't use anymore. DOS makes it very easy to erase files, but it has no provision to unerase, or restore, them. Use the DOS ERASE command with caution.

Erase a Single File

To erase a single file, just type in **erase** or **del** (for delete) and follow it with the name of the file you want to erase. Put your DOS Startup disk copy in drive A. Because it is a copy and you know that everything on it is also on the original DOS Startup disk, you can safely erase files. Nevertheless, we want to emphasize caution again. Data and programs are most frequently lost as the result of an accidentally or carelessly entered ERASE command than from any other cause. The original 5¼-inch diskette that comes with PC-DOS when you purchase it from IBM is permanently write-protected. It has no open square notches on the left edge. For MS-DOS, however, the 5¼-inch diskette is usually not write-protected. Upon opening MS-DOS, you should immediately cover the notch on the left edge with a write-protect tab. Then you will not be able to delete any files from it with the ERASE command. The copy of the DOS disk you made, however, is not write-protected, so you can erase files from it. Again make sure that your DOS Startup disk copy is in drive A, and enter this command to erase the FORMAT.COM file:

> **erase format.com**

Now enter this directory command to see what you've done:

> **dir format.com**

The file is now gone, so your screen should look like Figure 2.16.

Erasing Several Files All at Once

By using the global file name characters * and ?, you can tell DOS to erase several files with a single ERASE command. In fact, you can even wipe out every file on the whole disk. Although this is often useful to clear off a disk, it should be used with care. Make sure that your DOS Startup disk copy is in drive A, and enter this command:

> **erase *.***

Because this is a potentially disastrous command if entered by mistake, DOS will ask you if you're sure you want to do this. If you enter **y** for yes, DOS will go ahead and erase everything. If you say **n** for no, DOS will immediately cancel the

Figure 2.16   Erasing a File

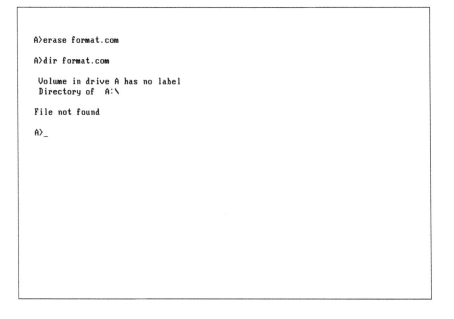

```
A>erase format.com

A>dir format.com

 Volume in drive A has no label
 Directory of   A:\

File not found

A>_
```

ERASE command. You will only get this chance to back out, however, if you use the *.* designation. If you enter **erase *.exe**, DOS does not ask you if you're sure and immediately deletes all files with an extension of EXE. So again, *be careful* with the ERASE command!

Answer **y** to erase all the files and enter **dir** to examine the disk directory. Your screen should look like Figure 2.17.

Figure 2.17   Erasing All the Files

```
A>erase *.*
Are you sure (Y/N)?y

A>dir

 Volume in drive A has no label
 Directory of   A:\

File not found

A>_
```

Displaying a Text File

So far, you've learned quite a bit about manipulating files with DOS. You haven't, however, yet looked inside one. The DOS TYPE command lets you display the contents of a file on the screen. Although TYPE will work with almost any file, unless it's a text file all you'll see is gibberish on the screen. A text file is one that is produced by a text editor or word processing program. Unfortunately, none of the files on the DOS disks are text files; they are all program files or system files. So we're going to use an interesting application of the COPY command to create a sample text file. Then we'll show you how to display that file on your screen and print it out.

Create a Sample Text File

DOS has an interesting feature that lets you treat certain devices, such as the keyboard/screen combination or the printer, as if they were files. These devices are given reserved names that you can use as if they were file names. For example, the keyboard and screen together are given the reserved name CON, which stands for console. Similarly, the primary printer connected to the computer can be referred to as PRN. You can use these *device names* in DOS commands as if they were file names.

We're going to use this feature along with the COPY command to create a text file. Put the new diskette you first formatted into disk drive A and enter this command:

copy con readme.txt

This command tells DOS to take everything you now type at the keyboard and copy it into a new file named README.TXT. Type the following text, pressing the **Enter** key at the end of each line:

This is a sample text file created to demonstrate the
use of the DOS TYPE and PRINT commands. A text file is
simply a file that contains only letters, numbers,
punctuation marks, and other symbols that appear on the
keyboard. Normally, text files are created with a text
editor or word processing program. You can, however,
create small text files directly from DOS by using the
COPY command with the device name CON. When you are
finished entering text, you must press the F6 function
key and then the Enter key to generate an end-of-file
code and have DOS copy the text file to your disk.

As the paragraph says, when you are finished entering the last line, press the **F6** function key and then press the **Enter** key. This inserts the DOS end-of-file code and completes the COPY command. Now enter **dir** to confirm that you have created the file on your disk. At this point, your screen should look like Figure 2.18.

Figure 2.18   Creating a Text File

```
A>copy con readme.txt
This is a sample text file created to demonstrate the
use of the DOS TYPE and PRINT commands.  A text file is
simply a file that contains only letters, numbers,
punctuation marks, and other symbols that appear on the
keyboard.  Normally, text files are created with a text
editor or word processing program.  You can, however,
create small text files directly from DOS by using the
COPY command with the device name CON.  When you are
finished entering text, you must press the F6 function
key and then the Enter key to generate an end-of-file
code and have DOS copy the text file to your disk.
^Z
        1 File(s) copied

A>dir

 Volume in drive A has no label
 Directory of  A:\

README   TXT      595  7-14-88  11:54a
        1 File(s)     308224 bytes free

A>_
```

Issue the TYPE Command

There's now a file named README.TXT on your disk in drive A. You can see the contents of this file by using the DOS TYPE command. To use the TYPE command, simply enter **type** followed by the name of the file you wish to display. Enter this command to see what's in the file README.TXT:

type readme.txt

DOS will then display the contents of README.TXT on your screen, as shown in Figure 2.19.

Figure 2.19   Displaying a Text File

```
A>type readme.txt
This is a sample text file created to demonstrate the
use of the DOS TYPE and PRINT commands.  A text file is
simply a file that contains only letters, numbers,
punctuation marks, and other symbols that appear on the
keyboard.  Normally, text files are created with a text
editor or word processing program.  You can, however,
create small text files directly from DOS by using the
COPY command with the device name CON.  When you are
finished entering text, you must press the F6 function
key and then the Enter key to generate an end-of-file
code and have DOS copy the text file to your disk.

A>_
```

Printing a Text File

Most text files eventually wind up on paper; after all, the end product of word processing is usually a hard-copy document. The DOS PRINT command lets you send a text file directly to the printer, instead of displaying it on the screen. You'll need a printer for this lesson, as well as the diskette with the README.TXT file you just created.

Put the DOS Operating Disk in Drive A

Unlike TYPE, the PRINT command is an external command that resides on the DOS Operating diskette. (DOS versions prior to 3.30 have the PRINT command on the diskette labeled DOS.) So, you must first put the disk containing the PRINT command into drive A. If your computer has two floppy drives, put the disk containing README.TXT in drive B.

Turn on Your Printer

Before you can print a file, your printer must be turned on. Make sure that the power is on and that the printer is on line, that is, connected to your computer.

Issue the PRINT Command

To use the PRINT command, just type PRINT followed by the name of the file you want to print. You can preface the name of the file by the letter of the disk drive on which it is stored. Even if your computer has only one floppy drive, enter this command:

print b:readme.txt

After you do this, DOS will ask you to supply the following:

```
Name of list device [PRN]:
```

This rather cryptic request allows you to tell DOS which printer to use if you have more than one connected to your computer. The expression [PRN] means that unless you tell it otherwise, DOS will send the output to the default printer, which has the device name PRN. If you have only one printer, then it is the default printer. All you have to do here is just press the **Enter** key. DOS will ask you to supply the list device only the first time you use PRINT for any given computer session.

If you have a B floppy drive in your computer, PRINT will inform you that it's currently printing README.TXT and your printer should be merrily pounding away (unless, of course, it's a laser or ink-jet printer). Figure 2.20 shows what you should see on your screen.

If your computer only has one floppy drive, then DOS will ask you to do the following:

```
Insert diskette for drive B: and strike any key when ready.
```

Figure 2.20   Printing a Text File

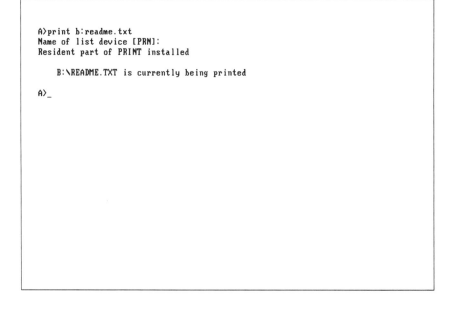

```
A>print b:readme.txt
Name of list device [PRN]:
Resident part of PRINT installed

    B:\README.TXT is currently being printed

A>_
```

This is an example of a handy DOS feature. If you have only an A drive, and you issue a command that refers to drive B, DOS will temporarily pretend that drive A is drive B. It will then ask you to insert into drive A the disk you would have put into drive B if you had a drive B. So, if you have only one floppy drive, put the README.TXT disk in drive A when you get this message and press any key to finish the printing process.

The end result of this PRINT command will be a printout of the text in file README.TXT that you saw on your screen (see Figure 2.19) when you used the TYPE command.

Running a Program

This lesson won't really teach you anything new, because you've been running programs throughout this entire chapter. Every time you entered a DOS command, you were running a program. Remember: files with an EXE or COM extension are executable programs that you can run.

Insert the Appropriate Disk

Just as you have to put the appropriate DOS disk in drive A when you want to use an external command, you must make sure a program is stored on a disk in one of your drives when you want to run the program. For example, to run an application program such as WordPerfect, you must have its disk in the A or B drive. Or, if your computer has a hard disk, you could run the program off the C drive provided that a copy resides there. If your computer is connected to a local area network, you could run the program if it's stored on your network's server disk. DOS must be able to find a program before it can be run.

Switch to the Appropriate Drive, if Necessary

For example, if you have two floppy drives, the DOS disk in A, and the application's program disk in B, you could switch to drive B as you learned earlier (see Figure 2.7). The alternative to switching drives is to preface the program name you enter with the letter of the drive on which the program's file is stored.

Type the Program Name and Press the Enter Key

As you now know, you invoke an external DOS command by entering its name along with any necessary file names and other information. In this sense, application programs such as WordPerfect are the same as DOS external commands; all you have to do to run them is type the name of the EXE or COM file in which they're stored and press the **Enter** key. So, for example, to run the WordPerfect program off your current default drive, just type **wp** and press the **Enter** key. Or, if your default drive is A and the WordPerfect disk is in drive B, you could enter **b:wp** from the A drive to run the program. When you do either of these, DOS will load the WordPerfect program into primary memory and begin executing it.

Working with Subdirectories

As you can imagine, people who use microcomputers extensively often generate large numbers of files. Before hard disks became common, users had many different floppy disks on which to store their files. Organizing files meant physically organizing diskettes by keeping them well-labeled and storing them in subdivided boxes, racks, or cabinets. Once hard disks became common, however, operating systems had to devise a better method of organizing large numbers of files. Even a modest 20-megabyte hard disk can store thousands of different files. Looking for a particular file among hundreds or thousands of files is time consuming and tedious. Consequently, most microcomputer operating systems, including DOS, have evolved a *hierarchical* method of organizing files into groups. Such a system allows you to cluster files into orders or ranks, each subordinate to the one above. These groups of files, called **subdirectories**, are like file folders that can be nested within one another. Disks can be organized into subdirectories, each of which can contain files and other subdirectories.

Subdirectories are invaluable tools for organizing programs and data files on high-capacity storage devices. In addition, subdirectories make it easier for the operating system to locate a particular file because large numbers of files are divided into smaller groups. Although subdirectories are almost always found on hard disks, they are occasionally used on floppy disks, too. DOS includes commands that let you create, access, and remove subdirectories.

With DOS, every disk has a single main directory, known as the **root directory**. DOS automatically creates a root directory on every disk you format. This is the directory you are in when you first boot up DOS or when you first change your default drive. The root directory itself has no name, but it's represented by a backslash (\).

Create a Subdirectory

Let's create a subdirectory on the new floppy disk you have used previously (the one with README.TXT on it). Put this disk into drive A, and enter this command:

md a:\text

The internal DOS command MD or MKDIR (short for Make Directory) is used to create a new subdirectory. It is followed by the **path** of the new subdirectory. The path is an optional disk drive specifier followed by a list of subdirectory names, separated by backslashes. The rules for naming subdirectories are the same as the rules for naming files. The simplest path is a single backslash \, which represents the root directory of your current default drive. The command you just entered creates a subdirectory named TEXT on the disk in drive A. This subdirectory is one level below the root directory.

Change to the Subdirectory

Think of the subdirectory as a separate "sub-disk" on your disk. Enter **dir** to display a directory of your disk. Now enter the Change Directory (CD or CHDIR) command to move into your new subdirectory:

cd a:\text

Enter **dir** again and Figure 2.21 shows what you should see on your screen. The first DIR gives a directory listing of the root directory of the floppy disk. It contains the README.TXT file and the TEXT subdirectory. The second DIR gives a directory listing inside the TEXT subdirectory.

Figure 2.21   Changing to a Subdirectory

```
A>md a:\text

A>dir

 Volume in drive A has no label
 Directory of  A:\

README   TXT       595   7-14-88  11:54a
TEXT          <DIR>       7-14-88   2:31p
        2 File(s)    307200 bytes free

A>cd a:\text

A>dir

 Volume in drive A has no label
 Directory of  A:\TEXT

.             <DIR>       7-14-88   2:31p
..            <DIR>       7-14-88   2:31p
        2 File(s)    307200 bytes free

A>_
```

Copy a File to the Subdirectory

Right now, the TEXT subdirectory has no ordinary user files in it. You can, however, copy your own files to this subdirectory just as if it were a separate disk. For example, let's copy the README.TXT file from the root directory to the TEXT subdirectory. Enter this command:

copy a:\readme.txt

This command copies the file README.TXT from the root directory of drive A to your current subdirectory, which happens to be TEXT. Now enter **dir** and you'll see that a copy of README.TXT now also exists in the TEXT subdirectory. It's important to realize that there are two separate copies of README.TXT now on the disk: one in the root directory and one in the TEXT subdirectory.

Remove the Subdirectory

Once you're in a subdirectory, you can almost think of it as a separate disk. You can run programs from within a subdirectory. Many DOS commands that deal with files will operate only on the files in your current subdirectory unless you specify otherwise. For example, you can delete every file in a subdirectory without affecting any files in the root directory or any other subdirectories. For example, try entering this command:

erase *.*

Answer **y** for yes when the ERASE command asks if you are sure that this is what you want to do. DOS will erase every file in your current directory, the TEXT subdirectory. Enter **dir** to see that this is true. Now change back to the root directory by entering this command:

cd a:

Now enter another **dir** command and you will see that the README.TXT file in the root is still intact.

Just as you must occasionally delete unneeded files, sometimes subdirectories must be removed, too. Let's say that you are finished with the TEXT subdirectory and you want to remove it from your disk. To do this you must first erase any files inside the subdirectory and move out of the subdirectory. We've already done this. Now you can enter the Remove Directory command (RD or RMDIR) to remove the empty TEXT subdirectory from your disk:

rd a:\text

If you enter **dir**, you will see that the TEXT subdirectory has indeed been removed, and your disk is the same as it was when you began this section.

Using Batch Files

A **batch file** is a text file that contains a list of commands or programs to be run. Batch files are usually created with a text editor or word processing program, but you can easily create short ones using the COPY command method we outlined on page 51. In DOS, every batch file must have an extension of BAT. Once it has been created, a batch file is invoked by typing its file name and pressing the **Enter** key. When this is done, DOS executes each command or program listed in the batch file, one at a time. DOS includes features that enable experienced users to construct complex and very helpful batch files. Even if you never actually make your own batch files, you will undoubtedly use some made by others or included with application packages. As an example, let's create and use a simple batch file.

Create the Batch File

As we said, batch files are usually created with a text editor or word processor. Short ones, however, can be easily created with the COPY command. At this point, you should still have the floppy disk with the README.TXT file on it in drive A. Enter this command to create a new batch file named SHOW.BAT on your current disk:

copy con show.bat

Now you can enter the text that will go inside the file SHOW.BAT. Type the following three commands, pressing the Enter key after each one:

cls
dir
type readme.txt

Finally, press the **F6** function key to generate the end-of-file code and then press the **Enter** key. Enter **dir** to examine the current contents of your disk and see that the batch file has indeed been created. Your screen should look like Figure 2.22.

Figure 2.22   Creating a Batch File

```
A>copy con show.bat
cls
dir
type readme.txt
^Z
        1 File(s) copied

A>dir

  Volume in drive A has no label
  Directory of  A:\

README    TXT       595   7-14-88   11:54a
SHOW      BAT        27   7-15-88    9:14a
          2 File(s)    307200 bytes free

A>_
```

Use the Batch File

Running a batch file is just like executing a command or running an application program. You type its filename (without the extension) and press the Enter key. To run your newly created batch file, simply type **show** and press the **Enter** key. Figure 2.23 shows the result.

Figure 2.23   Using a Batch File

```
A>dir

 Volume in drive A has no label
 Directory of  A:\

README   TXT      595   7-14-88  11:54a
SHOW     BAT       27   7-15-88   9:14a
         2 File(s)    307200 bytes free

A>type readme.txt
This is a sample text file created to demonstrate the
use of the DOS TYPE and PRINT commands.  A text file is
simply a file that contains only letters, numbers,
punctuation marks, and other symbols that appear on the
keyboard.  Normally, text files are created with a text
editor or word processing program.  You can, however,
create small text files directly from DOS by using the
COPY command with the device name CON.  When you are
finished entering text, you must press the F6 function
key and then the Enter key to generate an end-of-file
code and have DOS copy the text file to your disk.

A>
A>_
```

Most commands and programs that you can run directly from the DOS prompt can be put inside a batch file. Batch files allow you to automate frequently executed series of commands. They also allow experts to set up complex sequences of commands to be run by novices. For example, many new application programs must be installed on your system before you can use them. In some cases, this installation process can be quite involved. Most software developers, therefore, include one or more batch files that make the installation process much easier for users.

The AUTOEXEC.BAT File

The most commonly used batch file is a special one named AUTOEXEC.BAT—the auto-execute batch file. Whenever you boot up your computer, DOS searches the root directory of the current drive for this AUTOEXEC.BAT file. If there is no AUTOEXEC.BAT file present, DOS simply asks you to supply the current date and time, and then presents its prompt. If, on the other hand, AUTOEXEC.BAT is found, the batch file is automatically executed. Since the AUTOEXEC.BAT file is automatically invoked every time you boot up your computer, it is ideal for listing any commands and programs you always run when you first turn on your machine. For example, if there is a subdirectory that you always use, you could put a CD (Change Directory) command in the AUTOEXEC.BAT to move into that subdirectory. Most DOS users eventually set up their own AUTOEXEC.BAT files or have someone else help them do so.

Summary

In this chapter of the *Software Guide*, you've learned several of the most frequently used DOS commands. To be sure, we haven't covered every DOS command or discussed every feature of this rich and powerful operating system. Most computer users, however, find that they primarily spend their time running application programs such as Lotus 1-2-3. Their direct interaction with DOS is, for the most part, on the level of the commands and procedures we've introduced in this chapter. To learn even more about DOS, consult one of the many books completely devoted to the subject. Or, refer to the documentation provided by IBM and Microsoft: the *DOS User's Guide* and the *DOS Reference* manual.

Exercises

Multiple Choice

Choose the best selection to complete each statement.

_____ 1. An operating system is a(n)
    (a) hardware component of a mainframe computer system.
    (b) application program that produces text files.
    (c) set of programs that lets you use your computer's hardware and software resources.
    (d) system of procedures for operating a computer.

_____ 2. Transient routines or external commands are
    (a) kept in primary memory until the computer is shut off.
    (b) kept on disk and loaded into memory only when needed.
    (c) kept in ROM (read-only memory) chips.
    (d) used once then deleted.

_____ 3. The driving force behind each new DOS release has usually been
    (a) the addition of a new disk drive capability.
    (b) an effort to improve the user interface.
    (c) an attempt to eliminate all bugs.
    (d) an effort by IBM and Microsoft to make more money.

_____ 4. Upwardly compatible means that
    (a) you cannot take advantage of the new version's abilities.
    (b) all old software versions must be upgraded.
    (c) new hardware must be purchased to use the new version.
    (d) operations that worked with former versions work with the new version.

5. A command is a(n)
   - (a) combination of hardware switch settings.
   - (b) operating system directive issued to a user.
   - (c) application package instruction.
   - (d) word or abbreviation that tells DOS to run a program.

6. To boot DOS with the power off
   - (a) insert the DOS disk and turn on the power.
   - (b) hold down the Control, Alternate, and Delete keys at the same time.
   - (c) turn the power on and issue the boot command.
   - (d) turn the power on and kick the computer.

7. Pressing Ctrl-Alt-Del will
   - (a) invoke a DOS transient routine.
   - (b) delete a file.
   - (c) reboot DOS without having to shut off the computer.
   - (d) execute an application program.

8. The DOS directory command is
   - (a) DIRECT.
   - (b) LIST.
   - (c) DIR.
   - (d) CATALOG.

9. The two parts of a DOS file name are
   - (a) a disk drive designation and a disk sector number.
   - (b) a primary file name and an optional extension.
   - (c) a primary file name and a creation date.
   - (d) a primary extension and the size in bytes.

10. Files with COM and EXE extensions usually designate
   - (a) external commands and executable program files.
   - (b) command files and extension files.
   - (c) configuration files and batch files.
   - (d) BASIC and FORTRAN files.

11. Pressing Ctrl-Num Lock or Pause will
   - (a) echo input and output to the printer.
   - (b) print the screen.
   - (c) cancel a command.
   - (d) temporarily halt screen scrolling.

12. To change the default disk drive
   - (a) put a new disk in drive A.
   - (b) type the new disk drive designation and press **Enter**.
   - (c) open up the computer and replace the faulty drive.
   - (d) issue the DIR command.

13. To display a disk and memory status report, enter
   - (a) status.
   - (b) dir.
   - (c) chkdsk.
   - (d) diskcopy.

14. Formatting a diskette does not
   - (a) check the diskette for bad sectors.
   - (b) wipe out all data on the diskette.
   - (c) mark off the space into sectors.
   - (d) sort files in the directory.

15. To format a system diskette you must
   - (a) reboot the system.
   - (b) use the /s parameter with the FORMAT command.
   - (c) enter the COPY command.
   - (d) purchase a master diskette from IBM.

_____ 16. One way to copy every file from disk drive A to B is to
       (a) enter copy a:*.* b:.   (c) enter copy a: b:.
       (b) enter dir a: b:.   (d) use the REN command.

_____ 17. To make an exact copy of an entire diskette, use
       (a) COPY.   (c) DIR.
       (b) DISKCOPY.   (d) Ctrl-Alt-Del.

_____ 18. Entering the command del *.* will
       (a) reboot the system.   (c) rename all files on the disk in the
       (b) copy all files to the disk in the   default drive.
          default drive.   (d) erase all files from the disk in the
                   default drive.

_____ 19. To display a text file on your screen use the
       (a) PRINT command.   (c) TYPE command.
       (b) DISKCOPY command.   (d) Ctrl-Num Lock key.

_____ 20. To run a program or batch file you must
       (a) type its filename and press the   (c) press Ctrl-Break.
          Enter key.   (d) first make a backup copy.
       (b) reboot DOS.

Fill-In

1. A disk operating system has many utilities for dealing with the _____ that are stored on disks.

2. _____ is usually used with IBM computers while _____ is usually used with compatible computers such as those made by Compaq, AT&T, Tandy, and Zenith.

3. Booting DOS refers to the process of loading the disk operating system into _____.

4. In many cases, when you first boot DOS it asks you to enter the _____ and the _____.

5. The _____ command can be used to list the names, sizes, and creation dates and times of all the files on a disk.

6. A file's primary filename can have from one to _____ characters in it.

7. File name extensions are often used to _____ files.

8. You can press the _____ key to cancel a command if you haven't pressed the Enter key yet.

9. You can press _____ to cancel a command before it finishes normally.

10. The DOS _____ indicates the current default disk drive.

11. The _____ command can tell you how much memory is installed in your computer.

12. A diskette must be _____ before it can be used to store program and data files.

13. The _____ command can be used to duplicate one or more files on the same or on different disks.

14. _____ file name characters can be used to refer to several files at the same time.

15. The DISKCOPY command will automatically _____ the target diskette if it's brand new.

16. The REN command can be used to _____ one or more file names.

17. To remove a file from a disk, you would enter _____ or _____ followed by the file's name.

18. The TYPE command lets you display _____ files on your screen.

19. You could use the _____ command to produce a hard copy of a text file.

20. The DOS commands used to create, change to, and remove subdirectories are _____, _____, and _____.

Short Problems

1. If you have access to a diskette other than the DOS floppies, produce a directory listing of the files on it. If you have a printer, try using Ctrl-PrtSc to turn on printer echoing before you issue the directory command so that you can get a hard copy.

2. When you booted DOS, you were asked to supply the date and time. Two DOS commands, DATE and TIME, tell you the current date and time and let you change these settings. Try the DATE and TIME commands. If you don't want to change the date and time settings, just press the **Enter** key when asked for the new date or time. Notice how DOS automatically figures out and displays the day of the week.

3. Use the * global file name character to produce a directory listing of all the files on the DOS Startup disk with an EXE extension.

4. Use the * global file name character to produce a directory listing of all the files on the DOS Startup disk whose names begin with the letter K.

5. Use the ? global file name character to produce a directory listing of all the files on the DOS Startup disk that have an E as the second letter of their primary filenames.

6. You've probably noticed the "Volume in drive A has no label" message DOS gives when it displays a directory of the DOS disk. The FORMAT command has an option that lets you specify a name for a disk, or volume label as DOS calls it. Try formatting a blank disk with this command:

   format b:/v

   If you have only one floppy drive, enter this instead:

   format a:/v

The /V is an optional parameter that tells the FORMAT command to ask you for a volume label. Think up a name of 11 characters or less and enter it when FORMAT tells you to. When you're done, check the disk's directory to see your volume label displayed.

7. DOS versions 3.0 and newer have a command that lets you supply or change a volume label without having to reformat a disk. If you have DOS 3.0 or newer try using the LABEL command on the new disk you've just formatted. Note that you can't change the label of the original DOS disk because it's write-protected.

8. If you don't know what DOS version you have, enter **ver**. This command displays the number of the DOS version you are using.

9. Another way to find out the volume label of a disk is to use the VOL command. Enter **vol a:**. This command displays the volume label (if there is one) of the disk in drive A.

10. It is possible to display a text file on your screen by using the COPY command instead of the TYPE command. In certain cases, DOS can refer to its peripheral devices as if they were files. There are several file names that have a special meaning to DOS. These are called DOS device names. For example, CON refers to the console, or the keyboard and screen. Put the disk with your README.TXT file in drive A and enter this command:

   copy readme.txt con

   You should see the text of file README.TXT displayed on your screen just as if you used the TYPE command.

11. Just as CON is a DOS device name that refers to the keyboard and screen, PRN is a DOS device name that refers to the printer. Try using the COPY command to get a printout of the README.TXT file.

12. The DIR command has two optional parameters that can be useful when looking at disks with lots of files on them. The /P parameter will automatically pause the display when the screen is full and let you press a key to continue. The /W parameter will display the directory in a wide format across the screen, omitting the sizes and creation dates and times so that more file names will fit at once. Put your DOS Startup disk in drive A and try entering these options:

   dir /p
   dir /w

3

Introduction to BASIC

Learning Objectives

After reading this chapter you should understand:

- What programming languages are, and what they are used for
- What source files, compilers, and interpreters are
- The general format of a BASIC program
- The general format of a line of BASIC code
- How to specify a numeric variable
- How to create a numeric expression using BASIC operators
- How to specify a string variable
- How to create string expressions
- What a system variable is
- How to document programs so they are readable and maintainable

Introduction

In Chapter 1, we introduced you to general concepts of microcomputer hardware and operation. In the second chapter, you were introduced to DOS, the operating system that controls the operation of IBM and IBM-compatible microcomputers. Now that you have some familiarity with the microcomputer and how it operates, we turn to the BASIC programming language.

This chapter will introduce you to simple BASIC programming, describing the general format of a BASIC program, and introducing some BASIC program commands. After completing this chapter, you should have a good understanding of what variables are, how to specify them in certain BASIC commands, and their naming conventions. You will also learn how to insert comments in your programs so that the programs will be easy to read and maintain.

What Are Programming Languages?

As stated in the first chapter, a computer without software is not of much use. Software is the program or set of programs that tells the computer how to do various computing tasks (applications). Programming languages, such as BASIC, are the tools used to create software packages.

High-Level and Low-Level Languages

For any type of computer, there are two general categories of programming languages, low-level and high-level. **Low-level languages** are closer to "machine communication," that is, actual numbers or digits, while **high-level languages** correspond more closely to "human communication," using English words and mathematical formulas. Low-level languages are often used in the creation of system software. For example, DOS, the operating system discussed in Chapter 2, is written in a low-level language.

Machine language, consisting entirely of strings of 0's and 1's (corresponding to "off"s and "on"s), is one type of low-level language and the only language that the actual hardware can deal with.

Another type of low-level language, **assembly language**, uses symbols to specify computer instructions, constants, and data areas. Programs written in assembly language are translated into machine language through the use of an assembler. While assembly language programs do not look like machine language, they still look quite cryptic. Figure 3.1 is an example of an assembly language program written for an IBM-compatible microcomputer.

Figure 3.1   An Assembly Language Program

```
; This program calculates the sum of two numbers, subtracts a third number
  and stores the result in memory.
;
;
DATA      SEGMENT                        ; Define the data to be used.
;
NUMBER1 DW        20                     ; Store the 1st number (20) in memory.
NUMBER2 DW        35                     ; Store the 2nd number (35) in memory.
NUMBER3 DW        12                     ; Store the 3rd number (12) in memory.
RESULT  DW        ?                      ; Reserve a place in memory for the result.
;
DATA      ENDS
;
;
CODE      SEGMENT                        ; Describe the processing steps.
          ASSUME   CS:CODE,DS:DATA ; Tell computer where to find code and data.
;
          MOV      AX,NUMBER1            ; Move the 1st number into the accumulator.
          MOV      BX,NUMBER2            ; Move the 2nd number into the BX register.
          ADD      AX,BX                 ; Add the two and place result in accumulator.
          MOV      BX,NUMBER3            ; Move the 3rd number into the BX register.
          SUB      AX,BX                 ; Subtract 3rd number from previous sum.
          MOV      RESULT,AX             ; Move the result from accumulator into memory.
;
CODE      ENDS
          END
```

Low-level languages are useful because they allow fast and direct manipulation of storage, computer registers, and peripheral devices such as printers, but applications programmers have little use for them since they are usually hard to understand and tedious to write.

High-level languages, on the other hand, are widely used in the creation of application software. High-level languages have several advantages over low-level languages. They are much easier to read, understand, and maintain. Programs can be larger and more complex without becoming too complicated for the programmer to follow. Because of the Englishlike statements that high-level languages use, programming errors are much easier to find. In addition, high-level languages are usually uniform from one type of computer to the next, while low-level languages are machine-specific, that is, each type of computer has its own version of machine language. BASIC, FORTRAN, COBOL, PL/I, Pascal, and Ada are all examples of high-level languages.

Short History and Features of the BASIC Programming Language

The BASIC programming language was developed by Professors John Kemeny and Thomas Kurtz of Dartmouth College, in 1964. BASIC, an acronym for "*Beginners' All-purpose Symbolic Instruction Code*," was created for beginners in computer science. Although designed as a teaching tool, BASIC has been widely accepted, especially by microcomputer users. Programs written in BASIC on one computer can be copied to another computer system and run with little or no modification. Programs that run with little or no modification on several types of computers are called **portable** programs.

Before BASIC was devised, few accessible programming languages existed, and computing was more difficult in general. BASIC's most striking feature is its simplicity. It is very easy to learn and use. Users can often begin to write and run functional programs using only a few simple commands after only a few hours of instruction and practice. Derived from the earlier high-level programming languages FORTRAN and ALGOL, BASIC resembles a somewhat simplified version of FORTRAN. BASIC is an interactive language by design, that is, it permits the programmer to interact with the computer by entering, testing, or changing instructions. It is used for both computational (mathematical) and alphanumeric (textual) data-processing tasks, and has been extensively employed by users of all types of small computers. Pared-down versions of BASIC are even available for notebook and pocket-sized computers.

There are several different versions, or dialects, of BASIC. The most popular are Microsoft's BASIC and QuickBASIC, Borland International's Turbo BASIC, and True BASIC, a powerful, structured version of BASIC from its originators, Kemeny and Kurtz. BASICA, a version of BASIC written to run on IBM PCs, was quite popular, but it is being replaced by the many other versions. GWBASIC, the more popular extension of BASICA, also includes graphics capabilities. Fortunately, a core of certain BASIC features is common to almost every version. The Microsoft BASICs are upwardly compatible and therefore BASICA programs will run in GWBASIC and GWBASIC programs will run in QuickBASIC.

How Programming Languages Work

When you write a BASIC program to solve a problem, you'll be creating a set of instructions that will be input into an **interpreter** or **compiler** that will ultimately convert your program into a set of instructions to tell the computer what to do. The programs you'll be creating are known as **source files**. All high-level programming languages are based on the concept of reading a source file and converting this **source code** into **machine code** that the computer will understand. Source code is another name for the program in the source file. Machine code is the series of 1's and 0's that make up the language that a computer understands.

Programs are created with the use of an **editor**. An editor is a software program included as part of the computer's operating system. In this case, DOS allows you to enter programming language commands through a keyboard into the computer's memory.

Once the entire program has been input into the computer, the source file must be saved onto an auxiliary storage device, normally a magnetic disk. The source file or program must be stored before the computer is turned off if you wish to access the program after you restart your computer.

When the program is ready to be run, the programming language commands in your source file are translated into machine code that the computer can understand and execute. It is important to note that the computer does not execute the program you keyed into the computer using the editor, but executes a translated version of your program. A programming language can be translated into machine code using either a compiler or an interpreter. Figure 3.2 shows the progression of steps from entering the program to execution.

Compilers

Some programming languages rely on compilers to translate programs into machine code that the computer can understand. A compiler reads a whole source file to create another file, commonly referred to as an **object file** or **module**. Just as a source file contains programming language commands, a module contains machine language commands. A module can be run over and over again, eliminating the need to repeatedly translate a program into machine code. Microsoft's Quick-BASIC is an example of a BASIC compiler.

Interpreters

Some programming languages, including many popular versions of BASIC, rely on interpreters to perform the translation from a source file into machine code. Interpreters read a source file one line at a time, translating each line into machine code, and then executing the machine code for that line. For every line of a BASIC program you key in, the BASIC interpreter will read that single line into memory and translate the BASIC programming commands into machine code, allowing the computer to execute a program. GWBASIC, which this book is based on, is the BASIC interpreter that comes as part of MS-DOS.

Figure 3.2

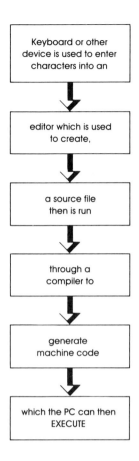

A BASIC Program

A BASIC program consists of several lines of information telling the GWBASIC interpreter, and ultimately the computer, what to do. The general format of a line within a BASIC program is a line number, followed by a BASIC command, followed by instructions, data, or other command-specific parameters, in the following form:

```
ln COMMAND parameters
```

where *ln* refers to a line number, *COMMAND* refers to a BASIC command, and *parameters* refers to additional command-specific instructions. Some simple examples of lines from a BASIC program follow.

```
10 LET SALARY = WAGE * HOURS
```

or

```
20 PRINT SALARY
```

You can see from the examples that each line begins with a number. This number identifies the line, and thus is called a **line number**. Line numbers are used by BASIC to determine the order of execution of commands within a program. Lines are always executed from the smallest line number up to the largest. Line numbers can be any whole number from 1 to 65528 (note that commas are not used in line numbers). It is good programming practice to use line numbers in increments of 10 to make a program easy to read and easy to modify. BASIC reads, interprets, and executes one line of BASIC code at a time, sequentially, based on line numbers. When you are keying in a BASIC program for the first time, you must specify a unique line number for every line of code in your program. (Note that in Quick-BASIC and some other new structured versions of BASIC the line numbers may be omitted.)

Following the line number in a BASIC program is the BASIC command. BASIC has a finite set of commands that direct the computer to perform various tasks to solve a problem. BASIC is easy to learn since all of the command names are Englishlike. For example, when you want to display information to the computer screen, you use the command PRINT, or when you want to gather information from a program user, you use the command INPUT. In the previous example, the command LET is used to instruct BASIC to assign a value to the variable, SALARY. The LET command is followed by a formula that calculates a salary, based on the values in the variables WAGE and HOURS. We'll discuss what variables are a little later on.

The final part of a BASIC program line is command-specific parameters. Depending on which command is specified on a line, there are additional items of information that are used by BASIC when the command gets interpreted and executed. In one of the lines of BASIC above, we want to display the value of a variable called SALARY, so we specify the variable name SALARY after the PRINT command.

Let's look at a small BASIC program. The following sample program solves a simple salary computation problem. John Doe earns $4.50 per hour. He works 8 hours a day and 5 days a week.

```
10 ' THIS SAMPLE BASIC PROGRAM COMPUTES WEEKLY SALARY
20 LET SALARY = 4.5 * 8 * 5
30 LET NAM$ = "John Doe"
40 PRINT NAM$" makes $"SALARY"per week."
50 END
```

Let's examine each line of the program.

Comments

Line number 10 is a program comment. Comments are very important in programs because they can describe what task a program does or what problem a program solves. Comments are also a good way of describing how a program operates. Special considerations and operational notes should be included within the program as comments. Comments allow others to use and understand your programs, and serve to remind you about the structure of your own programs, making changes and improvements easier. Comments are an essential element of good programming style. (Good programming style will be discussed more fully later in this chapter and in other chapters.)

The single quote after the line number identifies the rest of the line as a comment. Alternatively, the comment could be written as

```
10 REM THIS SAMPLE PROGRAM COMPUTES WEEKLY SALARY
```

or

```
10 REM THIS SAMPLE PROGRAM
15 REM COMPUTES WEEKLY SALARY
```

In this case, the BASIC command REM is used to identify the rest of the line as a comment. (See box for more explanation of the REM command.)

The REM Command

Purpose   To insert a comment into a program

Format   ln REM text   OR   ln ' text
where *ln* is a valid line number

Examples   10 REM This is a comment
               20 ' This is another comment
               30 PRINT SALARY   ' And yet another comment

Notes   Comments are not executed by BASIC; they are only displayed when listing or editing a program. REM and a single quote (') are interchangeable. A single quote can be placed anywhere after a line number, in which case all text on that line following the quote will be considered a comment.

Comments can also be placed toward the end of a line, after some other BASIC command. The single quote can be used anywhere on any line of a BASIC program, after the line number, to instruct BASIC that the rest of the line is a comment and is not to be executed.

Assignment Statements

Let's continue looking at our sample program.

```
20 LET SALARY = 4.5 * 8 * 5
30 LET NAM$ = "John Doe"
```

The lines numbered 20 and 30 are **assignment statements**. These statements assign values to SALARY and NAM$ respectively. Specifying 4.5 * 8 * 5 instructs BASIC to compute the product of the numbers 4.5, 8, and 5 (a salary of $4.50 times the 8 hours in a normal working day times the 5 days in a normal work week). The product, in this case 180, will be assigned to the variable SALARY. The asterisk, used here to indicate multiplication, is a numerical operator; numerical operators will be discussed later in this chapter.

"John Doe" in quotes shows how character (text) information gets assigned. Double quotes begin and end all character sequences (or strings) when they are specified in BASIC commands. Later in this chapter, we will discuss assignment statements in detail.

PRINT Statement

Line number 40 displays a message to the screen, consisting of message text and the values assigned to NAM$ and SALARY.

```
40 PRINT NAM$" makes $"SALARY"per week."
```

When the program is executed, line 40 will cause BASIC to display on the PC screen:

```
John Doe makes $ 180     per week.
```

The PRINT command displays output to the screen. The PRINT command will be described in detail in the next chapter.

END Command

The last line of the program contains the word END.

```
50 END
```

When executed, the END command causes BASIC to stop interpretation of the program and return to BASIC edit mode (see box for more detail).

The END Command

Purpose   To cause BASIC to stop the interpretation of a program

Format   ln END
where *ln* is a valid line number

Example   330 END

Notes   Any commands on lines following the END command will not be executed. It is good programming practice to place the END command at the bottom of your program.

Multiple Statements on One Line

The sample program above could have been written with multiple BASIC statements on a line, as in the following.

```
10 'THIS SAMPLE BASIC PROGRAM COMPUTES WEEKLY SALARY
20 LET SALARY = 4.5 * 8 * 5 : LET NAM$ = "John Doe"
30 PRINT NAM$" makes $"SALARY"per week." : END
```

The use of the colon within a BASIC program instructs BASIC that more than one statement is specified on the line. While the program will appear to be shorter, it is not easier to understand, and is actually less readable. Good programming style suggests you specify each BASIC statement on a separate numbered line.

Variables

When learning BASIC or any other programming language, it is important to understand the fundamental concept of variables. A **variable** is a name that identifies a location in computer memory where a value resides. Think of a variable as a nameplate on a mailbox: the nameplate identifies a particular mailbox, in essence pointing to the letters or information that are contained in the box.

Lines 20 and 30 of the sample salary program above contain examples of two variables, SALARY and NAM$, which are assigned certain values (4.5 * 8 * 5 and John Doe, respectively), via the LET command. See box for a summary of the LET command.

The LET Command

Purpose   To assign a value to a variable

Format   ln LET variablename = value
where *ln* is a valid line number, *variablename* is the name of a variable, and *value* is the expression that will be assigned

Examples   20 LET WAGE = 45 * .23
50 WAGE = RATE + .567

Note   The LET qualifier does not need to be specified in an assignment statement; if LET is not specified, there is no difference in the assignment of the value to the variable.

Assignment Statements in BASIC

BASIC statements that give a value to a variable are known as assignment statements. An assignment statement requires a simple variable on the left side of the equals sign ("="), and a numeric or character expression on the right-hand side.

In the sample program above, there were two assignment statements. One calculated a number and assigned it to the variable SALARY, and one created a **string** of characters (John Doe), and assigned it to the variable NAM$. We'll discuss string variables in more detail later, so let's first concentrate on assigning values to numeric variables.

Numeric Variables

Line 20 in the example above calculates the value of the variable SALARY by multiplying 4.5 (the wage rate) by 8 (the hours worked per day), and then multiplying that result by 5 (the number of days worked per week). Similarly, the line could have been written in a more expanded format:

```
110 LET WAGEPERHOUR = 4.5
120 LET HRSPERDAY = 8
130 LET DAYSPERWEEK = 5
140 LET SALARY = WAGEPERHOUR * HRSPERDAY * DAYSPERWEEK
```

The BASIC statements above give the same result as line 20 did, except that by expanding the statement into multiple statements, we can get a better understanding of what the program is really doing. We are describing what is going on in the program by using **descriptive variables**. Descriptive variables are variables whose names represent the value or values that the variable can hold. Descriptive variables are no different than ordinary variables except that their names are more informative.

Variables such as WAGEPERHOUR or DAYSPERWEEK are also examples of variables used to hold a single value throughout the execution of a program. These variables can be used to perform other operations (for example, to calculate the daily salary, or determine raises, taxes, or retirement benefits). The assignment of the value would only have to be done in one place and the variable could be used in as many statements as needed. Using variables such as WAGEPERHOUR is much easier than explicitly entering the same value throughout the entire program.

Variable names for numeric values can be up to 40 characters long, but must begin with an alphabetic character. The second through the fortieth characters can be any alphabetic or numeric characters, or periods. Variable names can and should be as descriptive as possible to help make the program easier to understand. However, you cannot use reserved BASIC keywords as variable names. Refer to Appendix C for a full list of reserved BASIC keywords.

The use of an invalid variable name will cause the error message "Syntax error in ln" to be displayed when you attempt to run the program (*ln* refers to the line number of the program with the invalid variable). Attempting to assign a value to a BASIC keyword will result in the error message "Illegal function call in ln," or in the error message "Syntax error in ln."

Error messages generated by the BASIC interpreter indicate that the execution of your program can no longer continue, and will describe what the error condition is and the line number of your program where BASIC encountered the problem.

Table 3.1 gives some invalid and valid examples of numeric variable names. The range of values that can be assigned to a numeric variable varies, depending on the size and characteristics of the value. For example, if the value is a whole number between $-32,768$ and $+32,767$, it will be stored in *integer* format. If the number is outside of this range and has seven or fewer digits, or if the number contains a decimal point and has seven or fewer digits, the value will be stored in *single precision* format. Generally, you do not need to be concerned with the way that the PC stores a number. The PC, however, will run calculations with integers much faster than calculations involving single precision numbers.

Table 3.1   Valid and Invalid Numeric Variable Names

Variable Name	Valid/Invalid	Explanation
PAYMENT	Valid	
PAY&RAISE	Invalid	"&" character not allowed
1CHECK	Invalid	Variable must start with alphabetic character
A.VERY.LONG.VARIABLE.NAME	Valid	
A.REALLY.REALLY.LONG.VARIABLE.NAME.DEFINED	Invalid	Variable name cannot exceed 40 characters in length
MY VARIABLE	Invalid	Spaces are not allowed in a variable name
STOCK-ITEM.1	Invalid	Dashes are not allowed in a variable name

Numerical Operators

A numeric expression or calculation that is to be assigned to a variable can consist of either numbers *or* variables that have previously been assigned numeric values. Also, a numeric expression can consist of numbers, numeric variables, and any one of the following operators. An **operator** is a symbol that denotes an arithmetic operation between two numbers. Table 3.2 lists a number of common BASIC numerical operators.

The normal order of operations within a numeric expression in BASIC is: items in parentheses, exponentiation, negative numbers indicated by the minus

Table 3.2   BASIC Numerical Operators

Operator	Description
+	Addition operator. Adds two numbers together. 3 + 2 would result in 5
−	Subtraction operator. Subtracts number specified after operand from first number specified. 4 − 3 would result in 1
*	Multiplication operator. Multiplies two numbers. 4 * 5 would result in 20
^	Exponentiation operator. Raises the first number specified to the power of the second number. 2 ^ 3 would result in 8 (similar to 2 * 2 * 2)
/	Division operator. Divides number specified after operand into first number specified. 14/2 would result in 7
−	Negative number indicator. If specified immediately before a number, the indicator tells BASIC that the number is negative. −8 is a negative 8
( )	Parentheses are used to change the way BASIC interprets an expression. Use parentheses around an expression when you wish to override the normal order of operations

sign (*not* indicating subtraction), multiplication and division, and addition and subtraction. If a numerical expression includes only multiplication and division or only addition and subtraction, the operators are evaluated from left to right. If the expression includes all four operations, all multiplication and division will be evaluated before any addition or subtraction. Expressions within parentheses are always evaluated first, before any other operation; for expressions enclosed within parentheses that are themselves enclosed within parentheses, the expression enclosed by the innermost set of parentheses gets evaluated first. (For example, in the numeric expression (4 * (10 + 5)), the expression (10 + 5) gets evaluated first (15), which is then multiplied by 4 to obtain a value of 60.)

The use of parentheses within an expression forces a change in the way BASIC will interpret the expression. In some instances, you may want to use parentheses to alter the interpretation of an expression instead of allowing BASIC to perform the interpretation using the default order of operations as described above. The following example indicates why you would want to use parentheses in certain cases. Assume that you want to calculate the division of one number with the sum of two other numbers: 10/(2 + 3). Specifying RESULT = 10/2 + 3 will yield the incorrect value of 8, instead of the expected value of 2. Specifying the assignment using parentheses in this case makes a difference: RESULT = 10/(2 + 3). Table 3.3 gives more examples of how BASIC evaluates numerical expressions.

Table 3.3   Numerical Expressions and Their Results*

BASIC Expression	Value of Expression
A + B * C + D	39
(A + B) * C + D	44
(A + B) * (C + D)	152
A + (B * C) − D	33
((A + B) * C) + D	44
A * B/C − D	29
A * B/(C + D)	8.75
A * (B/C) + D	41
A * (B/(C + D))	8.75
A * ((B/C) + D)	65
A + B ^ C/D	37.667
(A + B) ^ C/D	60.167
(A + B) ^ (D/C)	6859

*Assume that the variables have been assigned the values: A = 5, B = 14, C = 2, D = 6

Assigning values to variables is very important. It is not mandatory that variables in a numeric expression on the right-hand side of the equals sign be assigned a value prior to the assignment statement, but failure to assign a value to such a variable will cause BASIC to assign it the value of 0. Obviously, if you do not assign a value to a variable, your program will not yield the expected results. You should always assign values to variables within your program, before using them in a numeric expression.

String Variables

String variables are another type of variable you will use when programming in BASIC. Whereas numeric variables contain numeric data, string variables contain alphanumeric text (the text may contain letters or numbers or any other characters that exist on the PC keyboard). Numbers in string variables are used descriptively, such as in a street address, rather than in calculations. String variables are widely used in programs that manipulate and display strings of characters, such as name or address data, program messages, or other text.

String or character variables follow the same rules as those described for numeric variables, with a few exceptions. String variables must end with a dollar sign ("$"). Including the dollar sign, the maximum length of a string variable name is 40 characters. The variable name must start with an alphabetic character. Up to 255 characters may be assigned to a string variable. Table 3.4 gives some examples of valid and invalid string variable names. A string variable of length 0 is considered a null or empty string.

Table 3.4   Valid and Invalid String Variable Names

Variable Name	Valid/Invalid	Explanation
COMPONENT$	Valid	
COMPONENT.TYPE	Invalid	Variable name must end with $
1CHECK	Invalid	Variable must start with alphabetic character and end with $
A.VERY.LONG.VARIABLE.NAM$	Valid	
A.REALLY.REALLY.LONG.VARIABLE.NAME.DEFIN$	Invalid	Variable name cannot exceed 40 characters in length
MY VARIABLE	Invalid	Spaces are not allowed in a variable name. String variable name must end with $
STOCK-ITEM$	Invalid	Dashes are not allowed in a variable name
OFFICE$CODE	Invalid	Dollar sign not allowed in middle of variable name, only at the end of the name

A value is assigned to a string variable in several ways. If a string of text is to be directly assigned to a string variable, the text is enclosed in double quotes. The quotes tell BASIC where the beginning and end of the text is. As shown in our sample SALARY program above, the name "John Doe" is assigned to a string variable called NAM$. (Notice that we did not use NAME$, as NAME is a reserved keyword in BASIC. String variables follow many of the same restrictions that numeric variables follow—no keywords or system commands can be used as variable names.)

The BASIC statement 10 LET NAM$ = "John Doe" could also be expanded to the following lines.

```
10 LET FIRST.NAM$ = "John"
20 LET LAST.NAM$ = "Doe"
30 LET NAM$ = FIRST.NAM$ + " " + LAST.NAM$
```

In this example, we merged or **concatenated** two smaller character strings to produce a larger character string. The plus signs indicate concatenation of the two string variables FIRST.NAM$ and LAST.NAM$, with a string constant, " ", a blank space. Had we not used the string constant, the variable NAM$ would be assigned "JohnDoe". In our sample salary program we did not use plus signs, but relied on specifying the spaces between variables directly when issuing the PRINT command. You may have also noticed that different kinds of variables (a numeric and a string variable) were specified together on the PRINT command.

When assigning values to a string variable, you can only specify string variables, string constants, and the string concatenation symbol ("+") on the right side of the equals sign. You can assign numeric digits, as long as they are part of a string constant (enclosed in double quotes). However, you cannot assign a number to a string variable. For instance, the assignment STREET.ADDRESS$="123" + "Main Street" is valid, but STREET.ADDRESS$= 123 + " Main Street" is not.

Attempting to assign different kinds of variables or constants together in an assignment statement is a **type violation**. If you attempt to assign a numeric variable to a string variable, or vice versa, BASIC will display the error message "Type mismatch on ln" when you attempt to run the program. Table 3.5 gives examples of valid and invalid assignments.

Table 3.5   Valid and Invalid Assignments to String Variables

Assignment	Valid/Invalid	Explanation
PRINT$ = "Test"	Invalid	PRINT is a reserved keyword and cannot be used as a string variable name
EMPLOYEE$ = Jim Doe	Invalid	Must enclose string value in double quotes
COUNTRY.ENG$ = "Canada"	Valid	
FOOD = "Big-Mac"	Invalid	Variable name is not a string variable name
ZIP.CODE$ = "06410" + 7	Invalid	Cannot specify a numeric constant in a string expression
PART.TYPE$ = "Left-handed " + WIDGET$	Valid	

If a string variable does not get assigned a value through an assignment statement, BASIC will assign a null value to the variable; this would be similar to assigning the variable a value of "".

Character string manipulation can be accomplished through the use of various functions in BASIC. These functions, and other useful functions, will be examined in greater detail in Chapter 10.

System Variables

All of the variables described so far are examples of **user-defined variables**; that is, the programmer creates the name and defines the usage of the variable. Another kind of variable, **system variables**, is provided with BASIC to aid in BASIC programming.

System variables can only be used on the right side of an assignment expression, to assign a value to a user-defined variable. System variables cannot be on the left side of an assignment statement since they hold system information that cannot be changed. System variables are very handy for extracting system-related information.

DATE$ and TIME$ Variables

Two examples of system variables that BASIC provides are the DATE$ and TIME$ variables. The DATE$ string variable returns the current date from the computer's internal clock, the TIME$ string variable returns the current time. Together, these variables allow a program to use the current date and/or time in the formatting of reports, with user-entered or program-generated data, for information within a program menu display, or other uses.

The following sample program demonstrates the use of the DATE$ and TIME$ variables. This program, when run, will display the current date and time to the user.

```
10 ' Sample program to display the current date and time
20 PRINT "It is now "TIME$" on "DATE$"."
30 END
```

Executing this program will display, for instance:

```
It is now 12:00:01 on 11-19-1990.
```

BASIC provides many other system variables to ease your programming tasks. Refer to the MS-DOS BASIC manual for more information on these and other system variables.

A Word on Programming Style

Although you have not yet learned the information necessary to create intricate and powerful BASIC programs, we take this opportunity to present an important programming philosophy: programs should be well documented. Programs are documented by means of comments and descriptive variable names.

As noted before in this chapter, you can enter comments into a program by using the REM statement or using a single quote anywhere after the line number on a BASIC program line. Comments are extremely useful in conveying information that wouldn't otherwise be apparent. A recently written program may make sense to you, but later on, when you or someone else tries to understand the logic and flow of your program, the lack of proper comments will make the task much more difficult. Keep in mind that your program can never be too well documented.

Comments in a program are not executed by the interpreter; they are only visible when you are editing or listing a BASIC program. Their presence becomes

all the more important, though, when you have to make modifications or en-
hancements to a program.

A well-documented program should have several lines of comments at the beginning of the program describing such information as:

- The author of the program
- The date when the program was created
- Dates and descriptions of when the program was modified
- A brief description of the purpose of the program
- Any restrictions and/or dependencies of the program, mentioning limitations
  of the program (maximum length of a name entered into the program, for
  example)
- Descriptions of what internal subroutines and functions do (functions and
  subroutines will be covered in later chapters)

A program that is self-documenting can be achieved through the liberal use of
comments throughout, as well as using meaningful, descriptive variable names.
To a computer, the use of a variable name only identifies a location in memory, but
variable names should be meaningful for the people creating, maintaining, and
using the program. Variable names such as A123 or J$ or X3C2 are not meaning-
ful. Attempt to use Englishlike variable names wherever possible to convey the
true meaning of values that a variable may contain.

Summary

- A programming language is a programming tool used to create software packages. There are two types of programming languages, low-level and high-level
  languages.
- Low-level languages are used to create system software, like the DOS operating system. Machine language and assembly language are examples of low-
  level languages.
- High-level languages are used to create application software, and are commonly used by most programmers. FORTRAN, PL/I and BASIC are all examples of high-level languages.
- BASIC was developed by Professors John Kemeny and Thomas Kurtz of
  Dartmouth College to aid in the education of students in computer science and
  programming.
- A source file is a group of commands, written in a programming language, to
  instruct the computer to perform a task.
- An editor is a program that allows a programmer to enter a source file into the
  computer through the keyboard.
- A compiler is a program that reads in the programming language commands
  specified in a source file, and translates it into machine code that the computer
  can understand. The machine code a compiler generates from reading a
  source file is called an object file or module.
- Some programming languages, like BASIC, rely on interpreters, which read in
  a line of a source file at a time, translate the single line into machine code, and
  instruct the computer to execute the generated machine code. GWBASIC,
  which comes as part of MS-DOS, is an example of an interpreter.

- A BASIC program contains several BASIC statements, each of which has a unique line number.
- BASIC commands must always be preceded by a line number that is unique to the program.
- The REM statement or a single quote (') can be used to document the content and operation of a BASIC program.
- A variable is a name that identifies a location in computer memory where a value resides.
- Numeric variables are used to hold numeric data; a numeric variable name can be up to 40 alphanumeric characters (including periods), but must start with an alphabetic character.
- The range of integer values that can be assigned to a numeric variable can be any number between −32,768 and 32,767. If the value is outside of this range and has seven or fewer digits, or if the value has a decimal point and has seven or fewer digits, the value will be stored in single precision format.
- The order of operation of operators within a numeric expression is items within parentheses first, followed by exponentiation, the negative number indicator, multiplication and division, and addition and subtraction. For an expression with several operators of equal rank, the operators are evaluated from left to right.
- String variables are used to hold string data; a string variable name can be up to 40 alphanumeric characters or periods, but must start with an alphabetic character and end with a dollar sign ($).
- A string variable can contain from 0 to 255 characters.
- A string variable of length 0 is considered an empty or null string.
- String concatenation is the only operation that can be specified within a string expression.
- System variables are used to extract system-related information. The DATE$ and TIME$ functions are two examples of system variables that contain string data of the current date and time, respectively.
- A well-written program should have plenty of useful comments and descriptive variables.

Exercises

True or False

_____ 1. A portable program is software you can carry around in your shirt pocket.

_____ 2. A number is stored in single precision format if it has seven or fewer digits and contains a decimal point.

_____ 3. BASIC is considered a low-level language.

_____ 4. You do not need to specify an END statement in your program, although it is good practice to specify one.

_____   5. BASIC is an interpreter.

_____   6. BASIC creates modules from source files.

_____   7. You don't always have to specify line numbers in a program.

_____   8. You don't always have to specify LET before an assignment statement.

_____   9. A single quote can be used in place of the REM statement to specify comments.

_____   10. Always assign values to system variables at the beginning of your program.

Fill-In

1. Machine languages and assembly languages are both examples of _____ languages.

2. Programs that can be run on several types of computers with little or no change are called _____.

3. A program can be translated into machine language through either a _____ or _____.

4. A _____ is used to identify a value stored in memory.

5. _____ is the type of format used by the PC to store a number that is greater than +32,767, but has seven or fewer digits.

6. Words that cannot be used to represent variables in a BASIC program are known as _____.

7. The order of operation for a BASIC expression can be changed from the default order through the use of _____.

8. Two strings are _____ to produce one larger string.

9. Two examples of system variables that are provided in BASIC are _____ and _____.

10. _____ are lines of BASIC code that are not executed by the interpreter, but provide information about the program.

Short Answer

1. What are the advantages of high-level programming languages over low-level programming languages?

2. What are the differences between a compiler and an interpreter?

3. What are the purposes of comment statements in a BASIC program?

4. What is a variable?

5. Describe the order of operation in which a numeric expression is evaluated in BASIC.

Programming Problems

1. State whether the following variable names are valid or invalid. If they are invalid, state why.

   (a) AVERAGES   (e) 1a$
   (b) FIRST NAME$ (f) price-quoted
   (c) COST.OF.DOING.BUSINESS   (g) $Bank.Name$
   (d) a1   (h) last.name$

2. Evaluate the following (assume a = 1, b = 2, c = 3, and d = 4).

   _____   (a) a + b − c * d

   _____   (b) (a * b) ^ 2 − (−4) + c

   _____   (c) c ^ a * a ^ d * b/a

   _____   (d) d / b * c − a

   _____   (e) 5 * b * (d − a)/b

4

Introducing Microsoft's BASIC

Learning Objectives

After reading this chapter you should understand:

- How to start a BASIC session
- How to input, change, and display BASIC programs
- How to save, load, list, and run BASIC programs
- How to print BASIC programs

After reading Chapter 3, you should understand the general format of a BASIC program, as well as some general BASIC commands such as REM and END. This chapter will introduce the Microsoft BASIC interpreter you'll be using to key in programs and run them.

Introducing Microsoft's BASIC

The following is a list of some common variations of BASIC. Ask your instructor which BASIC interpreter is on your computer system. Then to invoke BASIC, key in the name of the BASIC interpreter at the DOS prompt and press the **Enter** key.

Some commands to invoke BASIC on different systems are:

BASIC
BASICA
GWBASIC

If BASIC is found on disk, the screen of the PC will clear and a screen similar to the one shown in Figure 4.1 will be displayed.

The BASIC program is on the second of the two floppy disks that make up the DOS system. You must have the DOS Supplemental Programs diskette inserted into the default floppy drive before you can start up a BASIC session.

After starting up BASIC, you will notice a copyright prompt displaying the version of BASIC you are using, followed by the word "OK." The "OK" informs you that BASIC has been successfully loaded by the PC and is ready to accept BASIC system commands.

Figure 4.1

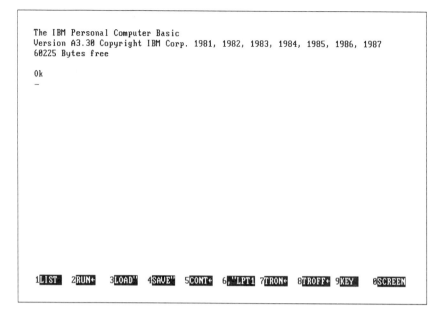

```
The IBM Personal Computer Basic
Version A3.30 Copyright IBM Corp. 1981, 1982, 1983, 1984, 1985, 1986, 1987
60225 Bytes free

Ok
–
```

```
1LIST  2RUN←  3LOAD"  4SAVE"  5CONT←  6,"LPT1 7TRON← 8TROFF← 9KEY   0SCREEN
```

The Format of the BASIC Screen

Let's look at the format of the BASIC screen displayed in Figure 4.1 after invoking the BASIC command. At the top of the screen, you'll see the words "BASIC" followed by a number. The number indicates the version of BASIC you are currently running. In Figure 4.1, the version is 3.30.

The next line of the screen displays a copyright notice, and the next line displays "60225 Bytes free." This message tells you that with the BASIC program loaded into the memory of the PC, there are 60,225 bytes of storage left. In other words, the BASIC program has 60,225 characters of storage to use when you begin a BASIC session. The amount of storage available will vary, depending on the type of PC you use.

The word "OK," which appears on the fourth line of Figure 4.1, informs you that BASIC is ready to accept commands. The cursor will be located directly beneath "OK." Except for the last line of the BASIC screen, all other lines are used to display and edit a BASIC program. The underscore (_) on the fifth line of Figure 4.1 indicates where the flashing cursor is located. If you type in anything at this point, the characters you key in will be displayed where the underscore is located. If you press the Enter key, the cursor will jump to the next line on the screen, in this case the sixth line of the display.

The last line of the screen displays a series of BASIC system commands. These commands can be invoked using the function keys. The function keys, which we introduced in Chapter 1, allow you to issue some commonly used BASIC system commands with one keystroke rather than having to repeatedly key in the commands letter for letter.

BASIC System Commands

LET, REM, and PRINT are examples of BASIC programming commands that you can include in a BASIC program. These commands must be preceded by a line number. BASIC also provides several commands which we'll refer to as **system commands**. BASIC system commands are *external to your program*; they help you create and modify your programs. These commands allow you to edit, list, or run a BASIC program, as well as many other operations. BASIC system commands differ from BASIC programming commands in that when you issue a system command, you do not precede it with a line number; also, BASIC will immediately perform a system command for you. We will introduce the following system commands in this chapter: NEW, RUN, LIST, LLIST, EDIT, DELETE, RENUM, SAVE, LOAD, FILES, SYSTEM, CLS, and KEY.

Program Design and Development

When writing programs, it is important to think through the process first, before writing any code. A commonly-used method of program layout is pseudocode, an Englishlike description of the problem to be solved. From pseudocode, a graphic representation, known as a flowchart, can be created to ensure that the process in the program is well-structured and flows efficiently. From a flowchart, a program can easily be written.

This book includes flowcharts and pseudocode for some of the programs in the text. Refer to Appendix A on program design and development for more information.

Introductory BASIC Session

Before we get into the details of specific BASIC commands, let's create and enter a simple program to illustrate some features of BASIC. The following program will perform a simple calculation of weekly salary, and display the results on the PC console. When translated into a BASIC source file, the program looks like the following, with the flowchart and pseudocode used for planning this program in Figure 4.2. Before entering the program displayed below, we should first make sure that no other BASIC program is loaded into memory.

The NEW Command

The NEW command is used to eliminate any traces of previous BASIC programs in the computer's memory. It is always a good idea to issue the NEW command before entering a BASIC program; failure to do so could result in having lines inserted in your program from the last BASIC program in memory (for a summary of the NEW command, see the box).

Figure 4.2

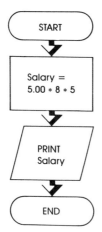

Program: Calculate salary
Set salary to product of 5 times 8 times 5
Display salary
End: Calculate salary

The NEW Command

Purpose   To clear computer memory of any previous BASIC program

Format   NEW

Notes   You do not need to issue this command unless you are keying in a new program. Any program currently in memory gets cleared without saving. *If a program resides in memory and has not been saved prior to issuing the NEW command, the program will be lost.*

If you want to clear memory of any BASIC programs, key in the word **new** or **NEW** (case doesn't matter) and then press the **Enter** key. Your screen should now look something like Figure 4.3. Notice how BASIC displays the word "OK" after you enter the NEW command; BASIC is ready to accept another command.

Entering a BASIC Program into the PC

With no BASIC program residing in memory, you are ready to key in a BASIC program. To enter the sample program on page 88, you key in each line, and then press the Enter key when you have typed in the entire line. You need not be concerned whether letters are typed in uppercase or lowercase; BASIC will understand lines of BASIC whether they are in upper, lower, or mixed case.

If you keyed in the program correctly, your screen should look like Figure 4.4. Notice in Figure 4.4 that there is a space before and after each BASIC command. When keying in a program, you must ensure that there is at least one space before and after each BASIC command. For readability, you can enter more than one space between (but not within) line numbers, BASIC commands, variables, and

Figure 4.3

```
The IBM Personal Computer Basic
Version A3.30 Copyright IBM Corp. 1981, 1982, 1983, 1984, 1985, 1986, 1987
60225 Bytes free

Ok
new
Ok
─
```

```
1LIST   2RUN←   3LOAD"   4SAVE"   5CONT←   6,"LPT1 7TRON←   8TROFF← 9KEY      0SCREEN
```

numbers. For instance, line 30 of our sample program could have been keyed in any of the following ways:

```
30    salary=5.00*8 *5
30 SALARY= 5.00 * 8 * 5
30 salary=5.00*8*5
30 SALARY = 5.00 * 8 * 5
```

but cannot be keyed in any of these ways:

```
3 0 S A L ARY = 5.  00 * 8 *5
30 S A L a r y = 5 . 0 0 * 8 * 5
30 SALARY = 5 . 00*8*5
30SALARY=5.00*8*5
```

Figure 4.4

```
The IBM Personal Computer Basic
Version A3.30 Copyright IBM Corp. 1981, 1982, 1983, 1984, 1985, 1986, 1987
60225 Bytes free

Ok
new
Ok
10 rem This is a sample BASIC program which calculates
20 rem salary.
30 salary = 5.00 * 8 * 5
40 print salary
50 end
─
```

```
1LIST   2RUN←   3LOAD"   4SAVE"   5CONT←   6,"LPT1 7TRON←   8TROFF← 9KEY      0SCREEN
```

Although Figure 4.4 shows the program entered in order by line number, it is not necessary to key in programs precisely by line number. For instance, we could have keyed in line 20 before line 10. If you forget to type in a line of a program or if you keyed in a line incorrectly, you can key the entire line in again. If you key in the same line several times, BASIC will use the last occurrence of the line that you typed in. If lines are entered out of line number order, BASIC will reorder them before execution.

Let's see how BASIC runs the program in Figure 4.4.

Running a BASIC Program

Once your BASIC program has been keyed in, the RUN command must be issued in order for the computer to interpret and execute the program's commands. The RUN command can be issued repeatedly to execute a program that is in memory, avoiding the need to reload or reenter the program (see box).

The RUN Command

Purpose   To instruct BASIC to begin interpretation and execution of the program currently in memory

Format   RUN

Note   Execution of the program begins sequentially starting with the line with the smallest line number.

You can also run a program by pressing the F2 function key, which will type the RUN command and execute it for you.

To begin execution of our sample program, we key in the word **run** and then press the **Enter** key (or press **F2**). If you keyed in the sample program correctly, after issuing RUN your screen would look something like Figure 4.5.

Figure 4.5

```
The IBM Personal Computer Basic
Version A3.30 Copyright IBM Corp. 1981, 1982, 1983, 1984, 1985, 1986, 1987
60225 Bytes free

Ok
new
Ok
10 rem This is a sample BASIC program which calculates
20 rem salary.
30 salary = 5.00 * 8 * 5
40 print salary
50 end
run
 200
Ok
_




1LIST  2RUN←  3LOAD"  4SAVE"  5CONT←  6 "LPT1 7TRON← 8TROFF← 9KEY   0SCREEN
```

After issuing the RUN command, BASIC read and interpreted every line of the program. The PRINT command on line 40 caused BASIC to display the value of the variable SALARY (200) on the screen. When line 50 of the program was executed, BASIC stopped interpretation of the program and displayed the "OK" prompt. When you see the "OK" prompt, you can issue the RUN command again to re-execute the program, or enter another BASIC system command.

Listing a BASIC Program

After keying in the BASIC program, you may want to view all lines, in numerical order. The BASIC system command LIST allows you to do just that. To list the entire program on the screen, type **LIST** and then press the **Enter** key. Note that the appearance of the program will vary depending which BASIC interpreter is used. The BASIC program that is currently keyed into the computer will be LISTed or scrolled up on the screen, followed by the "OK" prompt, meaning that the LIST command is finished, and that BASIC is ready to accept another command.

If you keyed in the sample salary program displayed in Figure 4.4, and then issued the LIST command, you might notice that some of the words you typed in are now in uppercase, even if you originally keyed the entire program into BASIC in lowercase. BASIC automatically puts command names and variable names in uppercase, even if you key them in lowercase. Any characters that you enclose in double quotes or any characters in a comment, however, are not translated to uppercase. You need not be concerned with uppercase and lowercase when you key in a program except when you key in a character string enclosed within double quotes, to be assigned to a string variable or to be the parameter of a PRINT command. For example, if you want the words "this is an example" to be displayed or printed in lowercase, you must enter them in lowercase, enclosed in double quotes.

If your program is more than one screen long (more than 23 lines), the entire program may scroll by too quickly to be read. In this case, if you wish to freeze the screen temporarily, press the **Control** and **Numlock** keys simultaneously. When you want to allow BASIC to resume the listing of the program, press any other key.

If you only want to display certain lines of your program, you can enter the LIST command with a line number range, for example, LIST 200-300. This will display all lines whose line numbers fall between and including 200 through 300. A summary of the LIST command is given in the box on the next page.

To display one line of the BASIC program, you can specify a single line number after the LIST command. You can press the F1 function key to have BASIC type out the LIST command for you. You must then press the **Enter** key to issue the LIST command.

If we issued the LIST command after running our sample salary program, we would see the screen as shown in Figure 4.6.

The LIST Command

Purpose   To display part or all of a program on the computer screen

Format   LIST <first ln>-<last ln>
where *ln* is a valid line number

Examples   LIST
LIST 20
LIST 230-400
LIST -50
LIST 2000-

Notes   Pressing function key F1 will invoke the LIST command for you. If LIST is
issued without any parameters, the entire program is displayed on the computer screen. If
LIST is issued with a line number followed by a dash and no other line number, the entire
program starting at the specified line number is displayed.

Figure 4.6

```
Ok
list
10 REM This is a sample BASIC program which calculates
20 REM salary.
30 SALARY = 5! * 8 * 5
40 PRINT SALARY
50 END
Ok
_
```

```
1LIST   2RUN←   3LOAD"   4SAVE"   5CONT←   6,"LPT1  7TRON←  8TROFF←  9KEY    0SCREEN
```

Printing a BASIC Program

If you wish to have a paper printout of your program to save or to show to others,
BASIC provides the LLIST command, which functions exactly the same as the
LIST command, except that output is sent to a printer rather than to the screen
(see box). Again, a range of lines or even a single line of the BASIC program can
be printed.

The LLIST Command

Purpose   To print part or all of a program on an attached printer

Format   LLIST <first ln>-<last ln>
where *ln* is a valid line number

Examples   LLIST
LLIST 20-500
LLIST 300
LLIST -60
LLIST 400-

Note   LLIST operates exactly like the LIST command except that all output is
displayed on the attached printer.

Changing a BASIC Program

Unless you are a perfect typist and programmer, you will undoubtedly make typo-
graphical errors that must be fixed. You may also wish to make changes and en-
hancements to an existing program. There are several ways that you can change a
BASIC program once it is entered into the PC.

The EDIT Command

The EDIT command is helpful when you know specifically which lines need
changes. EDIT can also be used to easily duplicate lines in a program. The following box summarizes the EDIT command.

The EDIT Command

Purpose   To display a line of a program and position the cursor under the first
character of the line to allow editing

Format   EDIT <ln>
where *ln* is a valid line number

Example   EDIT 40

Note   Instead of using the EDIT command, you can also type over a line that is displayed on the screen and then press the Enter key to make changes.

To edit line 140 of a BASIC program, you would type **EDIT 140**. BASIC responds by typing the specified line to the screen. The blinking cursor will be located directly under the first number (in this case, "1") of the line number. You
can move the cursor by using the cursor movement keys, and modify any part of
the line by merely typing over what needs to be changed. You can use the Insert
and Delete keys (the 0 and "." keys on the numeric keypad) to insert characters on

the line or to delete unwanted characters, and then press the **Enter** key to make changes.

We can use the EDIT command to change our sample salary program so that it displays a higher salary by changing line 30 of the program. Immediately after entering **EDIT 30**, our BASIC screen would look like Figure 4.7. The program is now in Edit mode for line 30.

Using the cursor movement keys, position the cursor under the 5 of 5.00, and type **10.0** over 5.00, changing the wage rate from 5 to 10. After making the change, press the **Enter** key to inform BASIC of the change. The screen should look like Figure 4.8.

Figure 4.7

```
Ok
list
10 REM This is a sample BASIC program which calculates
20 REM salary.
30 SALARY = 5! * 8 * 5
40 PRINT SALARY
50 END
Ok
edit 30
30 SALARY = 5! * 8 * 5




1LIST 2RUN+ 3LOAD" 4SAVE" 5CONT+ 6,"LPT1 7TRON+ 8TROFF+ 9KEY 0SCREEN
```

Figure 4.8

```
Ok
list
10 REM This is a sample BASIC program which calculates
20 REM salary.
30 SALARY = 5! * 8 * 5
40 PRINT SALARY
50 END
Ok
edit 30
30 SALARY = 10.0 * 8 * 5
_




1LIST 2RUN+ 3LOAD" 4SAVE" 5CONT+ 6,"LPT1 7TRON+ 8TROFF+ 9KEY 0SCREEN
```

Issuing the RUN command at this point would cause the program to display a higher salary, 400.

If you wish to duplicate a line several times quickly, then instead of keying in the line several times, we can use the EDIT command in the following fashion.

Suppose we wanted to change our salary program so that it displayed another salary. In this case, we would want to duplicate lines 30 and 40, which calculate and then display SALARY. First, let's duplicate line 30 to make line 41. You would issue the EDIT command and the line number **30**. This would display line 30 of the program in Edit mode. Type over the 30 with **41**, move the cursor past the equals sign, type **15.0**, and then press the **Enter** key. You have entered a new line into the program without keying the whole line over again.

If you change a line number while typing over a displayed line and press the Enter key, the original line will be retained, the cursor will move to the first position of the next line, and a new line with the specified line number will have been inserted into your program. The original line that you typed over will remain in your program but will not be displayed until you issue the LIST command to display it.

If you entered the LIST command at this point, your program would look like the following:

```
10 REM This is a sample BASIC program which calculates
20 REM salary.
30 SALARY = 10.0 * 8 * 5
40 PRINT SALARY
41 SALARY = 15.0 * 8 * 5
50 END
```

The same technique could be used again, by issuing **EDIT 40** and changing 40 to 42. After pressing **Enter**, if you issued the LIST command, the program would look like the following.

```
10 REM This is a sample BASIC program which calculates
20 REM salary.
30 SALARY = 10.0 * 8 * 5
40 PRINT SALARY
41 SALARY = 15.0 * 8 * 5
42 PRINT SALARY
50 END
```

Running the program after these lines are duplicated would result in 400 and 600 being displayed on the PC screen.

You can also change lines that appear on the screen by moving the cursor up to the line to be changed, changing the desired characters on the line, and then pressing the **Enter** key. As long as you do not change the line number, only the specified characters will be replaced. When you are through typing over lines to make changes, you can press the **Enter** key repeatedly until the blinking cursor is on an empty line toward the bottom of the screen. When the cursor is on an empty line, you can then issue a BASIC system command, or key in more lines of your program.

The DELETE Command

If you entered a line in the program that was not meant to be included in the program, you can delete that line in several ways. You can type the line number of the line to be deleted, with no other text after the line number, and press **Enter**. BASIC will delete that line from the program. You can also delete a line or group of lines by using the BASIC system command DELETE (see box).

The DELETE command will delete a single line or group of lines. DELETE is similar to the LIST command in how you specify which lines you want deleted.

If we duplicated lines 30 and 40 in our sample salary program above, and now wanted to delete lines 30 and 40, we could either issue **DELETE 30-40**, or we could type **30**, press **Enter**, type **40** and press **Enter**.

The DELETE Command

Purpose   To delete a line or group of lines of a program from memory

Format   DELETE <first ln>-<last ln>
Where *ln* is a valid line number

Examples   DELETE 300
DELETE -30
DELETE 50-
DELETE 10-70

Notes   If "first ln" only is specified followed by a dash, all lines from the specified line number to the end of the program are deleted. Likewise, specifying a dash before "last ln" will delete all lines from the beginning of the program up to and including the specified line number.

Renumbering the Lines in Your BASIC Program

In our sample salary program above, we used EDIT to duplicate lines 30 and 40 and create lines numbered 41 and 42. If we wanted to insert another command line between lines 41 and 42, we would not be able to do so without reentering the program specifying different line numbers. The RENUM command instructs BASIC to renumber your program, thus allowing you to insert more lines if necessary (see summary in box).

The RENUM command renumbers a BASIC program, depending on the increment values you wish to use. It is good practice to number lines in your program starting with 10 and thereafter upward in increments of 10 or 20. By using an increment value of 10 or more, you'll be able to add lines between existing lines of the program.

To renumber the program we entered above, issue **renum 10** or just **renum**. RENUM will then renumber all lines of the program, the first line being renumbered to 10, after which all other lines would be numbered in ascending increments of 10 as indicated in Figure 4.9.

The RENUM Command

Purpose   To renumber a range of lines or all lines within a program in memory

Format   RENUM <starting ln>,<target ln>,<increment>
where *ln* is a valid line number

Examples   RENUM
RENUM 10,10
RENUM 200,10,50
RENUM 100,,20
RENUM ,,30

Notes   If you only specify RENUM, the program will be renumbered starting at line 10, in increments of 10. All references in the program to line numbers will also be changed automatically if necessary.

Figure 4.9

```
Ok
list
10 REM This is a sample BASIC program which calculates
20 REM salary.
30 SALARY = 10! * 8 * 5
40 PRINT SALARY
41 SALARY = 15! * 8 * 5
42 PRINT SALARY
50 END
Ok
renum 10
Ok
list
10 REM This is a sample BASIC program which calculates
20 REM salary.
30 SALARY = 10! * 8 * 5
40 PRINT SALARY
50 SALARY = 15! * 8 * 5
60 PRINT SALARY
70 END
Ok
_

1LIST   2RUN←   3LOAD"   4SAVE"   5CONT←   6,"LPT1  7TRON←  8TROFF←  9KEY   0SCREEN
```

Saving a BASIC Program

BASIC programs are not automatically stored in the computer. After you have keyed in or changed a BASIC program, you must save the program so that you can later change or run the program again without having to rekey the program into the computer.

When you turn off your computer, the program you have been working on will be erased from the computer's memory unless you transfer it to a secondary storage device, such as a floppy diskette or a hard disk. In order to save a BASIC program to disk, use the BASIC SAVE command. The SAVE command will save the program currently in memory to a disk file, under the name that you specify.

Let's call the example program we've been using SALARY. To save a BASIC program in memory as SALARY on the B disk of a two-disk system, you would type **save "b:salary"** and then press the **Enter** key. Note the use of the double quotes ("). The double quotes are used to identify the DOS file name to BASIC; you need only specify a double quote at the beginning of the file name, unless you use the "A" option of the SAVE command (see box below), when you must specify a double quote at the end of the file name. You could have also entered **save "b:salary.bas** to perform the same function. If you wanted to save a BASIC program as SALARY2.BAS on the A disk, you would issue **save "a:salary2.bas**. Failure to use a double quote before the file name results in the BASIC error message "Type mismatch" displayed on the PC screen. If you need to review DOS file names, refer to Chapter 2.

BASIC programs that are saved without specifying a file extension (the one- to three-character suffix which goes after the period) will be automatically given the file extension of BAS. If you typed **save "b:myprog"**, the saved program would be stored on the disk in the B drive as the DOS file MYPROG.BAS. This will allow you to identify and load BASIC programs more easily.

The SAVE Command

Purpose   To save the current program in memory onto a hard disk or diskette

Format   SAVE "<drive:filespec.ext>",<A>

Examples   SAVE "MYPROG"
SAVE "MYPROG
SAVE "A:SALARY.BAS"
SAVE "ACCOUNT",A

Notes   The default file extension is .BAS. If you specify A after the file specification, the program will be saved in ASCII format so that you can use the DOS commands TYPE and PRINT with it. The double quote that follows the file name does not need to be specified, as long as you do not specify the "A" option.

BASIC programs are stored in a special format on disk, which prevents them from being used in such DOS commands as TYPE or PRINT. If you want to save BASIC programs so that you can use TYPE or PRINT with them, then use the "A" option as described in the box. Specifying "A" will force BASIC to save the BASIC program in ASCII format on disk. However, programs stored in ASCII format take up more space on disk than if the programs were stored without using the "A" option. (ASCII, which stands for *American National Standard Code for Information Interchange*, is a standard character code set used for information storage on many different kinds of computers, particularly personal computers. Files stored in ASCII format on one type of computer can be easily exchanged with other computers that use ASCII.)

You can have the computer type out SAVE " for you by pressing the F4 function key.

Displaying the Names of Files on a Disk from BASIC

In order to see the names of programs you have stored in a disk, you can display the names of files by typing in using the BASIC system command FILES. FILES is similar to the DOS command DIR described in Chapter 2. The names of all files on the current disk directory are displayed by entering FILES. To list all files on another disk, type in the FILES command followed by a space, double quotes, the disk drive identifier (A, B, C, etc.) followed by a colon and ending with double quotes. To see a listing of the files on the B drive, for example, enter **files "b:"**.

Figure 4.10 shows a sample of what your screen might look like after you have listed the files on the diskettes in the A and B drives. If you are sitting at your terminal, use the FILES command to see what files already exist on your disks (see box for a summary of the FILES command).

Remember, if you do not specify a file extension on any BASIC file command, the default file extension of .BAS is used. If any other file extension is used, it must be explicitly used when loading, listing, or performing any BASIC file command.

Figure 4.10

```
Ok
files "a:"
A:\
PREFACE .WS5        PREFACE .COR        FLOWCH  .WS5
 1440768 Bytes free

Ok
files "b:"
B:\
SAMPLE  .BAS        SALARY  .BAS        SIMPLE  .BAS        MYPROG  .BAS
PAYROLL .BAS
 357376 Bytes free

Ok
_




1LIST   2RUN↵   3LOAD"   4SAVE"   5CONT↵   6,"LPT1 7TRON↵  8TROFF↵ 9KEY    0SCREEN
```

The FILES Command

Purpose   To display the names of all files on a disk or diskette

Format   FILES "<drive:filespec.ext>"

Examples FILES
              FILES "A:"
              FILES "*.BAS"

Note   Issuing FILES "*.BAS" will display all BASIC programs on the default disk drive.

Loading a File from a Disk into BASIC

When you want to load a BASIC program from disk into memory, use the LOAD command. The LOAD command locates the specified file on disk, clears out memory (erasing any program that was residing in memory), and copies the program from disk to memory. After successful execution of the LOAD command, use the LIST command to verify that the desired program was loaded. The box below summarizes the LOAD command.

The LOAD Command

Purpose   To read a program from a disk or diskette, and load it into memory

Format   LOAD "<drive:filespec.ext>"

Examples   LOAD "SAMPLE"
LOAD "SAMPLE
LOAD "A:SALARY.BAS"
LOAD "MYPROG.BAS"

Note   If no file extension is specified, the default file extension .BAS will be used in the file name.

Let's assume that we want to load a program with the file name of MESSAGE.BAS, located on the disk in the B drive. To load the file, we enter **load "b:message"** (notice that BASIC must have a double quote before the file name).

If you had saved the file as MESSAGE.PRO, then you would have to specify the entire file name when issuing the LOAD command. If you do not specify a file extension, BASIC automatically assumes that the file extension is .BAS.

There is no need to enter the NEW command before you load a file. Any program already existing in the computer's memory is erased when another BASIC program is loaded. After the program is successfully loaded, issue the RUN command (or press the F2 function key) to run the program.

Function key F3 will type out LOAD ", after which you enter the file name of the BASIC program you wish to load.

The CLS Command

Similar to the DOS CLS command, the BASIC CLS command clears the screen of all text and moves the cursor to the top left-hand corner of the screen. The CLS command does not clear any program in memory, but rather erases all lines on the screen, so that the screen is not cluttered. You can use the CLS command at any time during a BASIC session to clear the screen. For example, assume your screen looks something like Figure 4.11.

Figure 4.11

```
Ok
list
10 REM This is a sample BASIC program which calculates
20 REM salary.
30 SALARY = 10! * 8 * 5
40 PRINT SALARY
41 SALARY = 15! * 8 * 5
42 PRINT SALARY
50 END
Ok
renum 10
Ok
list
10 REM This is a sample BASIC program which calculates
20 REM salary.
30 SALARY = 10! * 8 * 5
40 PRINT SALARY
50 SALARY = 15! * 8 * 5
60 PRINT SALARY
70 END
Ok
_

1LIST  2RUN←  3LOAD"  4SAVE"  5CONT←  6,"LPT1 7TRON←  8TROFF← 9KEY   0SCREEN
```

If you type **cls** and then press the **Enter** key, your screen would then look like Figure 4.12.

Figure 4.12

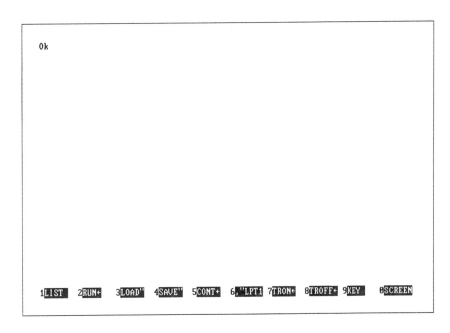

```
Ok










1LIST  2RUN←  3LOAD"  4SAVE"  5CONT←  6,"LPT1 7TRON←  8TROFF← 9KEY   0SCREEN
```

The KEY Command

The KEY command can be used to turn the function key display at the bottom of the screen off and on. Entering KEY OFF turns the display off, while KEY ON turns the display back on. When the function key display is turned off, you can still use the function keys; only the display is turned off. The KEY command comes in handy if you want to display one more line of a program on the screen, rather than have the function key display on the bottom of the screen.

Function key F9 is defined to type out the word KEY. You can then type the word **on** or **off** followed by pressing the **Enter** key to turn the function key display menu on or off.

Exiting BASIC

To exit the BASIC program, you issue the SYSTEM system command. SYSTEM will immediately exit the BASIC program and return you to DOS (indicated by the change to the DOS prompt). Note that any program that is in memory at the time you enter SYSTEM will be lost if it has not been saved; be careful to save any program you are working on before issuing SYSTEM (see box below).

The SYSTEM Command

Purpose   To exit the BASIC program and return to the DOS prompt

Format   SYSTEM

Notes   Any program that exists in memory when the SYSTEM command is executed is not saved. Make sure you have saved any programs before issuing the SYSTEM command.

Refer to the DOS BASIC Reference manual for detailed information on the BASIC system commands introduced in this chapter, as well as other BASIC system commands.

Summary

■ BASIC is an interpreter that reads one line of a source file at a time, translating a BASIC command into machine-code instructions that the computer can understand.

■ The GWBASIC command is used from MS-DOS to start a BASIC session.

■ The RUN command is used to instruct BASIC to begin interpretation of the program currently loaded into memory.

■ The NEW command is used to clear out any BASIC program currently loaded into memory.

■   The LIST and LLIST commands are used to display the lines of a BASIC program to the computer screen and printer, respectively.

■   The EDIT command is used to modify existing lines within a BASIC program. EDIT can also be used to duplicate lines within a program.

■   The DELETE command is used to delete a single line or group of lines from a BASIC program.

■   The RENUM command is used to renumber the lines in a BASIC program.

■   The SAVE command is used to save a program from computer memory to disk.

■   The LOAD command is used to load a program from disk or diskette to computer memory, so that it can be listed, edited, or run.

■   The FILES command is used to list a file or group of files on disk. FILES works in a similar fashion to the DOS DIR command.

■   The SYSTEM command is used to end the BASIC session, so that you can issue DOS commands.

■   The CLS command is used to clear the PC screen while in a BASIC session.

■   The KEY command is used to remove or display the settings of function keys on line 25 of the PC screen while in a BASIC session.

Exercises

True or False

_____   1. The "OK" prompt in a BASIC session tells you that you can enter another command.

_____   2. Always issue the NEW command before you save a program.

_____   3. You must always enter your program in uppercase.

_____   4. You must have a space before and after every command name.

_____   5. The LLIST command is used to display programs on your PC screen line by line.

_____   6. Once you've entered a program into the PC, there is no way you can resequence line numbers.

_____   7. Use the CLS system command to clear memory of all BASIC programs.

_____   8. The KEY command automatically keys in programs for you.

_____   9. You cannot issue the RUN command twice on a program successively.

_____   10. When entering a BASIC system command, you should always specify the line number after the command name.

Fill-In

1. Commands that are not used in the program but rather help you manipulate the BASIC environment are known as _____.

2. The _____ command clears out any program in memory and allows you to start entering a new program.

3. The _____ command is used to display all or select lines of a BASIC program to the screen, while the _____ command will write the same information to a printer.

4. To resequence lines of code and provide a constant increment of line numbers after lines have been inserted or deleted from the program, the _____ command is provided in BASIC.

5. The SAVE command copies the BASIC program from memory and stores it on a secondary storage device such as a _____ or a _____.

6. The default file extension for a file saved using SAVE "NEWPROG would be _____.

7. The FILES command in BASIC is similar to the _____ command in DOS.

8. The LOAD command loads a BASIC program from disk into _____.

9. Similar to the DOS command, the BASIC _____ command clears data off the screen.

10. To exit the BASIC environment and return to DOS, enter the _____ command.

Short Answer

1. What is the purpose of the RENUM command and when should you use it?

2. Name two ways that BASIC allows you to duplicate a program line without typing the entire line in.

3. Name two ways that BASIC allows you to delete lines from a BASIC program.

4. If you key in a BASIC program during a BASIC session, run the program, and then issue the CLS command, what will happen? What happens if you then issue the SYSTEM command?

5. If you key in a BASIC program during a BASIC session, run the program, and then issue the FILES command, what happens? What happens if you then issue the LOAD command?

6. Imagine that you have keyed in a BASIC program that is 50 lines long and is numbered from 10 to 500, in increments of 10. You wish to look at lines 200 through 400, but if you just enter the LIST command with no parameters, the program scrolls by too quickly. Describe three ways that you can avoid this problem.

Programming Problems

1. In the lines below, identify which lines are valid and invalid. For the lines that are invalid, explain why.

   (a) 100 20 REM This is a test
   (b) 1230 SALARY = (90.4 * (45 − STATE.TAX)/56) + BONUS + AWARD
   (c) 350
   (d) 23010'THIS PORTION OF THE PROGRAM CALCULATES INCOME TAX

2. Assume that the lines shown below are keyed in during the start of a BASIC session. What will be displayed on the screen if the LIST command were then issued?

   ```
   10 REM This is a sample BASIC program
   10 REM This is a sample BASIC program which calculates
   20 REMSALARY
   20 REM SALARY
   50 END
   40 PRINT SALARY
   30 SALARY=5*8*5
   ```

3. Assume that the lines shown below are keyed in during the start of a BASIC session. What will be displayed if the LIST command is then issued?

   ```
   10 'this is a test program to calculate three salaries
   20 'calculate salary
   30 salary = 5 * 8 * 40
   20
   25 print salary
   22 salary = 56 * 8 * 1
   27 salary = 43 * 23 * 1
   35 print salary
   40 print salary
   50 end
   50
   50 end
   ```

5

Input and Output Using BASIC

Learning Objectives

After reading this chapter you should understand:

- What the INPUT command does and how to use it
- How to specify prompts with the INPUT command
- What the PRINT command does, and how to use it

- How to use separators in the PRINT command to provide simple formatting of output
- What a print zone is
- What the BASIC commands CLS and KEY do

Introduction

This chapter will introduce you to the concepts of input and output within a BASIC program. When you complete this chapter, you should have a good understanding of how information is fed into a program, and how information is displayed by one.

The programs in earlier chapters used information embedded within the programs in assignment statements. Most large programs in any programming language are not normally written in this fashion; they allow the user to input information (data) during the running of the program, through commands like the INPUT command.

The INPUT Command

INPUT can be used by a BASIC program to gather data for use within the program. The INPUT command is used to prompt the user for information to be supplied for later use in assignment statements and in PRINT statements.

Let's look at our weekly salary program to understand the use of the INPUT command. The flowchart and pseudocode used for planning the program appear in Figure 5.1.

Figure 5.1

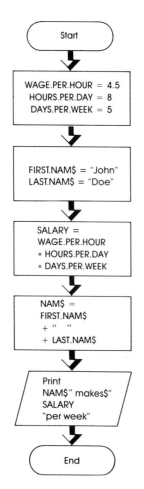

Program: Calculate weekly salary
Set Wage.Per.Hour to 4.5
Set Hours.Per.Day to 8
Set Days.Per.Week to 5
Set First.Name to John
Set Last.Name to Doe
Set salary to product of Wage.Per.Hour times
    Hours.Per.Day times Days.Per.Week
Set name to concatenation of First.Name, blanks,
    and Last.Name
Display name makes salary per week.
End: Calculate weekly salary

```
 10 'Sample program to calculate weekly salary
 20 LET WAGE.PER.HOUR = 4.5
 30 LET HOURS.PER.DAY = 8
 40 LET DAYS.PER.WEEK = 5
 50 LET FIRST.NAM$ = "John"
 60 LET LAST.NAM$ = "Doe"
 70 SALARY = WAGE.PER.HOUR * HOURS.PER.DAY * DAYS.PER.WEEK
 80 NAM$ = FIRST.NAM$ + " " + LAST.NAM$
 90 PRINT NAM$" makes $"SALARY"per week."
100 END
```

This program displays the weekly salary of Mr. John Doe for one particular week. While the program may be useful for Mr. Doe, it is not flexible or very useful except to describe how BASIC programs work. The program will calculate and display the same salary for the same person every time it is run. If instead of using assignment statements we had some method of getting the same information from the user, and if we could enter different values for the variables each time we ran the program, the program would be much more useful.

The INPUT command does just that. Replacing assignment statements in the program above with INPUT statements, the program can be used by anyone. Let's do this and see what happens when we run it. Notice also the changes in the flowchart and pseudocode for this program (Figure 5.2.).

Figure 5.2

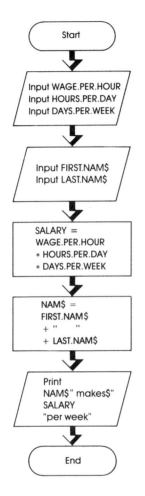

Program: Calculate weekly salary
READ Wage.Per.Hour
READ Hours.Per.Day
READ Days.Per.Week
READ First.Name
READ Last.Name
Set salary to product of Wage.Per.Hour times
    Hours.Per.Day times Days.Per.Week
Set name to concatenation of First.Name, blanks,
    and Last.Name
Display name makes salary per week.
END: Calculate weekly salary

```
10 'Sample program to calculate anyone's weekly salary
20 INPUT WAGE.PER.HOUR
30 INPUT HOURS.PER.DAY
40 INPUT DAYS.PER.WEEK
50 INPUT FIRST.NAM$
60 INPUT LAST.NAM$
70 SALARY = WAGE.PER.HOUR * HOURS.PER.DAY * DAYS.PER.WEEK
80 NAM$ = FIRST.NAM$ + " " + LAST.NAM$
90 PRINT NAM$" makes $"SALARY"per week."
100 END
```

This program has changed the assignment statements to INPUT statements. When the new program is run, the user will be prompted for information, as shown in the following:

```
Ok
run
? 10.50
? 8
? 5
? Jane
? Doe
Jane Doe makes $ 420 per week.
Ok
```

When the program is run, BASIC will interpret each INPUT command, type a prompt in the form of a question mark, and wait for the user to enter information. The user will be prompted with a question mark five times, and he or she must enter information of the correct type (character or numeric) in response to each prompt. After all information required by the five INPUT statements is entered correctly, the program calculates the weekly salary and displays a message with a full name and weekly salary.

Failure to input the correct type of data will result in the error message "?Redo from start" to be displayed on the screen. If the user presses the ENTER key without entering any information, BASIC will assign a value of 0 to numeric variables, and the null string to string variables. Notice that the user running the program must reply correctly to each of the five INPUT prompts before the program displays the salary message. Also notice that the values of the variables that appear in each INPUT command do not need to be predefined in the program; the user will assign a value to each variable when running the program.

The INPUT Command

Purpose   To assign values to variables by prompting the user for numeric or string data

Format   ln INPUT <msg text> <delimiter> <variable list>
where *ln* is a valid line number, *msg text* is the text of the INPUT message prompt enclosed within double quotes, *delimiter* is either a comma or semicolon (used only if msg text is supplied), and *variable list* is a list of variables that will be assigned values

Examples   10 INPUT AGE
20 INPUT "What is your age"; AGE
30 INPUT "Enter name, rank, serial number", NAM$,RANK$,SN

Notes   If no msg text is supplied, BASIC uses a ? to prompt. If a comma is used as a delimiter, no question mark is displayed; if a semicolon is used, a question mark is appended to the end of the msg text. If multiple variables are specified, the user must supply the same number of values, separated by commas.

The sample program using INPUT is much better than its predecessor, which used assignment statements. However, the user running the program can easily get confused when replying to the INPUT prompts. First, what does a question mark really mean? Second, it may seem obvious that the program needs information to continue, but what kind of information? Third, the user must answer five input prompts correctly. It would be much nicer if the program had more specific INPUT prompts.

The default INPUT prompt is a "?", but this prompt can be changed by the programmer to suit the user's needs. In the program above, instead of prompting the user with a "?", using meaningful prompts like "Please enter your hourly wage:" would make the program much easier to use. To use your own prompt, you can specify a message for each INPUT command by typing a character string enclosed in double quotes. Thus, line 20 of the previous program can be rewritten in the following manner:

```
20 INPUT "Please enter your hourly wage: ",WAGE.PER.HOUR
```

When this line is executed, rather than displaying a question mark, BASIC will display:

```
Please enter your hourly wage:
```

The use of a comma to separate the prompt message from the variable to be assigned a value prevents BASIC from displaying a question mark at the end of the prompt message. If we wanted BASIC to display a question mark at the end of a prompt message, we would specify a semicolon as a separator. For instance:

```
20 INPUT "What is your hourly wage"; WAGE.PER.HOUR
```

would return the following prompt:

```
What is your hourly wage?
```

In addition, instead of using three INPUT commands to gather the hourly wage, hours per day worked, and days worked per week, we could issue a single INPUT command that would prompt for all three values. The rules for specifying the message text remain the same, except that now we specify all three variables, separated by commas, as in:

```
20 INPUT "Enter wage, hours/day, days/week:", WAGE,HRS,DAYS
```

BASIC would display the input prompt, after which the user would have to specify the hourly wage, hours per day, and days per week worked, all separated with commas.

You can specify both numeric and string variables together in INPUT commands; the position of variables specified on the INPUT command variable list determines the order and type of data with which the user must respond. The following example shows a program that uses INPUT to get both numeric and string data.

```
Ok
10 'Sample program using 1 INPUT command to capture different
20 'kinds of data
30 INPUT "Enter your name and your hourly wage:",NAM$,WAGE
40 WEEKLY.SALARY = WAGE * 40
50 PRINT NAM$" makes $"WEEKLY.SALARY"during a 40 hour week."
60 END
```

Its output looks like the following:

```
run
Enter your name and your hourly wage:Jim Doe,15.00
Jim Doe makes $ 600 during a 40 hr week.
Ok
```

You'll find the INPUT command is useful for programs that involve small amounts of data to be keyed in by a user. In a later chapter, we'll see how to input large amounts of data into a program without having to prompt the user to key values into the PC.

The PRINT Command

The following sections describe the use of the PRINT command to produce output on the screen, and some ways that you can format this output so that it is easy to read and understand.

PRINT allows the programmer to display the values of variables generated or calculated by the program. PRINT can also be used to display informative messages or text while the program is running, to inform the user of what the program is doing. The discussion of PRINT in this chapter, as well as all references to output, describe information that is displayed on the PC screen. Sending output to an attached printer will be described in a later chapter.

How the PRINT Command Operates

The PRINT command is very similar to the INPUT command in the way variables or string constants are specified after the command. The PRINT command replaces each variable specified with the variable's value in memory, and then displays all values along with any string constants that are specified.

The simplest example of the PRINT command is when it is specified with no parameters at all. Specifying 200 PRINT in a program will print a blank line. Printing blank lines is useful when displaying sizable amounts of data, to visually separate parts of the program.

PRINT can also be used to display informative text during the running of a program. String constants can be specified by the PRINT command, with the string of characters enclosed by double quotes. We could insert PRINT commands in our salary program to describe what the program is doing in different sections.

```
10 'Sample program using 1 INPUT command to capture different
20 'kinds of data
30 PRINT "Entering information gathering section:"
40 PRINT
50 INPUT "Enter your name and your hourly wage:",NAM$,WAGE
60 PRINT "Entering information calculation section:"
70 PRINT
80 WEEKLY.SALARY = WAGE * 40
90 PRINT "Entering report section:"
100 PRINT
110 PRINT NAM$" makes $"WEEKLY.SALARY"during a 40 hour week."
120 END
```

Running this program would display the text specified by each PRINT command with each string constant on a separate line. Here is an example of a program that uses PRINT to display several messages.

```
Ok
run
Entering information gathering section:

Enter your name and your hourly wage:Jack Doe,12.75
Entering information calculation section:

Entering report section:

Jack Doe makes $ 510 during a 40 hr week.
Ok
```

Although the complexity of the sample salary program doesn't really warrant the use of messages to describe what the program is doing, the method of placing PRINT commands that just display a string constant can be useful in larger, more sophisticated programs.

We've already seen examples of programs that display variables using the PRINT command. String and numeric variables can be specified together, by one PRINT command. Our sample salary program demonstrates just that:

```
110 PRINT NAM$" makes $"WEEKLY.SALARY" during a 40 hr week."
```

When BASIC interprets line 110, it will replace the variables NAM$ and SALARY with their corresponding values in memory, and then display the line. The string constants in the PRINT command above, "makes $" and "during a 40 hr week." do not get translated by BASIC; whenever you enclose any text with double quotes in a PRINT command, BASIC will display exactly the text you specify.

Positioning Text Using the PRINT Command

The examples of PRINT above did not use the special formatting capabilities that BASIC offers. Lines to be displayed on the screen were formatted by the user (notice the use of spaces in the string constant " makes $"). By specifying certain characters in the PRINT command, we can change the way the output looks on the screen. The concepts that get introduced in the following section are also applicable to displaying output on a printer.

We introduce the concept of **print zones** here to understand the formatting features that the PRINT command provides.

Typically, each line of the PC display is 80 characters wide, of which all 80 spaces per line are available for BASIC to use for displaying information. BASIC breaks the first 70 spaces into 5 sections, each section being 14 spaces in length. Each of these 5 sections is called a print zone. Though the use of PRINT commands has not been of a tabular nature so far, in some instances you'll want to display data in evenly spaced columns. BASIC allows you to do this using print zones.

Let's look at a sample program that will print out a multiplication table of whole numbers up to 5.

```
Ok
10 'This sample program displays a multiplication table for
20 'numbers up to 5
30 '
40 PRINT "Multiplication table up to 5"
50 PRINT
60 PRINT 1 * 1, 1 * 2, 1 * 3, 1 * 4, 1 * 5
70 PRINT 2 * 1, 2 * 2, 2 * 3, 2 * 4, 2 * 5
80 PRINT 3 * 1, 3 * 2, 3 * 3, 3 * 4, 3 * 5
90 PRINT 4 * 1, 4 * 2, 4 * 3, 4 * 4, 4 * 5
100 PRINT 5 * 1, 5 * 2, 5 * 3, 5 * 4, 5 * 5
110 PRINT
120 END
```

The output from the program demonstrates the results of using a comma as a **separator** between items specified on each PRINT command.

```
run
Multiplication table up to 5

1            2            3            4            5
2            4            6            8            10
3            6            9            12           15
4            8            12           16           20
5            10           15           20           25

Ok
```

The first item on each PRINT command is printed starting in the first column (print zone). The comma between the first and second items causes BASIC to "tab" or space over to the next print zone before printing the next item. The use of commas as separators in the PRINT command creates an easy listing to read, as all items are evenly spaced in columns.

However, our multiplication program will not display output neatly if we print a table that has more than five columns. Since we only have five print zones to work with, attempting to specify a sixth or greater item on each PRINT command would cause the output to wrap around.

```
10 'This sample program displays a multiplication table for
20 'numbers up to 6.  This program does not PRINT the data
30 'correctly.
40 PRINT "Multiplication table up to 6"
50 PRINT
60 PRINT 1 * 1, 1 * 2, 1 * 3, 1 * 4, 1 * 5, 1 * 6
70 PRINT 2 * 1, 2 * 2, 2 * 3, 2 * 4, 2 * 5, 2 * 6
80 PRINT 3 * 1, 3 * 2, 3 * 3, 3 * 4, 3 * 5, 3 * 6
90 PRINT 4 * 1, 4 * 2, 4 * 3, 4 * 4, 4 * 5, 4 * 6
100 PRINT 5 * 1, 5 * 2, 5 * 3, 5 * 4, 5 * 5, 5 * 6
110 PRINT 6 * 1, 6 * 2, 6 * 3, 6 * 4, 6 * 5, 6 * 6
120 PRINT
130 END
```

The output shows what happens if you specify more than five print zones.

```
run
Multiplication table up to 6

1               2               3               4               5
6
2               4               6               8               10
12
3               6               9               12              15
18
4               8               12              16              20
24
5               10              15              20              25
30
6               12              18              24              30
36

Ok
```

Because there are only five print zones per line, BASIC displayed the value of
the sixth item of each PRINT command on a separate line. To avoid having the
sixth item displayed on a separate line, we should use a semicolon instead of a
comma as a separator. Changing our program to use semicolons produces this
result:

```
Ok
10 'This sample program displays a multiplication table for
20 'numbers up to 6.  This program uses semi-colons as
30 'separators between items on each PRINT command.
40 PRINT "Multiplication table up to 6"
50 PRINT
60 PRINT 1 * 1; 1 * 2; 1 * 3; 1 * 4; 1 * 5; 1 * 6
70 PRINT 2 * 1; 2 * 2; 2 * 3; 2 * 4; 2 * 5; 2 * 6
80 PRINT 3 * 1; 3 * 2; 3 * 3; 3 * 4; 3 * 5; 3 * 6
90 PRINT 4 * 1; 4 * 2; 4 * 3; 4 * 4; 4 * 5; 4 * 6
100 PRINT 5 * 1; 5 * 2; 5 * 3; 5 * 4; 5 * 5; 5 * 6
110 PRINT 6 * 1; 6 * 2; 6 * 3; 6 * 4; 6 * 5; 6 * 6
120 PRINT
130 END
```

In the following output, the use of semicolons has allowed us to print more than
five items per line. We can probably display seven, eight, or more items per line.
Note that the displayed values are no longer in tabular format.

```
run
Multiplication table up to 6

1  2  3  4  5  6
2  4  6  8  10  12
3  6  9  12  15  18
4  8  12  16  20  24
```

```
5   10   15   20   25   30
6   12   18   24   30   36
```

Ok

When using commas to separate items in a PRINT command, you must also consider the length of each value in each variable that you specify. Study the flowchart and pseudocode in Figure 5.3, and then consider the program.

Figure 5.3

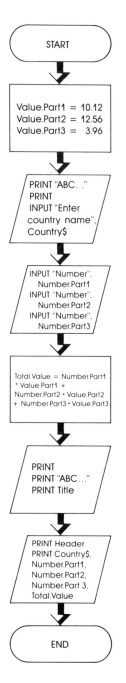

Program: Worldwide inventory program
Set value Part1 to 10.12
Set value Part2 to 12.56
Set value Part3 to 3.96
Display program title
READ country name
READ number of items of Part1
READ number of items of Part2
READ number of items of Part3
Set total value to sum of products of value of part times
    number of part
Display report title
Display column headings
Display country name, number of items of Part1, Part2,
    Part3 and total value
End: Worldwide inventory program

```
10 REM World-wide inventory program for ABC Incorporated
20 REM
30 REM This program gathers input such as country name, number of items
40 REM of part types 1, 2, and 3 in stock, and then generates total value
50 REM of all parts in that warehouse.  All information is then displayed
60 REM to user.
70 REM
80 REM Step 1: Initialize constants
90 REM
100 VALUE.PART1 = 10.12
110 VALUE.PART2 = 12.56
120 VALUE.PART3 = 3.96
130 REM
140 REM Step 2: Gather information from user.
150 REM
160 PRINT "ABC Incorporated - Worldwide Inventory Report Program"
170 PRINT
180 INPUT "Enter country name: ", COUNTRY$
190 INPUT "Enter number of items of part type 1 in stock: ",NUMBER.PART1
200 INPUT "Enter number of items of part type 2 in stock: ",NUMBER.PART2
210 INPUT "Enter number of items of part type 3 in stock: ",NUMBER.PART3
220 REM
230 REM Step 3: Calculate total value of all parts in remote warehouse.
240 REM
250 TOTAL.VALUE = NUMBER.PART1 * VALUE.PART1 + NUMBER.PART2 * VALUE.PART2
260 TOTAL.VALUE = TOTAL.VALUE + NUMBER.PART3 * VALUE.PART3
270 REM
280 REM Step 4: Display information for user
290 REM
300 PRINT
310 PRINT "ABC Incorporated - Inventory Report for "COUNTRY$
320 PRINT
330 PRINT "Country name","Number-PART1","Number-PART2","Number-PART3","Value"
340 PRINT
350 PRINT COUNTRY$,NUMBER.PART1,NUMBER.PART2,NUMBER.PART3,TOTAL.VALUE
360 PRINT
370 END
```

If we run the program and enter a country name that is less than 14 characters long, the program will display inventory information in tabular format:

```
Ok
run
ABC Incorporated - Worldwide Inventory Report Program

Enter country name: France
Enter number of items of part type 1 in stock: 90
Enter number of items of part type 2 in stock: 451
Enter number of items of part type 3 in stock: 2783
```

```
ABC Incorporated - Inventory report for France
Country name   Number-PART1   Number-PART2   Number-PART3   Value
France         90             451            2783           17596.04
Ok
```

If we run the program and enter a country name that is 14 or more characters long, however, the program will display inventory information in tabular format, but the information will not be aligned correctly:

```
Ok
run
ABC Incorporated - Worldwide Inventory Report Program

Enter country name: United Kingdom
Enter number of items of part type 1 in stock: 345
Enter number of items of part type 2 in stock: 234
Enter number of items of part type 3 in stock: 1123

ABC Incorporated - Inventory report for United Kingdom

Country name   Number-PART1   Number-PART2   Number-PART3   Value
United Kingdom                345            234            1123
   10877.52
Ok
```

We can see in the program above that by entering a country name of United Kingdom (more than 14 characters) the number of parts of type 1 is displayed where we would expect the number of parts of type 2 to be. Likewise, the number of parts of type 2 is displayed where we would expect the number of parts of type 3 to be. The number of parts of type 3 is displayed in the Value position, and the total value of all parts is displayed on the next line. We could change the program to use semicolons as separators, but the program would still generate nontabular reports. In Chapter 9, we will introduce you to advanced concepts that will allow you to use semicolons as separators and produce easy-to-read tabular reports.

The comma is used not only for separating items on a PRINT statement, but also can be used to print several items of data on a single line, using multiple PRINT statements. Our salary program could be rewritten in the following manner:

```
Ok
10 'Sample program using multiple PRINT commands to print one
20 'line of information - name and calculated weekly salary.
30 INPUT "Enter your name and your hourly wage:",NAM$,WAGE
40 WEEKLY.SALARY = WAGE * 40
50 PRINT NAM$,
60 PRINT " makes $",
70 PRINT WEEKLY.SALARY,
80 PRINT " during a 40 hour week."
90 END
```

This program produces the following output:

```
run
Enter your name and your hourly wage: Joe Doe,11
Joe Doe       makes $          440        during a 40 hr week.
Ok
```

The commas at the end of lines 60, 70, and 80 instruct BASIC to print each line on the same line, if there is space. The comma specifies not only that the next PRINT statement will begin printing on the same line, but that a skip to the next print zone will be performed as well. Specifying semicolons instead of commas at the end of lines 60, 70, and 80 would have instructed BASIC to print all data on the same line with no skipping to the next print zone.

Printing Numerical Expressions

When specifying items in a PRINT command, you should be aware of when to use and not to use numerical expressions. For instance, suppose we have a simple program to determine the discount rebate on a sale item:

```
10 'Calculate discount rebate on sale item
20 PCOFF = .25        ' Sale items are 25 percent off price
30 INPUT "Enter unit price, number of units: ",UNITPRICE,UNITS
40 PRICE = UNITPRICE * UNITS
50 PRINT "Discount is "PRICE * PCOFF
60 END
```

In this program, the user supplies an item's normal price and the number of items bought. On line 50, we are displaying the sale rebate in PRICE * PCOFF. Because the program ends after the PRINT statement, there is really no need to assign PRICE * PCOFF to a variable; the expression PRICE * PCOFF is only used in the PRINT command.

However, if the program were to do more calculations, particularly with the sale rebate, it would make more sense to create a variable called DISCOUNT, as in the following example:

```
10 'Calculate discount rebate on sale item and perform
20 'other calculations
30 PCOFF = .25        ' Sale items are 25 percent off price
40 INPUT "Enter unit price, number of units: ",UNITPRICE,UNITS
50 PRICE = UNITPRICE * UNITS
60 DISCOUNT = PRICE * PCOFF
70 PRINT "Discount is "DISCOUNT
80 PRICE = PRICE - DISCOUNT
90 PRINT "Cost of item is "PRICE
100 END
```

Other BASIC Commands Useful in Information Display

The CLS Command

CLS, as noted in Chapter 4, can be used as a BASIC system command to clear the screen while inputting, editing, or listing a BASIC program while in a BASIC session. You can also include the CLS command within a program, as a programming command, to clear the computer screen.

It is important for a program to be easy to use and easy to understand. Program input and output to and from the computer screen can often look cluttered and confusing to the end user; prompts for input, output of program results, plus other program-generated messages can all too often be overwhelming.

When large quantities of information are displayed to the user on the PC screen, you can use the CLS command to clear the screen of information that no longer needs to be displayed. Proper use of the CLS command can make a program display only the pertinent data that need to be on the PC screen at any given time (see box).

The CLS Command

Purpose   To clear the BASIC screen of all output

Format   ln CLS
where *ln* is a valid line number

Example   20 CLS

The KEY Command

The KEY command, like CLS, can improve the way a program displays information on the computer screen. When in a BASIC session, the bottom line of the display describes what the function keys do. During the execution of a BASIC program, these definitions are not necessary, and should be turned off to avoid screen clutter. KEY OFF will prevent the function key definitions from being displayed on line 25. KEY ON will redisplay the function key definitions (see box).

The KEY Command

Purpose   To turn the function key display on line 25 of the PC screen on or off

Format   ln KEY <setting>
where *ln* is a valid line number, and *setting* is either ON or OFF

Examples   30 KEY OFF
                1120 KEY ON

Note   The KEY command is sometimes used with the CLS command at the beginning and end of a program to make program output easier to read.

If your program displays more than a few lines of information, than it is good programming practice to include the following statement at the beginning of a BASIC program:

```
20 CLS : KEY OFF
```

and the following statement just before the end of a program:

```
100 CLS : KEY ON
```

Here is a sample weekly salary program that uses the CLS and KEY commands.

```
Ok
10 'Sample weekly program which calculates 3 weekly salaries.
20 CLS : KEY OFF
30 INPUT "Enter your name and your hourly wage:",NAM$,WAGE
40 WEEKLY.SALARY = WAGE * 40
50 PRINT NAM$" makes $"WEEKLY.SALARY"during a 40 hour week."
60 PRINT
70 INPUT "Press the ENTER key for second run",DUMMY$
80 CLS
90 INPUT "Enter your name and your hourly wage:",NAM$,WAGE
100 WEEKLY.SALARY = WAGE * 40
110 PRINT NAM$" makes $"WEEKLY.SALARY"during a 40 hour week."
120 PRINT
130 INPUT "Press the ENTER key for third run",DUMMY$
140 CLS
150 INPUT "Enter your name and your hourly wage:",NAM$,WAGE
160 WEEKLY.SALARY = WAGE * 40
170 PRINT NAM$" makes $"WEEKLY.SALARY"during a 40 hour week."
180 PRINT
190 INPUT "Press the ENTER key to end the program.",DUMMY$
200 CLS : KEY ON
210 END
```

Line 20 in the program above will clear the screen and turn the key definitions off. Line 200, immediately before the END statement in the program, will clear the screen once again, and turn the key definitions on again. By including the CLS and KEY commands, your programs will display data in a professional manner. The program above, when run, will first display the following screen:

```
Enter your name and your hourly wage: Jean Doe, 6.66
Jean Doe makes $ 266.4 during a 40 hour week.

Press the ENTER key for second run:
```

The INPUT command specifying DUMMY$ is used to pause the screen so that the user can see the output before the screen is cleared. As soon as the user presses the Enter key, the second screen will be displayed.

```
Enter your name and your hourly wage: Jan Doe, 10.00
Jan Doe makes $ 400 during a 40 hour week.

Press the ENTER key for third run:
```

As soon as the user presses the Enter key, the third and final screen of the program will appear.

```
Enter your name and your hourly wage: Janet Doe,30
Janet Doe makes $ 1200 during a 40 hour week.

Press the ENTER key to end the program:
```

When the user presses the Enter key again, the screen will clear, the BASIC "OK" prompt will appear at the top left-hand corner of the screen, and the function key display will reappear on line 25 of the screen.

Summary

- The INPUT command is used to gather information for a program by prompting the user to enter the information through the keyboard.
- The standard INPUT prompt is a question mark, but can be tailored to suit the program's needs. INPUT prompts are specified by enclosing the prompt text in double quotes one space after the word INPUT.
- A single variable or many variables may be specified on an INPUT command. The user must enter enough information of a specific type (character or numeric) to assign information to each variable specified in the INPUT command.
- The PRINT command is used to display information on the PC screen.
- BASIC can display information on 80 spaces of each line on the PC screen. The first 70 spaces are broken up into 5 print zones of 14 spaces each.
- Specifying a comma as a separator between items in a PRINT command will cause each item to be displayed, if it fits, in a single print zone.
- To print more than five items on one line, a space or semicolon must be used as the separator for items in the PRINT command.
- If you specify a comma after the last item in a PRINT command, BASIC will attempt to place the items of the next PRINT command in the next zone on the same line.
- If you specify a semicolon after the last item on a PRINT command, BASIC will attempt to place the items of the next PRINT command in the next space on the same line.
- The CLS command, like the BASIC CLS system command, can be used within a program to clear the BASIC screen. This command is of great use in programs that display large quantities of information.
- The KEY command, like the BASIC KEY system command, can be used within a program to clear the 25th line of the BASIC screen, which displays the settings of the function keys. The KEY command can also be used to turn the 25th line display on again.

Exercises

True or False

_____ 1. The INPUT command allows you to insert lines into a BASIC program.

_____ 2. If a numeric variable is followed by a string variable in an INPUT statement, when the INPUT statement is run the user must enter a number, and then the string information.

_____ 3. If the user presses the Enter key without typing any information when prompted to enter information by an INPUT command, BASIC will assign a zero to numeric variables and the null string to string variables specified on the INPUT statement.

_____ 4. The default INPUT prompt is a question mark.

_____ 5. If you do not specify any parameters after the PRINT statement, BASIC will clear the screen.

_____ 6. Specifying a comma as a separator between items on a PRINT command will cause BASIC to begin printing the next item on a separate line.

_____ 7. Specifying a semicolon as a separator between items on a PRINT command will cause BASIC to begin printing the next item in the next print zone.

_____ 8. Specifying spaces as separators between items on a PRINT command will cause BASIC to print the items each on a separate line.

_____ 9. When placed in a BASIC program, the CLS command will clear the screen.

_____ 10. When placed in a BASIC program, the KEY ON command will turn on the function key display at the bottom of the screen.

Fill-In

1. Data can be assigned to variables by the user while the program is running by using the _____ command.

2. The default prompt in an INPUT statement is _____ .

3. The _____ command is used to display data to the screen.

4. A PRINT command followed by no parameters will print a _____ .

5. To display string constants on the screen using the PRINT command, it is necessary to enclose the text of the string in _____ .

6. Variables separated by commas in a PRINT statement will be printed in _____ .

7. In 80 character mode, there are _____ print zones and _____ characters per zone for each printed line.

8. Multiple PRINT statements can be used to print data on a single line, provided the PRINT statement ends in a _____ or _____.

9. To clear the screen of data from within a BASIC program, the _____ command is used.

10. To turn the function key display located at the bottom of the BASIC screen off or on during the execution of a BASIC program, the _____ command can be used.

Short Answer

1. What advantages does the use of the INPUT statement have over hard-coding values within a program?

2. What would cause a "?Redo from start" error message to be issued on an INPUT statement?

3. If the INPUT command did not have the capability of allowing you to specify a prompt message, is there any way you could display a prompt message for input?

4. When should you use commas as separators between items in a PRINT command? When should you use semicolons as separators between items in a PRINT command? Give examples.

Programming Problems

1. Write a program to calculate the hourly and weekly salary of an employee, given that every employee will work 40 hours per week, and that you know the yearly gross salary. Your program should be flexible enough to be used by anyone.

2. Write a program to determine the selling price of a product, assuming that the product is marked up 5.5% due to state tax and 20% due to retail markup. You should use the INPUT command to prompt for product name and product wholesale cost.

3. A local bank has asked you to write a program that will quickly display how much money a person could save if they opened a variable-time savings account. Using the INPUT command, write a program that gathers the customer's name, principal amount, and number of years the principal can be kept in the savings account, and calculates the amount of interest earned, assuming that the interest is compounded annually at 8.8%. The formula to calculate yearly compounded interest is: INTEREST = PRINCIPAL (1 + (interest rate/100)) ^ YEARS.

4. As a member of the land conservation commission of a small town, you have been selected to calculate the amount of tax revenue the commission will receive on the property taxes collected on certain large tracts of land owned by wealthy landholders. Write a program to help you perform this task. Input to the program should be the property owner's name and the assessed value of the land. Assume a tax rate of $20 per $1000 of property value, and that the commission gets 5.3% of all collected property taxes.

5. With the information supplied in Problem 3 above (the savings account/interest program), write a program that displays the interest earned for a year, the principal at the beginning of the year, and the principal with interest at the end of the year, for each year in a fixed 10-year period, given an interest rate of 9.1%. Your program should utilize print zones to present all information.

6

Decision Making

After reading this chapter you should understand:

- How and when to use the IF-THEN statement
- What the various BASIC relational operators are and how to use them
- How characters are stored in ASCII format and how to use the ASCII table to compare character strings.

- What complex conditions are and the order of precedence of the logical operators
- How to use the IF-THEN-ELSE statement
- What nested IF statements are and how they can be used for more complex condition evaluations

Introduction

An important part of most programs written for business applications is the capability to make decisions. The program asks a question, the question is answered, a decision is made based on the answer, and an output is returned. Very often, in all but the simplest of programs, the decisions will take the form: if a condition is true, then do one thing; if not, do something else. This chapter shows you how to make decisions within your BASIC program, and what to do based on the decision made.

IF-THEN Statements

The simplest form of decision making within the BASIC program is the IF-THEN statement. The IF-THEN statement allows you to evaluate a condition, and if the condition is true, execute a desired task. A summary of the IF-THEN statement is given in the box below.

The IF-THEN Statement

Purpose	To provide a way of executing an instruction based on the result of evaluating a condition

Format	ln IF <condition> THEN <statement>
where *ln* is a valid line number, *condition* is a true/false condition, and *statement* is a valid BASIC expression to be executed if the condition proves to be true

Example	100 IF A < 0 THEN LET A = A + 100
200 IF HOURS > 40
	THEN LET PAY = (RATE * 40) + 1.5 * (RATE * (HOURS − 40))

Notes	If the condition proves to be true, the BASIC statement of the THEN clause is evaluated, and the program continues with the next line number in sequence. If the condition proves to be false, the program skips the THEN expression and continues with the next line number in sequence.

Programming Note	IF-THEN statements often span more than one line in a BASIC program. This allows for longer, more involved expressions than most other BASIC commands require, as well as allowing the statement to be structured in a more readable fashion. To continue a single statement onto the next line, instead of pressing the Enter key to go to the next line, hold down the **Ctrl** key, and press the **Enter** key.

In the following example, the program will prompt the user for sales data and then print the sales report. See Figure 6.1 for the flowchart and pseudocode used in planning this program.

```
10 REM Program to print a salesman's sales for the
20 REM current day and the associated commissions.
30 LET AVERAGE.SALES = 300
40 INPUT "Enter salesman's name: ",SALESMAN$
50 INPUT "Enter sales district: ",DISTRICT$
60 INPUT "Enter today's sales: ",TODAYS.SALES
70 INPUT "Enter salesman's commission rate: ",RATE
80 REM Calculate salesman's commission
90 LET COMMISSION = RATE * TODAYS.SALES
100 REM Print out sales report
120 PRINT "Salesman","District","Sales","Commission"
130 PRINT SALESMAN$,DISTRICT$,TODAYS.SALES,COMMISSION
140 IF (TODAYS.SALES > AVERAGE.SALES)
      THEN PRINT "Congratulations! Great job!"
150 END
```

Figure 6.1

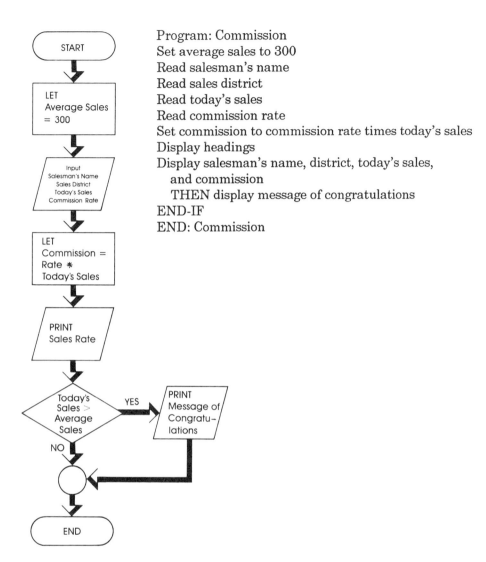

Program: Commission
Set average sales to 300
Read salesman's name
Read sales district
Read today's sales
Read commission rate
Set commission to commission rate times today's sales
Display headings
Display salesman's name, district, today's sales,
    and commission
    THEN display message of congratulations
END-IF
END: Commission

If the salesman had a better than average day (i.e., if sales were greater than 300) a short message of congratulations will be printed. If the sales for today were less than average, the program would continue on, skipping the THEN statement and executing the statement immediately following the THEN statement. This is what the program looks like when run:

```
run
Enter salesman's name: JONES
Enter sales district: NORTHEAST
Enter today's sales: 550
Enter salesman commission rate: .20

Salesman       District      Sales    Commission
 JONES         NORTHEAST      550       110
Congratulations!  Great job!
Ok
```

In this example, the sales of 550 is greater than the 300 average, so the message of congratulations is printed. If you had entered 250 for today's sales, you would get the following results:

```
run
Enter salesman's name: JONES
Enter sales district: NORTHEAST
Enter today's sales: 250
Enter salesman commission rate: .20

 Salesman      District    Sales   Commission
  JONES        NORTHEAST    250          50
Ok
```

The program skips over printing the message of congratulations and continues onto the next line, line 150.

Relational Operators

The conditional clause that determines whether the statement following the THEN gets executed is in the format described in the box below.

Valid Relational Operators

<	Less than
>	Greater than
=	Equal to
<=	Less than or equal to
>=	Greater than or equal to
<>	Not equal to

Format   value <relational operator> value
where *value* is any valid variable, constant, or character string and *relational operator* is one of the six valid relational operators

Examples   Given the following assignments; $a = 3, b = 2, c = 5$,

$a = b$	False
$b > 2$	False
$c > a$	True
$3 <> a$	False
$b <= c$	True
$b <= 2$	True

Note   The values separated by a relational operator must be of the same type. If a character and a numeric value are compared using a relational operator, the following message will occur: Type mismatch in <ln>.

Although the examples in the box use numeric values, the relational operators also work for character strings. Comparing character strings, however, is a little more confusing. For example, while it is very obvious that the character "3" would come before the character "9," and that the character "A" would come before the character"C," it gets a little confusing when special characters such as blanks, periods, and commas are compared with numbers and letters. For example does "1" come before "A," or "B" before "!"?

To understand these comparisons, it is necessary to understand how these values are ordered in the computer's memory. Characters are stored in memory in a binary format (as a series of 1's and 0's). These binary numbers are represented in BASIC by the ASCII (American Standard Code of Information Interchange) code, which is a 2-digit code representing each character as it is stored in memory. The ASCII code is a standard representation that can be used consistently with various operating systems and programming languages. As an example, the ASCII codes for several characters are listed below.

Character	ASCII Code
A	65
B	66
C	67
1	49
2	50
3	51
!	33
+	43
(blank)	32

For a complete list of the BASIC character set and the corresponding ASCII values, see Appendix C.

Thus, when you key in ABC123, the characters are stored in memory as 656667495051. By assigning each character as numeric value, it becomes possible to use relational operators with character strings. Character strings are compared character by character, from left to right, using their ASCII values. For example:

"ABC" = "AB"	False	"C" (67) does not equal a blank(32)
"+2B" = "-2B"	False	"+"(43) does not equal "-"(45)
"ABC" > "123"	True	"A"(65) is greater than "1"(49)
"?" < "G"	True	"?"(63) is less than "G"(71)

Complex Conditional Clauses

The conditional clauses that are evaluated by the IF-THEN statement can be made up of one or more conditions; multiple conditions are separated by **logical operators**. Logical operators allow the evaluation or negation of multiple conditions. The three logical operators available in BASIC are AND, OR, and NOT. The AND and OR operators join two or more conditional clauses, while NOT operates on single conditional clauses only.

AND

The logical operator AND compares two conditional clauses and returns a true value only if both conditional clauses prove to be true, or else a value of false is returned. For example, if we assume $a = 1$ and $c = 3$, then the statement $(a < 5)$ AND $(c = 3)$ would be evaluated as true, since $(a < 5)$ is true and $(c = 3)$ is also true. In the same way, the statement $(a < 0)$ AND $(c = 3)$ would be false, since $(a < 0)$ is false and $(c = 3)$ is true (if both conditions are not true, the expression is false). Likewise, if both conditions are false, the statement is false.

A **truth table** (see Table 6.1) is used to demonstrate the possible combinations and evaluations of conditions, in this case using the logical operator AND. In this table, X and Y represent conditional clauses and X *and* Y represents the evaluation of all possible combinations of X and Y.

Table 6.1   Truth Table for AND

X	Y	X AND Y
TRUE	TRUE	TRUE
TRUE	FALSE	FALSE
FALSE	TRUE	FALSE
FALSE	FALSE	FALSE

OR

The logical operator OR compares two conditional clauses and returns a true value if one *or* both of the conditional clauses prove to be true. If both of the conditional clauses prove false, then the resulting value is false. Using the example in which $a = 1$ and $c = 3$, $(a < 5)$ OR $(c = 3)$ would be true since $(a < 5)$ is true, and $(c = 3)$ is also true. The expression $(a < 0)$ OR $(c = 3)$ would also be true, since $(a < 0)$ is false, and $(c = 3)$ is true. One of the conditions is true, so the expression is also true. If both conditions are false, the expression is also false. The truth table (Table 6.2) demonstrates the results for conditions using the logical operator OR.

Table 6.2   Truth Table for OR

X	Y	X OR Y
TRUE	TRUE	TRUE
TRUE	FALSE	TRUE
FALSE	TRUE	TRUE
FALSE	FALSE	FALSE

NOT

The logical operator NOT works on a single condition and simply takes the opposite of the evaluation of the expression. If <condition> is true, then NOT<condition> is false. If <condition> is false, then NOT<condition> is true.

For example, if we assume that $a = 1$, NOT$(a < 5)$ would be false. Since $(a < 5)$ is true, then NOT$(a < 5)$ is false. Likewise, if $(a = 0)$ is false, then NOT$(a = 0)$ would be TRUE. Table 6.3 shows a truth table of the possibilities for the NOT logical operator.

Table 6.3 Truth Table for NOT

X	NOT(X)
TRUE	FALSE
FALSE	TRUE

Order of Operations for Logical Operators

A complex condition can be made up of several conditional clauses separated by a variety of ANDs, ORs, and NOTs. Since multiple ANDs, ORs, and NOTs can be used in a single condition, an order of precedence is necessary to determine which logical operator should be evaluated first (similar to the order of operation for numeric operators). For logical operators, the order of operations is as follows:

1. Expressions in parentheses
2. NOT
3. AND
4. OR

Of the logical operators, all the NOTS are evaluated first, then all the ANDS, and finally all the ORs. To change the default order of operation, use parentheses to specify which operator should be evaluated first. All operators in parentheses are evaluated first, just as with the numeric operators described in Chapter 4.

For example:

Assume $a = 1, b = 2, c = 3$

```
Evaluate: (a <> 1) AND NOT(b < 3) OR (c > a)          NOTs
   Step 1:                [FALSE]                      ANDs
   Step 2:   [FALSE] AND  [FALSE]                      ORs
   Step 3:         [FALSE]           OR  [TRUE]
   Result:                          [TRUE]
```

The result ends up to be true after evaluating all the NOTs first, followed by the ANDs, followed by the ORs.

```
Evaluate: (a <> 1) AND (NOT(b < 3) OR (c > a))        ()s
   Step 1:              (                      )       NOTs
   Step 2:              ([FALSE]               )       ORs
   Step 3:              ([FALSE]    OR  [TRUE])         ANDs
   Step 4:   [FALSE] AND (          [TRUE]    )
   Result:           [FALSE]
```

The result ends up to be false after evaluating the operators within the parentheses in order, the NOTs first, followed by the ORs, and then evaluating what is outside the parentheses, in this case the AND.

We can now expand the sales program we used earlier in this chapter to be more useful and flexible through the use of logical operators.

```
10 REM Program to print a salesman's sales for the
20 REM current day and the associated commissions based
30 REM on the profit made over cost of goods sold.
40 REM
50 REM Average sales, cost, and profit
60 LET AVERAGE.SALES = 300
70 LET AVERAGE.COST = 175
80 LET PROFIT = (AVERAGE.SALES/AVERAGE.COST) - 1
90 REM
100 REM Commission rates:
110 REM If sales above average and profit above average:
120 REM    Commission is 15%.
130 REM If sales above average but profit below average:
140 REM    Commission is 10%.
150 REM If sales below average but profit above average:
160 REM    Commission is 10%.
170 REM If sales below average and profit below average:
180 REM    Commission is 5%.
190 LET COM1 = .15
200 LET COM2 = .1
210 LET COM3 = .05
220 REM
230 REM Read in INPUT data:
240 INPUT "Enter salesman's name:  ",SALESMAN$
250 INPUT "Enter sales district:  ",DISTRICT$
260 INPUT "Enter today's sales:  ",TODAYS.SALES
270 INPUT "Enter cost of goods sold:  ",COST
280 REM
290 REM Calculate the salesman's commission.
300 LET TODAYS.PROFIT = (TODAYS.SALES/COST) - 1
310 IF (TODAYS.SALES > AVERAGE.SALES) AND (TODAYS.PROFIT > PROFIT)
      THEN LET RATE = COM1
320 IF (NOT(TODAYS.SALES > AVERAGE.SALES) AND (TODAYS.PROFIT > PROFIT)) OR
    ((TODAYS.SALES > AVERAGE.SALES) AND NOT(TODAYS.PROFIT > PROFIT))
      THEN LET RATE = COM2
330 IF NOT(TODAYS.SALES > AVERAGE.SALES) AND NOT(TODAYS.PROFIT > PROFIT)
      THEN LET RATE = COM3
340 COMMISSION = RATE * TODAYS.SALES
350 REM Print out sales report.
360 PRINT
370 PRINT "Salesman","District","Sales", "Rate","Commission"
380 PRINT SALESMAN$,DISTRICT$,TODAYS.SALES,RATE,COMMISSION
390 END
```

In this example, we use several complex conditions and logical operators to allow this program to calculate a commission based on the profit made on the sales and whether the day's sales were higher than average. When run, the results would look like this if the sales and profit are higher than average:

```
run
Enter salesman's name: JONES
Enter sales district: NORTHEAST
Enter today's sales: 500
Enter cost of goods sold: 200

Salesman        District      Sales        Rate           Commission
  JONES         NORTHEAST      500          .15                75
Ok
```

But if the sales are higher than average and profit is lower, the output would look like this:

```
run
Enter salesman's name: JONES
Enter sales district: NORTHEAST
Enter today's sales: 500
Enter cost of goods sold: 400

Salesman        District      Sales        Rate           Commission
  JONES         NORTHEAST      500          .1                 50
Ok
```

The output when the profit is higher than average and sales are lower would look like the following:

```
run
Enter salesman's name: JONES
Enter sales district: NORTHEAST
Enter today's sales: 250
Enter cost of goods sold: 100

Salesman        District      Sales        Rate           Commission
  JONES         NORTHEAST      250          .1                 25
Ok
```

Finally, if the sales and profit are lower than average, the result would be the following output:

```
run
Enter salesman's name: JONES
Enter sales district: NORTHEAST
Enter today's sales: 250
Enter cost of goods sold: 200

Salesman        District      Sales        Rate           Commission
  JONES         NORTHEAST      250          .05               12.5
Ok
```

IF-THEN-ELSE Statements

The IF-THEN-ELSE statement is a variation of the IF-THEN statement. It allows greater flexibility in the evaluation of a conditional clause because it allows a statement to be evaluated if the condition proves to be false, rather than just dropping down to the next line. The following summarizes IF-THEN-ELSE statements.

The IF-THEN-ELSE Statement

Purpose   To provide a way of executing an instruction based on the result of evaluating a condition.

Format   ln IF <condition> THEN <state1> ELSE <state2>
where *ln* is a valid BASIC line number, *condition* is true/false condition, *state1* is a valid BASIC expression to be executed if the condition proves to be true, and *state2* is a valid BASIC expression to be executed if the condition proves to be false

Examples   200 IF HOURS > 40
    THEN LET PAY = (RATE * 40) + 1.5 * (RATE * (HOURS − 40))
    ELSE LET PAY = (RATE * HOURS)

Notes   If the condition proves to be true, the THEN expression is evaluated, then the program continues with the next line number after the ELSE statement. If the condition proves to be false, the program skips the THEN expression and continues with the ELSE.

Programming Note   Remember that as with the IF-THEN statement, the Ctrl-Enter combination is used to continue a BASIC statement onto the next line.

The following program is a derivation of the example describing the IF-THEN statement. In this example, an ELSE clause has been added to be executed if the sales for the day are less than or equal to the average sales for a day.

```
 10  REM Program to print a salesman's sales for the
 20  REM current day and the associated commissions
 30  LET AVERAGE.SALES = 300
 40  INPUT "Enter salesman's name: ",SALESMAN$
 50  INPUT "Enter sales district: ",DISTRICT$
 60  INPUT "Enter today's sales: ",TODAYS.SALES
 70  INPUT "Enter salesman's commission rate: ",RATE
 80  REM Calculate salesman's commission
 90  LET COMMISSION = RATE * TODAYS.SALES
100  REM Print out sales report
110  PRINT
120  PRINT "Salesman","District","Sales","Commission"
130  PRINT SALESMAN$,DISTRICT$,TODAYS.SALES,COMMISSION
140  IF (TODAYS.SALES > AVERAGE.SALES)
        THEN PRINT "Congratulations!  Great job!"
        ELSE PRINT "Too Bad!  Try a little harder!"
150  END
```

The run for a sales value greater than 300 would be identical:

```
run
Enter salesman's name: JONES
Enter sales district: NORTHEAST
Enter today's sales: 550
Enter salesman commission rate: .20

Salesman      District    Sales   Commission
 JONES         NORTHEAST    550        110
Congratulations!  Great job!
Ok
```

If a sales value less than or equal to 300 is entered, then another message (less flattering) is printed following the sales report.

```
run
Enter salesman's name: JONES
Enter sales district: NORTHEAST
Enter today's sales: 250
Enter salesman commission rate: .20

Salesman      District    Sales   Commission
 JONES         NORTHEAST    250        50
Too Bad! Try a little harder!
Ok
```

Nested IF Statements

The expressions for the THEN and ELSE statements can themselves contain IF statements. This allows for a more complex and more controlled decision-making program. When the THEN or ELSE expression contains an IF-THEN or an IF-THEN-ELSE statement, it is called a **nested IF statement**. The nested IF statements follow the same rules as regular IF statements. The following example shows a nested IF statement on line 305. First, study Figure 6.2 for the flowchart and pseudocode used in planning the following program:

Figure 6.2

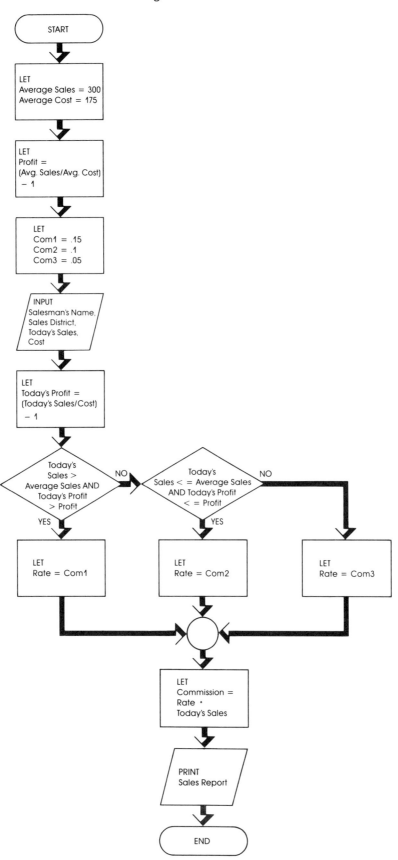

Program: Commission2
Set average sales to 300
Set average cost to 175
Set profit to average sales divided by average cost minus 1
Set Com1 to .15
Set Com2 to .1
Set Com3 to .05
READ salesman's name
READ sales district
READ today's sales
READ cost of goods sold
Set today's profit to today's sales divided by cost minus 1
IF today's sales are greater than average sales
      THEN set rate to Com1
      ELSE IF today's sales are less than or equal to average sales
         AND today's profit is less than or equal to profit
           THEN set rate to Com3
           ELSE set rate to Com2
      END-IF
END-IF
Set commission to rate times today's sales
Display headings
Display salesman's name, district, today's sales, and commission
END: Commission2

```
10 REM Program to print a salesman's sales for the
20 REM current day and the associated commissions based
30 REM on the profit made over cost of goods sold.
40 REM
50 REM Average sales, cost and profit
60 LET AVERAGE.SALES = 300
70 LET AVERAGE.COST = 175
80 LET PROFIT = (AVERAGE.SALES/AVERAGE.COST) - 1
90 REM
100 REM Commissions rates:
110 REM    If sales above average and profit above average:
120 REM       Commission is 15%.
130 REM    If sales above average but profit below average:
140 REM       Commission is 10%.
150 REM    If sales below average but profit above average:
160 REM       Commission is 10%.
170 REM    If sales below average and profit below average:
180 REM       Commission is 5%.
190 LET COM1 = .15
200 LET COM2 = .1
210 LET COM3 = .05
220 REM
230 REM Read in INPUT data
240 INPUT "Enter salesman's name: ",SALESMAN$
```

```
250 INPUT "Enter sales district: ",DISTRICT$
260 INPUT "Enter today's sales:  ",TODAYS.SALES
270 INPUT "Enter cost of goods sold:  ",COST
280 REM
290 REM Calculate the salesman's commission
300 LET TODAYS.PROFIT = (TODAYS.SALES/COST) - 1
305 IF (TODAYS.SALES > AVERAGE.SALES) AND (TODAYS.PROFIT > PROFIT) THEN RATE = COM1
    ELSE IF (TODAYS.SALES <= AVERAGE.SALES) AND (TODAYS.PROFIT <= PROFIT)
    THEN RATE = COM3 ELSE RATE = COM2
340 COMMISSION = RATE * TODAYS.SALES
350 REM Print out sales report
360 PRINT
370 PRINT "Salesman","District","Sales","Rate","Commission"
380 PRINT SALESMAN$,DISTRICT$,TODAYS.SALES,RATE,COMMISSION
390 END
```

The program shown here performs the exact same function as the program listed after the section on logical operators, but replaces lines 310, 320, and 330 with one nested IF statement in line 305. This program will give the same results for the same input data, as the earlier program (see page 132.)

A Word on Programming Style

One of the primary goals of this book is to teach you to write your BASIC programs in a clear, readable, and well-structured format. Since this chapter has focused on IF-THEN and IF-THEN-ELSE statements, we would like to take the opportunity here to stress the importance of presenting your IF statements in a clear, readable format. IF statements tend to span several lines and can become difficult to follow if not structured neatly. Consider for example the following nested IF statement:

```
100   IF (A < B) AND (B = C)
      THEN IF (A <> 0)
      THEN PRINT A;" Is not 0 and is < ";C
      ELSE PRINT A;" Equals 0, B = ";C
      ELSE IF (A = 0)
      THEN PRINT A;" Equals 0"
      ELSE PRINT A;" Not equal to 0"
```

In this format this line of code is difficult to read. Now let's indent some of the code to present it in a more structured manner. We indent so that the code more readily shows which statements are on the same level by their position in the line. For example, we line up all the THEN and ELSE clauses for one IF statement, and indent nested IF statements so it is easier to determine to which THEN or ELSE they belong. After a little cleaning up, the example above looks like this:

```
100   IF (A < B) AND (B = C)
         THEN IF (A <> 0)
                 THEN PRINT A;" Is not 0 and is < ";C
                 ELSE PRINT A;" Equals 0, B = ";C
         ELSE IF (A = 0)
                 THEN PRINT A;" Equals 0"
                 ELSE PRINT A;" Not equal to 0"
```

See how much easier this statement is to read when indented properly. Try to keep this in mind when coding IF statements or any statement that spans several lines.

Summary

- IF-THEN statements are used to evaluate a condition and execute a BASIC statement if that condition proves true.
- The relational operators for BASIC are:
  - <   Less than
  - >   Greater than
  - =   Equal to
  - <=   Less than or equal to
  - >=   Greater than or equal to
  - <>   Not equal to
- Character strings are stored and evaluated in ASCII format.
- The logical operators for BASIC are:
  AND   Returns a value of true if both conditions are true.
  OR   Returns a value of true if at least one condition is true.
  NOT   Returns the opposite value of the condition.
- The IF-THEN-ELSE statement will evaluate a condition, and execute the expression following the THEN if the condition is true, and execute the expression following the ELSE if the condition is false.
- Nested IF-THEN and IF-THEN-ELSE statements allow IF statements to be executed from within another IF statement.

Exercises

True or False

_____   1. One of the simplest forms of decision making within a BASIC program is the IF-THEN statement.

_____   2. The THEN section of an IF-THEN statement must begin with the next line number in sequence after the line number of the IF statement.

_____   3. Relational operators are only valid for comparisons of numeric variables and constants.

_____   4. The ASCII code is a standard representation for every character, and is used to keep a consistency between various operating systems and programming languages.

_____   5. The logical operator AND compares two conditional clauses and returns a value of true if neither of the two clauses is false.

_____ 6. The logical operator OR compares two conditional clauses and returns a value of false if either one or both conditions prove to be false.

_____ 7. The logical operator NOT compares two conditional clauses and returns a value of true if both conditions are false.

_____ 8. The order of evaluation of logical operators is always from left to right, unless a condition is enclosed in parentheses.

_____ 9. If the expression following the THEN or ELSE of an IF statement is itself an IF statement, it is called a nested IF statement.

_____ 10. It shows good programming techniques to left-justify all the lines in an IF-THEN and IF-THEN-ELSE statement to provide greater readability.

Fill-In

1. The _____ statement allows you to evaluate a condition, and if that condition is true, execute a desired task.

2. In coding an IF-THEN statement, if the line of code spans more than one line, a combination of the _____ and the _____ keys are depressed rather than pressing the Enter key.

3. The six symbols used to compare variables, constants, and character strings are known as _____ _____.

4. Characters are stored in a binary form in memory, and are represented by a two-character code known as the _____ _____.

5. _____ _____ allow the evaluation and negation of multiple expressions.

6. The logical operator _____ compares two conditional clauses and returns a value of false only if both of the conditions are false.

7. If <condition> is true, then NOT<condition> is _____.

8. A _____ _____ is used to diagram all the possible values of two clauses, joined by a logical operator.

9. The order of operation to evaluate an expression with logical operators would be: all the conditions in parentheses, followed by the logical operators in the order _____, _____, then _____.

10. The best way to structure an IF statement to make it more readable is to _____ the THEN and ELSE expressions.

Short Answer

1. What are the six BASIC relational operators and what are their purposes?

2. How are character strings compared using relational operators?

3. What is the purpose of the logical operators AND, OR, and NOT?

4. What are the differences between IF-THEN and IF-THEN-ELSE statements?

5. How does indenting code help to make IF statements more readable?

Programming Problems

1. Given the assignments $a = 2, b = 3, c = 0, d = 5$, evaluate whether the following relations are true or false.
   (a) $b = 3$
   (b) $(a - b) <> (d - (2 * b)$
   (c) $c <= 0$
   (d) $a + a > 4$
   (e) $0 = c + d - b - a$
   (f) $d + 2 < a + b$
   (g) $a + 5 >= b$

2. Using the ASCII code chart in Appendix C, evaluate whether the following relations are true or false.
   (a) "abcde" = "ABCDE"
   (b) "+123" <= "−123"
   (c) "?" > ">"
   (d) "A" <> "A"
   (e) "TRUE" > "FALSE"
   (f) "123" <= "321"
   (g) "+−@#" > "a"

3. Given the assignments $a = 3, b = 1, c = 0, d = 5$, evaluate the following expressions to be true or false.
   (a) $(a > 3)$ AND $(b = 1)$
   (b) NOT$(c > 5)$ OR NOT$(d = a)$
   (c) NOT$(a = 3)$ OR NOT $(b < 1)$ OR $(c <> 4)$ AND $(a = d)$
   (d) $((a <= 2)$ OR $(c = b))$ AND $(d = 5)$
   (e) $(d >= 2)$ AND NOT $(c <> 0)$

4. Write a BASIC program that will prompt for a student's name, and five exam grades, calculate an average exam score, and print out the corresponding letter grade, where an A is greater than or equal to 90, a B is greater than or equal to 80 but less than 90, etc.

5. Write a BASIC program to read in a customer's name and account number, the ending balances of the customer's checking and savings accounts, and whether or not the customer has direct deposit. The program should print out a heading, the name and account number, ending balances for the checking and savings accounts, and a total less a service fee. The service charge is $0.00 if the customer has over $1000 in checking or over $3000 in savings, $3.00 if the customer has direct deposit and over $300 in checking or over $500 in savings, and $5.00 otherwise.

6. Write a BASIC program to accept as input a part number, the quantity purchased, a unit price for that part, and the total number of that part available in stock. If the total purchase is greater than $1,000 and the quantity purchased depletes the supply in stock, give a 15% discount. If the total purchase exceeds $1000 or the number purchased depletes what is in stock (but not both), give a 10% discount. For any other case, no discount is given. Print out the total sale and any discounts given.

7. Write a BASIC program that accepts as input an employee name and whether he or she is salaried. If he or she is salaried, then prompt for the weekly salary. If he or she is not salaried, prompt for the number of hours worked and the hourly rate. If the number of hours exceeds 40, then pay time and a half for the hours in excess of 40. Then figure out the tax for both salaried and hourly work using the following rates:

greater than $3000	38%
between $2000 and $3000	32%
between $1000 and $2000	24%
less than $1000	20%

Print the employee name, gross pay, tax deductions and net pay.

7

Unconditional Branching

Learning Objectives

After reading this chapter you should understand:

- How to make unconditional branches in a BASIC program and the advantages and disadvantages of this type of branching
- What a subroutine is and how to call a subroutine from within a BASIC program

- The purpose of the GOTO statement.
- How to use the ON-GOSUB statement to develop user-friendly menus
- How to use the ON-GOTO statement to develop user-friendly menus

Introduction

Often in a BASIC program you will want to leave the normal flow of the program, execute a certain task, and then return to where you left the program. Leaving the normal flow of the program to execute statements at another section of the program is known as an **unconditional branching**. An unconditional branch allows you to choose a specific line number from which to continue processing. The program counter, which points to the current line number that is being executed, is changed to point to the line number specified by the branch. The program continues executing from this new line.

At one time, unconditional branching was considered a powerful and extremely useful tool in programming. It was widely used to interrupt the normal processing of program statements in sequential order by line number. The advantage of branching is that repetitive sections of code need to be coded only once, and the program can just branch to that section of code when necessary. These branches also provide the capability of executing involved procedures because they can be called based on the result of an IF statement. Over time, however, it has become evident that the use of unconditional branching can make programs more difficult to debug and enhance. Programmers began to notice that programs using many unconditional branches jumped around too much to trace errors, and this jumping around made the program even more susceptible to errors. There was a temptation for programmers to get sloppy, and instead of correctly handling difficult sections of code, to branch around in it. It became clear that while there was still a place for unconditional branching, care had to be taken to make sure this branching was done carefully and correctly. Since the intention of this book is to not only teach you to program in BASIC, but also to teach you good programming skills, we will try to identify and stress differences between proper and improper uses of unconditional branching.

Subroutines

Subroutines are independent groups of statements that are located outside of the logical sequence of execution of the main program, and which perform separate, limited functions. The main program branches to one of these subroutines to execute a specific task. Upon completion of this task the subroutine returns program execution to the statement immediately following the line from which the subroutine was called.

For example, suppose you have a program which, depending on the input, can print out one of twenty reports. Suppose also that each report has the same title page. A good use for a subroutine would be to print that title page. If the code were copied throughout the program it would be difficult to make a change in this title, since the change would have to be made in twenty different places. A subroutine could be used to print the title, and be called from all twenty parts of the program, returning execution to the calling section after the title is printed.

Care should be taken when creating a subroutine. A subroutine should perform a single task and return control to the main program. Subroutines should primarily be used for tasks that are executed frequently and are called from several places in the program, or when a subroutine would make the program more readable. Let's take a look at a sample program that could be more efficiently written using subroutines. The program below takes twelve months' worth of inventory data, and for each quarter produces three reports using three common inventory reporting methods. The first inventory method is the weighted average. This works by assuming that the value of the inventory at the end of the quarter is equal to the number of items left multiplied by the average cost of these items over the three months within the quarter. The second method we will use is the first-in first-out approach (FIFO). Using this method we assume that the items we have sold over the quarter were sold in the order in which they were purchased. If the price of the item increased over the quarter, the value of the inventory under the FIFO method would be greater than the weighted average at the end of the quarter. The third method we will use is the last-in first-out method (LIFO). Using the LIFO method, we assume that the items we sell first are the most recently purchased. This means that if the price of the items increased over the quarter, the value of the items left in the inventory at the end of the quarter would be less than the weighted average. Notice that since the same header appears on all twelve reports, many lines of code need to be written several times.

```
10 REM This program assumes a starting inventory of 0, and accepts data for 12
20 REM months on the number of Widgets purchased and the unit price
30 REM per Widget.  Then for each quarter, a report is made using three
40 REM common inventory methods:  Weighted Average, FIFO, and LIFO.
50 REM Three reports are printed for each quarter, one for each method used.
60 REM
```

```
 70 CLS
 80 INPUT "Number of Widgets purchased, unit price for JAN: ",WID1,PR1
 90 INPUT "Number of Widgets purchased, unit price for FEB: ",WID2,PR2
100 INPUT "Number of Widgets purchased, unit price for MAR: ",WID3,PR3
110 INPUT "Number of Widgets purchased, unit price for APR: ",WID4,PR4
120 INPUT "Number of Widgets purchased, unit price for MAY: ",WID5,PR5
130 INPUT "Number of Widgets purchased, unit price for JUN: ",WID6,PR6
140 INPUT "Number of Widgets purchased, unit price for JUL: ",WID7,PR7
150 INPUT "Number of Widgets purchased, unit price for AUG: ",WID8,PR8
160 INPUT "Number of Widgets purchased, unit price for SEP: ",WID9,PR9
170 INPUT "Number of Widgets purchased, unit price for OCT: ",WID10,PR10
180 INPUT "Number of Widgets purchased, unit price for NOV: ",WID11,PR11
190 INPUT "Number of Widgets purchased, unit price for DEC: ",WID12,PR12
200 REM
210 INPUT "Number of units in inventory at end of Q1: ",INV1
220 INPUT "Number of units in inventory at end of Q2: ",INV2
230 INPUT "Number of units in inventory at end of Q3: ",INV3
240 INPUT "Number of units in inventory at end of Q4: ",INV4
250 PRINT
260 REM
270 REM Initialize inventory for beginning of the year to 0
280 REM
290 WID.START = 0
300 WAVG.START = 0
310 FIFO.START = 0
320 LIFO.START = 0
330 REM
340 REM Calculate the number of units available for the first quarter
350 REM
360 NUMB.AVAL = WID.START + WID1 + WID2 + WID3
370 REM
380 REM Calculate Weighted Average inventory for Q1
390 REM
400 WAVG.GAFS = (WID.START * WAVG.START) + (WID1 * PR1) + (WID2 * PR2) + (WID3 * PR3)
410 WAVG.AVG.COST = WAVG.GAFS/NUMB.AVAL
420 WAVG.END.INV = INV1 * WAVG.AVG.COST
430 WAVG.START = WAVG.AVG.COST
440 REM
450 REM Calculate first-in first-out inventory for Q1
460 REM
470 FIFO.GAFS = (WID.START * FIFO.START) + (WID1 * PR1) + (WID2 * PR2) + (WID3 * PR3)
480 SOLD = NUMB.AVAL - INV1
490 IF SOLD <= WID.START
       THEN FIFO.END.INV = ((WID.START-SOLD)*FIFO.START)+(WID1*PR1)+ (WID2*PR2)
                         + (WID3*PR3)
500 IF (SOLD > WID.START) AND (SOLD <= WID.START + WID1)
       THEN FIFO.END.INV = ((WID.START + WID1 - SOLD) * PR1) + (WID2 * PR2) +
                         (WID3 * PR3)
510 IF (SOLD > WID.START + WID1) AND (SOLD <= WID.START + WID1 + WID2)
       THEN FIFO.END.INV = ((WID.START + WID1 + WID2 - SOLD) * PR2) + WID3 * PR3)
```

```
520 IF (SOLD > WID.START + WID1 + WID2) AND (SOLD <= WID.START + WID1 + WID2 + WID3)
      THEN FIFO.END.INV = ((WID.START + WID1 + WID2 + WID3 - SOLD) * PR3)
530 FIFO.START = FIFO.END.INV/INV1
540 REM
550 REM Calculate last-in first-out inventory for Q2
560 REM
570 LIFO.GAFS = (WID.START * LIFO.START) + (WID1 * PR1) + (WID2 * PR2) + ((WID3
                  - SOLD * PR3)
580 SOLD = NUMB.AVAL - INV1
590 IF SOLD <= WID3
      THEN LIFO.END.INV = (WID.START * LIFO.START) + (WID1 * PR1) + (WID2 * PR2)
                          + ((WID3 - SOLD) * PR3)
600 IF (SOLD > WID3) AND (SOLD <= WID3 + WID2)
      THEN LIFO.END.INV = (WID.START * LIFO.START) + WID1 * PR1) + ((WID3 +
                          WID2 - SOLD) * PR2)
610 IF (SOLD > WID3 + WID2) AND (SOLD <= WID3 + WID2 + WID1)
      THEN LIFO.END.INV = (WID.START * LIFO.START) + ((WID3 + WID2 + WID1 -
                          SOLD) * PR1)
620 IF (SOLD > WID3 + WID2 + WID1) AND (SOLD <= WID.START + WID3 + WID2 + WID1)
      THEN LIFO.END.INV = ((WID.START + WID1 + WID2 + WID3 - SOLD) * LIFO.START)
630 LIFO.START = LIFO.END.INV/INV1
640 WID.START = INV1
650 REM
660 CLS
670 PAGE.NO = 1
680 PRINT ,,"page ";PAGE.NO
690 PRINT
700 PRINT "XYZ Widget Supply Company"
710 PRINT "Dallas Distribution Center:
720 PRINT "Dallas, Texas"
730 PRINT
740 PRINT "Periodic Inventory Analysis"
750 PRINT "          Product:  Widget                 Part No:  A3234-34"
760 PRINT
770 PRINT "*******************************************************************"
780 PRINT
790 PRINT "Analysis Summary for Q1:"
800 PRINT
810 PRINT "                      Weighted Average Method"
820 PRINT
830 PRINT "              Goods Available for Sale         $";WAVG.GAFS
840 PRINT "              Less Ending Inventory           $";WAVG.END.INV
850 PRINT "              Cost of Goods Sold              $";WAVG.GAFS - WAGV.END
860 PRINT
870 PRINT
880 INPUT "Press ENTER to continue",TEMP$
890 CLS
900 PAGE.NO = 2
910 PRINT ,,"page ";PAGE.NO
920 PRINT
```

```
930 PRINT "XYZ Widget Supply Company"
940 PRINT "Dallas Distribution Center"
950 PRINT "Dallas, Texas"
960 PRINT
970 PRINT "Periodic Inventory Analysis"
980 PRINT "          Product: Widget              Part No:  A3234-34"
990 PRINT
1000 PRINT "****************************************************************"
1010 PRINT
1020 PRINT "Analysis Summary for Q1:"
1030 PRINT
1040 PRINT "                    First-In First-Out Method"
1050 PRINT
1060 PRINT "          Goods Available for Sale         $";FIFO.GAFS
1070 PRINT "          Less Ending Inventory           $";FIFO.END.INV
1080 PRINT "          Cost of Goods Sold             $";FIFO.GAFS-FIFO.END"
1090 PRINT
1100 PRINT
1110 INPUT "Press ENTER to continue",TEMP$
1120 CLS
1130 PAGE.NO = 3
1140 PRINT ,,"page ";PAGE.NO
1150 PRINT
1160 PRINT "XYZ Widget Supply Company"
1170 PRINT "Dallas Distribution Center"
1180 PRINT "Dallas, Texas"
1190 PRINT
1200 PRINT "Periodic Inventory Analysis"
1210 PRINT "          Product: Widget              Part No:  A3234-34"
1220 PRINT
1230 PRINT "****************************************************************"
1240 PRINT
1250 PRINT "Analysis Summary for Q1:"
1260 PRINT
1270 PRINT "                    Last-In First-Out Method"
1280 PRINT
1290 PRINT "          Goods Available for Sale      $";LIFO.GAFS
1300 PRINT "          Less Ending Inventory         $";LIFO.END.INV
1310 PRINT "          Cost of Goods Sold            $";LIFO.GAFS - LIFO.END
1320 PRINT
1330 PRINT
1340 INPUT "Press ENTER to continue",TEMP$
1350 CLS
1360 REM
1370 REM Calculate the number of units available for the second quarter
1380 REM
1390 NUMB.AVAL = WID.START + WID4 + WID5 + WID6
1400 REM
1410 REM Calculate Weighted Average Inventory for Q2
1420 REM
```

```
1430 WAVG.GAFS = (WID.START * WAVG.START) + (WID4 * PR4) + (WID5 * PR5) + (WID6 * PR6)
1440 WAVG.AVG.COST = WAVG.GAFS/NUMB/AVAL
1450 WAVG.END.INV = INV2 * WAVG.AVG.COST
1460 WAVG.START = WAVG.AVG.COST
1470 REM
1480 REM Calculate first-in first-out inventory for Q2
1490 REM
1500 FIFO.GAFS = (WID.START * FIFO.START) + (WID4 * PR4) + (WID5 * PR5) + (WID6 * PR6)
1510 SOLD = NUMB.AVAL - INV2
1520 IF SOLD <= WID.START
       THEN FIFO.END.INV = ((WID.START - SOLD) * FIFO.START) + (WID4 * PR4) +
                           (WID5 * PR5) + (WID6 * PR6)
1530 IF (SOLD > WID.START) AND (SOLD <= WID.START + WID4)
       THEN FIFO.END.INV = ((WID.START + WID4 - SOLD) * PR4) + (WID5 * PR5) +
                           (WID6 * PR6)
1540 IF (SOLD > WID.START + WID4) AND (SOLD <= WID.START + WID4 + WID5)
       THEN FIFO.END.INV = ((WID.START + WID4 + WID5 - SOLD) * PR5) +
                           (WID6 * PR6)
1550 IF (SOLD > WID.START + WID4 + WID5) AND (SOLD <= WID.START + WID4 +
     WID5 + WID6)
       THEN FIFO.END.INV = ((WID.START + WID4 + WID5 + WID6 - SOLD) * PR6)
1560 FIFO.START = FIFO.END.INV/INV2
1570 REM
1580 REM Calculate last-in first-out inventory for Q3
1590 REM
1600 LIFO.GAFS = (WID.START * LIFO.START) + (WID4 * PR4) + (WID5 * PR5) +
                 (WID6 * PR6)
1610 SOLD = NUMB.AVAL - INV2
1620 IF SOLD <= WID6
       THEN LIFO.END.INV = (WID.START * LIFO.START) + (WID4 * PR4) +
                           (WID5 * PR5) + ((WID6 - SOLD) * PR6)
1630 IF (SOLD > WID6) AND (SOLD <= WID6 + WID5)
       THEN LIFO.END.INV = (WID.START * LIFO.START) + (WID4 * PR4) +
                           ((WID6 + WID5 - SOLD) * PR5)
1640 IF (SOLD > WID6 + WID5) AND (SOLD <= WID6 + WID5 + WID4)
       THEN LIFO.END.INV = ((WID.START + WID4 + WID5 + WID6 - SOLD) *
                           LIFO.START)

1660 LIFO.START = LIFO.END.INV/INV2
1670 WID.START = INV2
1680 REM
1690 CLS
1700 PAGE.NO = 4
1710 PRINT ,,"page ";PAGE.NO
1720 PRINT
1730 PRINT "XYZ Widget Supply Company"
1740 PRINT "Dallas Distribution Center"
1750 PRINT "Dallas, Texas"
1760 PRINT
1770 PRINT "Periodic Inventory Analysis"
```

```
1780 PRINT "          Product:  Widget               Part No:  A3234-34"
1790 PRINT
1800 PRINT "*************************************************************"
1810 PRINT
1820 PRINT "Anaylsis Summary for Q2:"
1830 PRINT
1840 PRINT "                        Weighted Average Method"
1850 PRINT
1860 PRINT "          Goods Available for Sale        $";WAVG.GAFS
1870 PRINT "          Less Ending Inventory          $";WAVG.END.INV
1880 PRINT "          Cost of Goods Sold             $";WAVG.GAFS - WAVG.END
1890 PRINT
1900 PRINT
1910 INPUT "Press ENTER to continue",TEMP$
1920 CLS
1930 PAGE.NO = 5
1940 PRINT ,,"page ";PAGE.NO
1950 PRINT
1960 PRINT "XYZ Widget Supply Company"
1970 PRINT "Dallas Distribution Center"
1980 PRINT "Dallas, Texas"
1990 PRINT
2000 PRINT "Periodic Inventory Analysis"
2010 PRINT "          Product:  Widget               Part No:  A3234-34"
2020 PRINT
2030 PRINT "*************************************************************"
2040 PRINT
2050 PRINT "Analysis Summary for Q2:"
2060 PRINT
2070 PRINT "                   First-In First-Out Method"
2080 PRINT
2090 PRINT "          Goods Available for Sale        $";FIFO.GAFS
2100 PRINT "          Less Ending Inventory          $";FIFO.END.INV
2110 PRINT "          Cost of Goods Sold             $";FIFO.GAFS-FIFO.END

2120 PRINT
2130 PRINT
2140 INPUT "Press ENTER to continue",TEMP$
2150 CLS
2160 PAGE.NO = 6
2170 PRINT ,,"page ";PAGE.NO
2180 PRINT
2190 PRINT "XYZ Widget Supply Company"
2200 PRINT "Dallas Distribution Center"
2210 PRINT "Dallas, Texas"
2220 PRINT
2230 PRINT "Periodic Inventory Analysis"
2240 PRINT "          Product:  Widget               Part No:  A3234-34"
2250 PRINT
2260 PRINT "*************************************************************"
```

```
2270 PRINT
2280 PRINT "Analysis Summary for Q2:"
2290 PRINT
2300 PRINT "                    Last-In First-Out Method"
2310 PRINT
2320 PRINT "          Goods Available for Sale          $";LIFO.GAFS
2330 PRINT "          Less Ending Inventory            $";LIFO.END.INV
2340 PRINT "          Cost of Goods Sold               $";LIFO.GAFS-LIFO.END
2350 PRINT
2360 PRINT
2370 INPUT "Press ENTER to continue",TEMP$
2380 CLS
2390 REM
2400 REM Calculate the number of units available for the third quarter
2410 REM
2420 NUMB.AVAL = WID.START + WID7 + WID8 + WID9
2430 REM
2440 REM Calculate weighted average inventory for Q3
2450 REM
2460 WAVG.GAFS = (WID.START * WAVG.START) + (WID7 * PR7) + (WID8 * PR8) +
                (WID9 * PR9)
2470 WAVG.AVG.COST = WAVG.GAFS/NUMB.AVAL
2480 WAVG.END.INV = INV3 * WAVG.AVG.COST
2490 WAVG.START = WAVG.AVG.COST
2500 REM
2510 REM Calculate first-in first-out inventory for Q3
2520 REM
2530 FIFO.GAFS = (WID.START * FIFO.START) + (WID7 * PR7) + (WID8 * PR8) +
                (WID9 * PR9)
2540 SOLD = NUMB.AVAL - INV3
2550 IF SOLD <= WID.START
     THEN FIFO.END.INV = ((WID.START - SOLD) * FIFO.START) + (WID7 * PR7) +
                        (WID8 * PR8) + (WID9 * PR9)
2560 IF (SOLD > WID.START) AND (SOLD <= WID.START + WID7)
     THEN FIFO.END.INV = ((WID.START + WID7 - SOLD) * PR7) + (WID8 * PR8) +
                        (WID9 * PR9)
2570 IF (SOLD > WID.START + WID7) AND (SOLD >= WID.START + WID7 + WID8)
     THEN FIFO.END.INV = ((WID.START + WID7 + WID8 - SOLD) * PR8) +
                        (WID9 * PR9)
2580 IF (SOLD > WID.START + WID7 + WID8) AND (SOLD <= WID.START + WID7 + WID8 + WID9)
     THEN FIFO.END.INV = ((WID.START + WID7 + WID8 + WID9 - SOLD) * PR9)
2590 FIFO.START = FIFO.END.INV/INV3
2600 REM
2610 REM Calculate last-in first-out inventory for Q3
2620 REM
2630 LIFO.GAFS = (WID.START * LIFO.START) + (WID7 * PR7) + (WID8 * PR8) +
                (WID9 * PR9)
2640 SOLD = NUMB.AVAL - INV3
```

```
2650 IF SOLD <= WID9
     THEN LIFO.END.INV = (WID.START * LIFO.START) + (WID7 * PR7) +
                         (WID8 * PR8) + **WID9 - SOLD) * PR9)
2660 IF (SOLD > WID9) AND (SOLD <= WID9 + WID8)
     THEN LIFO.END.INV = (WID.START * LIFO.START) + (WID8 * PR8) +
                         ((WID9 + WID8 - SOLD) * PR8)
2670 IF (SOLD > WID9 + WID8) AND (SOLD <= WID9 + WID8 + WID7)
     THEN LIFO.END.INV = (WID.START * LIFO.START) + ((WID9 + WID8 + WID7 -
                         SOLD) * PR7)
2680 IF (SOLD > WID9 + WID8 + WID7) AND (SOLD <= WID.START + WID9 + WID8 + WID7)
     THEN LIFO.END.INV = ((WID.START + WID7 + WID8 + WID9 - SOLD) * LIFO.START)
2690 LIFO.START = LIFO.END.INV/INV3
2700 WID.START = INV3
2710 REM
2720 CLS
2730 PAGE.NO = 7
2740 PRINT ,,"page ";PAGE.NO
2750 PRINT
2760 PRINT "XYZ Widget Supply Company"
2770 PRINT "Dallas Distribution Center"
2780 PRINT "Dallas, Texas"
2790 PRINT
2800 PRINT "Periodic Inventory Analysis"
2810 PRINT "        Product:  Widget              Part No:  A3234-34"
2820 PRINT
2830 PRINT "******************************************************************"
2840 PRINT
2850 PRINT "Analysis Summary for Q3:"
2860 PRINT
2870 PRINT "                    Weighted Average Method"
2880 PRINT
2890 PRINT "        Goods Available for Sale        $";WAVG.GAFS
2900 PRINT "        Less Ending Inventory           $";WAVG.END.INV
2910 PRINT "        Cost of Goods Sold              $";WAVG.GAFS-WAVG.END
2920 PRINT
2930 PRINT
2940 INPUT "Press ENTER to continue",TEMP$
2950 CLS
2960 PAGE.NO = 8
2970 PRINT ,,"page ";PAGE.NO
2980 PRINT
2990 PRINT "XYZ Widget Supply Company"
3000 PRINT "Dallas Distribution Center"
3010 PRINT "Dallas, Texas"
3020 PRINT
3030 PRINT "Periodic Inventory Analysis"
3040 PRINT "        Product:  Widget              Part No:  A3234-34"
3050 PRINT
3060 PRINT "******************************************************************"
3070 PRINT
```

```
3080 PRINT "Analysis Summary for Q3:"
3090 PRINT
3100 PRINT "                    First-in First-out Method"
3110 PRINT
3120 PRINT "          Goods Available for Sale         $";FIFO.GAFS
3130 PRINT "          Less Ending Inventory            $";FIFO.END.INV
3140 PRINT "          Cost of Goods Sold               $";FIFO.GAFS - FIFO.END
3150 PRINT
3160 PRINT
3170 INPUT "Press ENTER to continue",TEMP$
3180 CLS
3190 PAGE.NO = 9
3200 PRINT ,,"page ";PAGE.NO
3210 PRINT
3220 PRINT "XYZ Widget Supply Company"
3230 PRINT "Dallas Distribution Center"
3240 PRINT "Dallas, Texas"
3250 PRINT
3260 PRINT "Periodic Inventory Analysis"
3270 PRINT "        Product:  Widget              Part No:  A3234-34"
3280 PRINT
3290 PRINT "*********************************************************************"
3300 PRINT
3310 PRINT "Analysis Summary for Q3:"
3320 PRINT
3330 PRINT "                    Last-In First-Out Method"
3340 PRINT
3350 PRINT "          Goods Available for Sale         $";LIFO.GAFS
3360 PRINT "          Less Ending Inventory            $";LIFO.END.INV
3370 PRINT "          Cost of Goods Sold               $";LIFO.GAFS-LIFO.END
3380 PRINT
3390 PRINT
3400 INPUT "Press ENTER to continue",TEMP$
3410 CLS
3420 REM
3430 REM Calculate the number of units available for the fourth quarter
3440 REM
3450 NUMB.AVAL = WID.START + WID10 + WID11 + WID12
3460 REM
3470 REM Calculate weighted average inventory for Q4
3480 REM
3490 WAVG.GAFS = (WID.START * WAVG.START) + (WID10 * PR10) + (WID11 * PR11) +
                  (WID12 * PR12)
3500 WAVG.AVG.COST = WAVG.GAFS/NUMB.AVAL
3510 WAVG.END.INV = INV4 * WAVG.AVG.COST
3520 WAVG.START = WAVG.AVG.COST
3530 REM
3540 REM Calculate first-in first-out inventory for Q4
3550 REM
```

```
3560 FIFO.GAFS = (WID.START * FIFO.START) + (WID10 * PR10) + (WID11 * PR11) +
                 (WID12 * PR12)
3570 SOLD = NUMB.AVAL - INV4
3580 IF SOLD <= WID.START
     THEN FIFO.END.INV = ((WID.START - SOLD) * FIFO.START) + (WID10 * PR10) +
                          (WID11 * PR11) + (WID12 * PR12)
3590 IF (SOLD > WID.START) AND (SOLD <= WID.START + WID10)
     THEN FIFO.END.INV = ((WID.START + WID10 - SOLD) * PR10) + (WID11 * PR11) +
                          (WID12 * PR12)
3600 IF (SOLD > WID.START + WID10) AND (SOLD <= WID.START + WID10 + WID11)
     THEN FIFO.END.INV = ((WID.START + WID10 + WID11 - SOLD) * PR11) +
                          (WID12 * PR12)
3610 IF (SOLD > WID.START + WID10 + WID11) AND (SOLD <= WID.START + WID10 +
                 WID11 + WID12)
     THEN FIFO.END.INV = ((WID.START + WID10 + WID11 + WID12 - SOLD) * PR12)
3620 FIFO.START = FIFO.END.INV/INV4
3630 REM
3640 REM Calculate Last-in First-out inventory for Q4
3650 REM
3660 LIFO.GAFS = (WID.START * LIFO.START) + (WID10 * PR10) + (WID11 * PR11) +
                 (WID12 * PR12)
3670 SOLD = NUMB.AVAL - INV4
3680 IF SOLD <= WID12
     THEN LIFO.END.INV = (WID.START * LIFO.START) + (WID10 * PR10) +
                          ((WID12 + WID11 - SOLD) * PR11)
3700 IF (SOLD > WID12 + WID11) AND (SOLD <= WID12 + WID11 + WID10)
     THEN LIFO.END.INV = (WID.START * LIFO.START) + ((WID12 + WID11 +
                          WID10 - SOLD) * PR12)
3710 IF (SOLD > WID12 + WID11) AND (SOLD <= WID12 + WID11 + WID10)
     THEN LIFO.END.INV = ((WID.START + WID10 + WID11 + WID12 - SOLD) *
                          LIFO.START)
3720 LIFO.START = INV4
3740 REM
3750 CLS
3760 PAGE.NO = 10
3770 PRINT ,,"page ";PAGE.NO
3780 PRINT
3790 PRINT "XYZ Widget Supply Company"
3800 PRINT "Dallas Distribution Center"
3810 PRINT "Dallas, Texas"
3820 PRINT
3830 PRINT "Periodic Inventory Analysis"
3840 PRINT "        Product: Widget              Part No:  A3234-34"
3850 PRINT
3860 PRINT "**********************************************************************"
3870 PRINT
3880 PRINT "Analysis Summary for Q4:"
3890 PRINT
3900 PRINT "                          Weighted Average Method"
3910 PRINT
```

```
3920 PRINT "            Goods Available for Sale        $";WAVG.GAFS
3930 PRINT "            Less Ending Inventory          $";WAVG.END.INV
3940 PRINT "            Cost of Goods Sold             $";WAVG.GAFS-WAVG.END
3950 PRINT
3960 PRINT
3970 INPUT "Press ENTER to continue",TEMP$
3980 CLS
3990 PAGE.NO = 11
4000 PRINT ,,"page ";PAGE.NO
4010 PRINT
4020 PRINT "XYZ Widget Supply Company"
4030 PRINT "Dallas Distribution Center"
4040 PRINT "Dallas, Texas"
4050 PRINT
4060 PRINT "Periodic Inventory Analysis"
4070 PRINT "        Product:  Widget              Part No:  A3234-34"
4080 PRINT
4090 PRINT "*****************************************************************"
4100 PRINT
4110 PRINT "Analysis Summary for Q4:"
4120 PRINT
4130 PRINT "                First-In First-Out Method"
4140 PRINT
4150 PRINT "            Goods Available for Sale        $";FIFO.GAFS
4160 PRINT "            Less Ending Inventory          $";FIFO.END.INV
4170 PRINT "            Cost of Goods Sold             $";FIFO.GAFS-FIFO.END
4180 PRINT
4190 PRINT
4200 INPUT "Press ENTER to continue",TEMP$
4210 CLS
4220 PAGE.NO = 12
4230 PRINT ,,"page ";PAGE.NO
4240 PRINT
4250 PRINT "XYZ Widget Supply Company"
4260 PRINT "Dallas Distribution Center"
4270 PRINT "Dallas, Texas"
4280 PRINT
4290 PRINT "Periodic Inventory Analysis"
4300 PRINT "        Product:  Widget              Part No:  A3234-34"
4310 PRINT
4320 PRINT "*****************************************************************"
4330 PRINT
4340 PRINT "Analysis Summary for Q4:"
4350 PRINT
4360 PRINT "                Last-In First-Out Method"
4370 PRINT
4380 PRINT "            Goods Available for Sale        $";LIFO.GAFS
4390 PRINT "            Less Ending Inventory          $";LIFO.END.INV
4400 PRINT "            Cost of Goods Sold             $";LIFO.GAFS-LIFO.END
4410 PRINT
```

```
4420 PRINT
4430 INPUT "Press ENTER to continue",TEMP$
4440 CLS
4450 END
```

Notice that in the above program, similar sections of code appear several times. The calculations for the weighted average, FIFO, and LIFO inventories are each repeated four times, once for each quarter. The PRINT statements for the page headings are repeated twelve times. All of this duplication can make a program very difficult to change or enhance, not to mention the extra time and effort of keying in or reading the same material over and over. Say, for example, you wanted to insert a street address for the XYZ Widget Supply Company to appear in the heading of each page of the report. This would mean that you would have to make the same change (add a PRINT statement) at twelve different locations. Since the code is so similar, it would be more efficient if the same lines of code could be specified once and used multiple times in the program. This would save time entering the code, make it faster when changes had to be made, and make the program on the whole much shorter, so that it would be easier to read and take up less space on disk. All of this can be accomplished with subroutines.

The GOSUB Statement

The GOSUB command is used to specify a line number where the subroutine begins, and to cause the program to begin executing at the first line in the subroutine. The process of branching to a subroutine from the main section of code is known as **calling a subroutine**. A subroutine can also be called from within another subroutine. A subroutine should not be called from within itself. The following box summarizes the GOSUB statement.

The GOSUB Statement

Purpose   To transfer execution to the subroutine starting at a specified line number

Format   ln GOSUB ln2
where *ln* is the current line number of the BASIC statement, and *ln2* is the starting line number in the desired subroutine

Examples   100 GOSUB 500

would start executing the subroutine starting at line number 500

Note   It is extremely important to make certain that the specified line number exists, and that it is the beginning of a subroutine.

The RETURN Statement

For every subroutine called, there has to be a way to get back to the main program. BASIC remembers where it left the main program when a subroutine is called. The RETURN statement is used to mark the end of the subroutine (see box).

The RETURN Statement

Purpose   To signal the completion of the subroutine and return control to the calling program

Format   ln RETURN
where *ln* is the starting line number in a BASIC subroutine

Examples   1000 RETURN

Notes   The RETURN statement should only be located in a subroutine. There can be several RETURN statements in a given subroutine.

When the RETURN statement is executed, the program continues executing at the line following the line that initially called the subroutine. There can be multiple RETURNs in a subroutine.

Let's see what our inventory program, along with its flowchart and pseudocode (Figure 7.1), looks like when rewritten using subroutines.

Figure 7.1

Program: Inventory
INPUT WID1, PR1
INPUT WID2, PR2
INPUT WID3, PR3
INPUT WID4, PR4
INPUT WID5, PR5
INPUT WID6, PR6
INPUT WID7, PR7
INPUT WID8, PR8
INPUT WID9, PR9
INPUT WID10, PR10
INPUT WID11, PR11
INPUT WID12, PR12
INPUT INV1
INPUT INV2
INPUT INV3
INPUT INV4

Set WID start to 0
Set WAVG start to 0
Set FIFO start to 0
Set LIFO start to 0
Set page number to 0
Set Numb.Aval to WID start plus WID1 plus WID2 plus WID3
Set quarter to Q1
Set W1 to WID1
Set W2 to WID2
Set W3 to WID3
Set P1 to PR1
Set P2 to PR2
Set P3 to PR3
Set INV to INV1
Execute subroutine weighted average
Execute subroutine FIFO
Execute subroutine LIFO
Set Numb.Aval to WID start plus WID4 plus WID5 plus WID6
Set quarter to Q2
Set W1 to WID4
Set W2 to WID5
Set W3 to WID6
Set P1 to PR4
Set P2 to PR5
Set P3 to PR6
Set INV to INV2
Execute subroutine weighted average
Execute subroutine FIFO
Execute subroutine LIFO
Set Numb.Aval to WID start plus WID7 plus WID8 plus WID9
Set quarter to Q3
Set W1 to WID7
Set W2 to WID8
Set W3 to WID9
Set P1 to PR7
Set P2 to PR8
Set P3 to PR9
Set INV to INV3
Execute subroutine weighted average
Execute subroutine FIFO
Execute subroutine LIFO
Set Numb.Aval to WID start plus WID10 plus WID11 plus WID12
Set quarter to Q4
Set W1 to WID10
Set W2 to WID11
Set W3 to WID12

Set P1 to PR10
Set P2 to PR11
Set P3 to PR12
Set INV to INV4
Execute subroutine weighted average
Execute subroutine FIFO
Execute subroutine LIFO
END: Inventory

Subroutine: Weighted average
Set method to "weighted average method"
Set GAFS to (WID start times WAVG start) plus (W1 times P1) plus
     (W2 times P2) plus (W3 times P3)
Set Avg.Cost to GAFS divided by Numb.Aval
Set End.Inv to INV times Avg.Cost
Set WAVG start to Avg.Cost
Execute subroutine: Output
END: Weighted average

Subroutine: FIFO
Set GAFS to (WID start times FIFO start) plus (W1 times P1) plus
     (W2 times P2) plus (W3 times P3)
Set sold to Numb.Aval minus INV
IF sold less than or equal to WID start
     THEN set End.Inv to ((WID start minus sold) times FIFO.Start)
          plus (W1 times P1) plus (W2 times P2) plus (W3 times P3)
END-IF
IF sold greater than WID.Start and sold less than or equal to
     WID.Start plus W1
     THEN set End.Inv to ((WID.Start plus W1 minus sold) times P1)
          plus (W2 times P2) plus (W3 times P3)
END-IF
IF sold greater than WID.Start plus W1 and sold less than or equal
     to WID.Start plus W1 plus W2
     THEN set End.Inv to ((WID.Start plus W1 plus W2 minus sold)
          times P2) plus (W3 times P3)
END-IF
IF sold greater than WID.Start plus W1 plus W2 and sold less than or
     equal to WID.Start plus W1 plus W2 plus W3
     THEN set End.Inv to ((WID.Start plus W1 plus W2 plus W3 minus
          sold times P3)
END-IF
Set FIFO.Start to End.Inv divided by INV
Set method to "first-in first-out method"
Execute subroutine output
END: FIFO

Subroutine: LIFO
Set GAFS to (WID start times LIFO start) plus (W1 times P1) plus
  (W2 times P2) plus (W3 times P3)
Set sold to Numb.Aval minus INV
IF sold less than or equal to W3
  THEN set End.Inv to (WID start times LIFO.Start)
    plus (W1 times P1) plus (W2 times P2) plus
    ((W3 minus sold) times P3)
END-IF
IF sold greater than W3 and sold less than or equal to W2 plus W3
  THEN set End.Inv to ((WID.Start times LIFO.Start) plus
    (W1 times P1) plus ((W3 plus W2 minus sold) times P2)
END-IF
IF sold greater than W3 plus W2 and sold less than or equal
  to W1 plus W2 plus W3
  THEN set End.Inv to ((WID.Start times LIFO.Start) plus
    ((W3 plus W2 plus W1 minus sold) times P1)
END-IF
IF sold greater than W3 plus W2 plus W1 and sold less than or
  equal to WID.Start W1 plus W2 plus W3
  THEN set End.Inv to (WID.Start plus W1 plus W2 plus W3)
   times LIFO.Start
END-IF
Set LIFO.Start to End.INV divided by INV
Set method to "last-in first-out method"
Execute subroutine output
END: FIFO

Subroutine: Output
Set page number to page number plus 1
Display page number
Display heading
Display report
INPUT anything to continue
END: Output

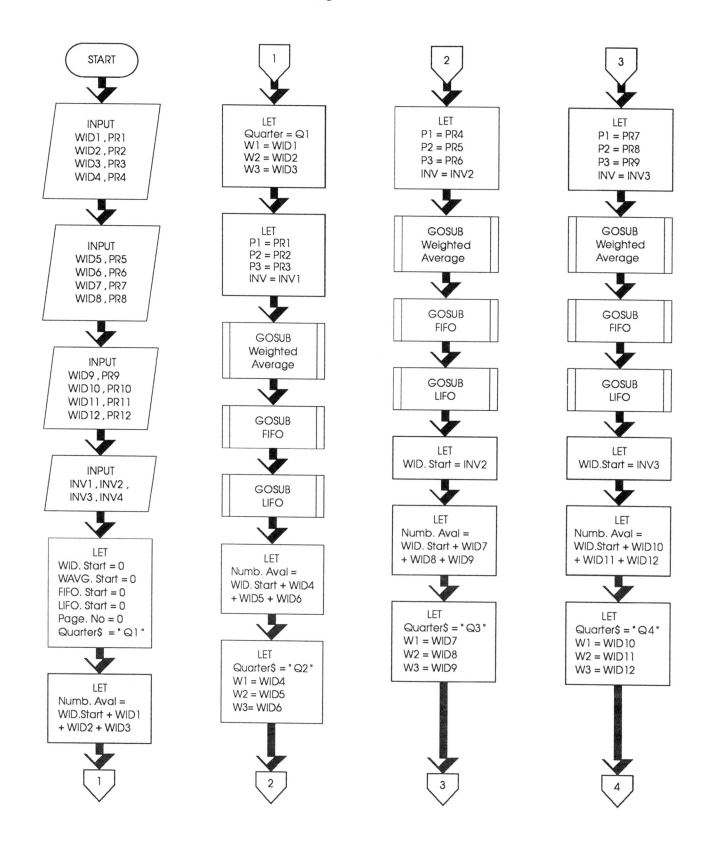

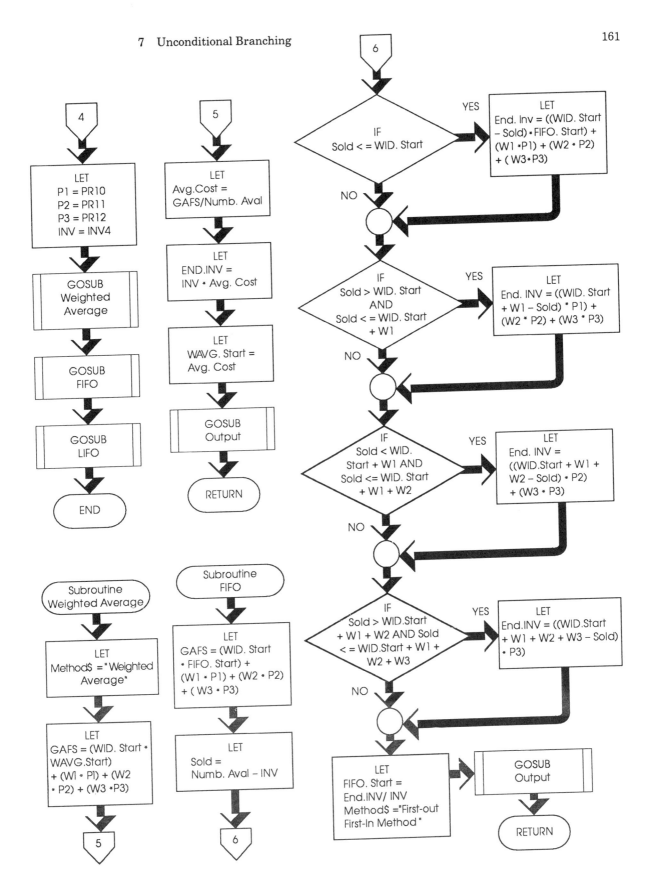

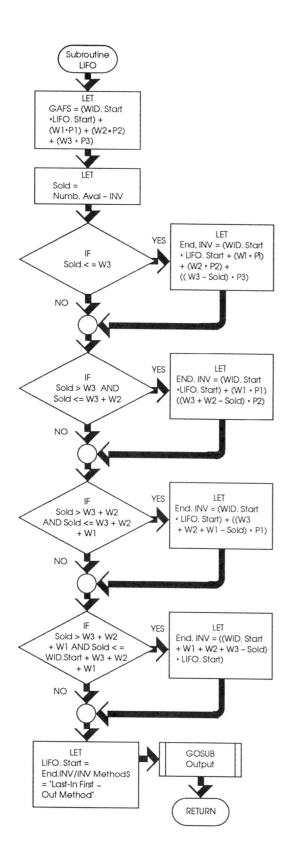

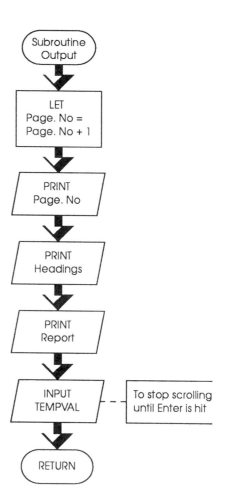

```
10 REM This program assumes a starting inventory of 0, and accepts data for 12
20 REM months on the number of Widgets purchased and the unit price
30 REM per Widget.  Then for each quarter, a report is made using three
40 REM common inventory methods:  Weighted Average, FIFO, and LIFO.
50 REM Three reports are printed for each quarter, one for each method used.
60 REM
70 REM Subroutines called:
80 REM          Weighted Average          starting at line 1120
90 REM          FIFO                      starting at line 1220
100 REM         LIFO                      starting at line 1340
110 REM         PRINT REPORT              starting at line 1460
120 REM
130 CLS
140 REM Prompt for INPUT values:
150 INPUT "Number of Widgets purchased, unit price for JAN: ",WID1,PR1
160 INPUT "Number of Widgets purchased, unit price for FEB: ",WID2,PR2
170 INPUT "Number of Widgets purchased, unit price for MAR: ",WID3,PR3
180 INPUT "Number of Widgets purchased, unit price for APR: ",WID4,PR4
190 INPUT "Number of Widgets purchased, unit price for MAY: ",WID5,PR5
200 INPUT "Number of Widgets purchased, unit price for JUN: ",WID6,PR6
210 INPUT "Number of Widgets purchased, unit price for JUL: ",WID7,PR7
220 INPUT "Number of Widgets purchased, unit price for AUG: ",WID8,PR8
230 INPUT "Number of Widgets purchased, unit price for SEP: ",WID9,PR9
240 INPUT "Number of Widgets purchased, unit price for OCT: ",WID10,PR10
250 INPUT "Number of Widgets purchased, unit price for NOV: ",WID11,PR11
260 INPUT "Number of Widgets purchased, unit price for DEC: ",WID12,PR12
270 REM
280 INPUT "Number of units in inventory at end of Q1: ",INV1
290 INPUT "Number of units in inventory at end of Q2: ",INV2
300 INPUT "Number of units in inventory at end of Q3: ",INV3
310 INPUT "Number of units in inventory at end of Q4: ",INV4
320 PRINT
330 REM
340 REM Initialize inventory for beginning of the year to 0
350 REM
360 WID.START = 0
370 WAVG.START = 0
380 FIFO.START = 0
390 LIFO.START = 0
400 PAGE.NO = 0
410 QUARTER$ = "Q1"
420 REM
430 REM
440 REM Run reports for first quarter
450 NUMB.AVAL = WID.START + WID1 + WID2 + WID3
460 QUARTER$ = "Q1"
470 W1 = WID1
480 W2 = WID2
490 W3 = WID3
500 P1 = PR1
```

```
510 P2 = PR2
520 P3 = PR3
530 INV = INV1
540 REM Calculate weighted average for Q1
550 GOSUB 1120
560 REM Calculate the FIFO inventory for Q1
570 GOSUB 1220
580 REM Calculate the LIFO inventory for Q1
590 GOSUB 1340
600 WID.START = INV1
610 REM Run reports for second quarter
620 NUMB.AVAL = WID.START + WID4 + WID5 + WID6
630 QUARTER$ = "Q2"
640 W1 = WID4
650 W2 = WID5
660 W3 = WID6
670 P1 = PR4
680 P2 = PR5
690 P3 = PR6
700 INV = INV2
710 REM Calculate the weighted average for Q2
720 GOSUB 1120
730 REM Calculate the FIFO inventory for Q2
740 GOSUB 1220
750 REM Calculate the LIFO inventory for Q2
760 GOSUB 1340
770 WID.START = INV2
780 REM Run reports for third quarter
790 NUMB.AVAL = WID.START + WID7 + WID8 + WID9
800 QUARTER$ = "Q3"
810 W1 = WID7
820 W2 = WID8
830 W3 = WID9
840 P1 = PR7
850 P2 = PR8
860 P3 = PR9
870 INV = INV3
880 REM Calculate the weighted average for Q3
890 GOSUB 1120
900 REM Calculate the FIFO inventory for Q3
910 GOSUB 1220
920 REM Calculate the LIFO inventory for Q3
930 GOSUB 1340
940 WID.START = INV3
950 REM Run reports for fourth quarter
960 NUMB.AVAL = WID.START + WID10 + WID11 + WID12
970 QUARTER$ = "Q4"
980 W1 = WID10
990 W2 = WID11
```

```
1000 W3 = WID12
1010 P1 = PR10
1020 P2 = PR11
1030 P3 = PR12
1040 INV = INV4
1050 REM Calculate the weighted average for Q4
1060 GOSUB 1120
1070 REM Calculate the FIFO inventory for Q4
1080 GOSUB 1220
1090 REM Calculate the LIFO inventory for Q4
1100 GOSUB 1340
1110 END
1120 REM Subroutine to calculate the weighted average
1130 REM Calculate weighted average inventory
1140 REM
1150 METHOD$ = "Weighted Average Method"
1160 GAFS = (WID.START * WAVG.START) + (W1 * P1) + (W2 * P2) + (W3 * P3)
1170 AVG.COST = GAFS/NUMB.AVAL
1180 END.INV = INV * AVG.COST
1190 WAVG.START = AVG.COST
1200 GOSUB 1460
1210 RETURN
1220 REM Calculate first-in first-out inventory
1230 REM
1240 GAFS = (WID.START * FIFO.START) + (W1 * P1) + (W2 * P2) + (W3 * P3)
1250 SOLD = NUMB.AVAL - INV
1260 IF SOLD <= WID.START
     THEN END.INV = ((WID.START - SOLD) * FIFO.START) + (W1 * P1) +
                    (W2 * P2) + (W3 * P3)
1270 IF (SOLD > WID.START) AND (SOLD <= WID.START + W1)
     THEN END.INV = ((WID.START + W1 - SOLD) * P1) + (W2 * P2) + (W3 * P3)
1280 IF (SOLD > WID.START + W1) AND (SOLD <= WID.START + W1 + W2)
     THEN END.INV = ((WID.START + W1 + W2 - SOLD) * P2) + (W3 * P3)
1290 IF (SOLD > WID.START + W1 + W2) AND (SOLD <= WID.START + W1 + W2 + W3)
     THEN END.INV = ((WID.START + W1 + W2 + W3 - SOLD) * P3)
1300 FIFO.START = END.INV/INV
1310 METHOD$ = "First-In First-Out Method"
1320 GOSUB 1460
1330 RETURN
1340 REM Calculate last-in first-out inventory
1350 REM
1360 GAFS = (WID.START * LIFO.START) + (W1 * P1) + (W2 * P2) + (W3 * P3)
1370 SOLD = NUMB.AVAL - INV
1380 IF SOLD <= W3
     THEN END.INV = (WID.START * LIFO.START) + (W1 + P1) + (W2 * P2) +
                    ((W3 - SOLD) * P3
1390 IF (SOLD > W3) AND (SOLD <= W3 + W2)
     THEN END.INV = (WID.START * LIFO.START) + (W1 * P1) + ((W3 + W2 -
                    SOLD)* P2)
```

```
1400 IF (SOLD > W3 + W2) AND (SOLD <= W3 + W2 + W1)
     THEN END.INV = (WID.START * LIFO.START) + ((W3 + W2 + W1 - SOLD) * P1)
1410 IF (SOLD > W3 + W2 + W1) AND (SOLD <= WID.START + W3 + W2 + W1)
     THEN END.INV = ((WID.START + W1 + W2 + W3 - SOLD) * LIFO.START)
1420 LIFO.START = END.INV/INV
1430 METHOD$ = "Last-In First-Out Method"
1440 GOSUB 1460
1450 RETURN
1460 REM Subroutine to print out the inventory reports
1470 REM This subroutine uses variables PAGE.NO, QUARTER$, GAFS, and
1480 REM END.INV to print out the three separate reports for each quarter
1490 REM
1500 CLS
1510 PAGE.NO = PAGE.NO + 1
1520 PRINT ,,"page ";PAGE.NO
1530 PRINT
1540 PRINT "XYZ Widget Supply Company"
1550 PRINT "Dallas Distribution Center"
1560 PRINT "Dallas, Texas"
1570 PRINT
1580 PRINT "Periodic Inventory Analysis"
1590 PRINT "          Product:  Widget            Part No:  A3234-34"
1600 PRINT
1610 PRINT "**********************************************************************"
1620 PRINT
1630 PRINT "Analysis Summary for ";QUARTER$;":"
1640 PRINT
1650 PRINT "                     ";METHOD$
1660 PRINT
1670 PRINT "          Goods Available for Sale         $";GAFS
1680 PRINT "          Less Ending Inventory            $";END.INV
1690 PRINT "          Cost of Goods Sold               $";GAFS-END.INV
1700 PRINT
1710 PRINT
1720 INPUT "Press ENTER to continue",TEMP$
1730 RETURN
1740 END
```

Note that in this new version we have accomplished several things by using subroutines. First, we have managed to create a functionally equivalent program while reducing the number of lines from 445 to 174. We also have made the program easier to debug and change. If we want to make a change in a particular section of code, we only have to make that change in one location. When we run this program we get the same results as we would with the first inventory program using no subroutines.

```
run
Number of Widgets purchased, unit price for JAN: 200,7.25
Number of Widgets purchased, unit price for FEB: 200,7.25
Number of Widgets purchased, unit price for MAR: 100,7.25
Number of Widgets purchased, unit price for APR: 75,7.50
Number of Widgets purchased, unit price for MAY: 100,7.75
Number of Widgets purchased, unit price for JUN: 50,8.00
Number of Widgets purchased, unit price for JUL: 100,8.00
Number of Widgets purchased, unit price for AUG: 125,8.25
Number of Widgets purchased, unit price for SEP: 100,8.25
Number of Widgets purchased, unit price for OCT: 100,8.50
Number of Widgets purchased, unit price for NOV: 50,8.75
Number of Widgets purchased, unit price for DEC: 100,9.00
Number of units in inventory at end of Q1: 75
Number of units in inventory at end of Q2: 100
Number of units in inventory at end of Q3: 50
Number of units in inventory at end of Q4: 10
```

```
                            page 1

XYZ Widget Supply Company
Dallas Distribution Center
Dallas, Texas

Periodic Inventory Analysis
        Product: Widget          Part No: A3234-34


**************************************************************

Analysis Summary for Q1:

                  Weighted Average Method

        Goods Available for Sale       $ 3625
        Less Ending Inventory          $ 543.75
        Cost of Goods Sold             $ 3081.25

Press ENTER to continue
```

```
                              page 2

XYZ Widget Supply Company
Dallas Distribution Center
Dallas, Texas

Periodic Inventory Analysis
        Product: Widget          Part No: A3234-34


*****************************************************************

Analysis Summary for Q1:

                First-In First-Out Method

        Goods Available for Sale         $ 3625
        Less Ending Inventory            $ 543.75
        Costs of Goods Sold              $ 3081.25

Press ENTER to continue
```

```
                                        page 3

XYZ Widget Supply Company
Dallas Distribution Center
Dallas, Texas

Periodic Inventory Analysis
        Product: Widget          Part No: A3234-34



*****************************************************************

Analysis Summary for Q1:

                Last-In First-Out Method

        Goods Available for Sale         $ 3625
        Less Ending Inventory            $ 543.75
        Costs of Goods Sold              $ 3081.25

Press ENTER to continue
```

```
        .           .           .
        .           .           .
        .           .           .
```

```
                              page 12

XYZ Widget Supply Company
Dallas Distribution Center
Dallas, Texas

Periodic Inventory Analysis
        Product: Widget           Part No: A3234-34



******************************************************************

Analysis Summary for Q4:

                  Last-In First-Out Method

        Goods Available for Sale         $ 2553.125
        Less Ending Inventory            $ 73.125
        Costs of Goods Sold              $ 2480

Press ENTER to continue

Ok
```

Care should be taken in using subroutines to be certain that they are readable and well documented. Consider the following when using a subroutine.

- A subroutine should be beneficial to a program, i.e., performing a task that would otherwise have to be coded in several locations in the same program.
- A subroutine should be well documented. The first line or lines of the subroutine should be comments that describe the purpose of the subroutine and what it does. Subroutines should also be documented in the program description of the main (or calling) program.
- Although subroutines can call other subroutines using a GOSUB statement, subroutines should not call themselves; nor should a subroutine within another subroutine call the primary subroutine. This can cause **recursion**, in which the program may go into an endless loop.
- Subroutines should be entered only through a GOSUB statement and left only through a RETURN statement. Subroutines should be placed after the main program and an END statement should be placed at the end of the main program and before the subroutines to make sure the program does not continue down into the subroutines.

The GOTO Statement

The GOTO statement allows branching from any point in a BASIC program to any other point. However, it does not "remember" where it left the main program nor return processing to the main program after it is executed. Frequent use of GOTO statements tends to create programs that are difficult to follow, debug, or change. Although the GOTO statement was very popular in the first decade or so after BASIC was developed, it is now used infrequently. This is because of the problems mentioned above and also because of the development of structured programming techniques. **Structured programming** is a set of guidelines that assist the programmer in creating a well-designed program. Structured programming will be discussed in great depth in Appendix A.

The problem with GOTO is that although it is a powerful command (one that allows the programmer to unconditionally branch to another section of the program), it also inhibits structured program flow. If GOTOs are used in a program, and the program is in any way complex, every time you want to delete a line, you must go through the entire program and make certain that there are no GOTO statements pointing to that line number. In a long program using GOTOs, if a certain section has to be changed, or even a line deleted, the programmer must trace back through the entire program, examining all possible routes to get to the changed section, and exhausting all possible branches to be certain the change doesn't affect anything else in the program. If, on the other hand, the programmer had used structured programming techniques, any change would mean the programmer would just have to examine the section immediately above the changed section, and the only section a change could affect would be immediately below the changed section.

Although GOTO statements are no longer in vogue and we discourage you from using them, they are still part of the BASIC programming language, and it is more than likely that you may come across them in someone else's program. The box below summarizes the features of the GOTO statement.

Let's take a look at an example using GOTOs. The flowchart and pseudocode are shown in Figure 7.2, and the program follows.

The GOTO Statement

Purpose   The GOTO statement shifts control of the program to a specified line number and the program continues executing normally from that point

Format   ln GOTO ln2
where *ln* is the line number of the current BASIC statement and *ln2* is the line number of the next line to be executed

Examples   100 GOTO 200
500 GOTO 999

Note   The line number specified following the GOTO command must exist or BASIC will display the message: "Undefined line number in *ln*."

Figure 7.2

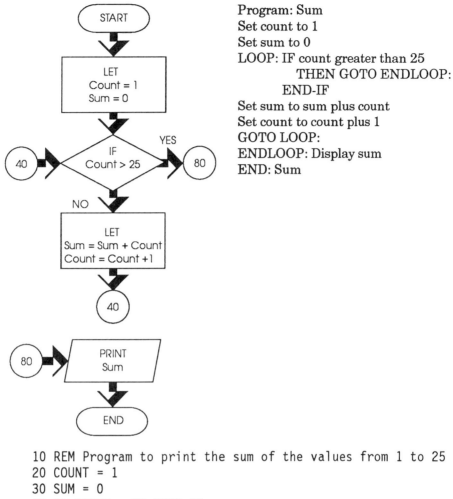

Program: Sum
Set count to 1
Set sum to 0
LOOP: IF count greater than 25
          THEN GOTO ENDLOOP:
        END-IF
Set sum to sum plus count
Set count to count plus 1
GOTO LOOP:
ENDLOOP: Display sum
END: Sum

```
10 REM Program to print the sum of the values from 1 to 25
20 COUNT = 1
30 SUM = 0
40 IF COUNT > 25 THEN 80
50 LET SUM = SUM + COUNT
60 LET COUNT = COUNT + 1
70 GOTO 40
80 PRINT "The sum of the numbers from 1 to 25 is";SUM
90 END
```

When run, the output will look like

```
run
The sum of the numbers from 1 to 25 is 235
Ok
```

The GOTO statement is sometimes used as a "quick and dirty" fix in a small, easily readable program. Otherwise, the GOTO statement has no place in well-written, structured programs. For this reason, this is the only chapter in which GOTO will be mentioned, and you will not see the GOTO statement used in any other section of this book. So remember, if you think you need to use a GOTO, think again. There is a better way.

The ON-GOSUB Statement

The decision-making process is ordinarily not limited to true or false conditions as provided by using the IF-THEN and IF-THEN-ELSE statements. Often a certain set of instructions are executed depending on a selection from a number of different choices. An example of such a choice would be the following menu:

Primary Option Menu

1. Enter New Sales Data
2. Generate Monthly Sales Report
3. Calculate Commission by Salesperson
4. Print Salesperson's Commission Check
5. Generate Sales Report by District
6. Graph Sales by Quarter
7. Graph Sales by Year
8. Exit

    Select One = = = >

In this menu, depending on the number selected, one of eight tasks will be executed. While a series of nested IF statements could be used to handle the input, a program containing ON-GOSUB is more efficient.

The ON-GOSUB statement allows you to branch to one of several subroutines depending on a given input. One of the primary uses of the ON-GOSUB statement is in the development of menus. A **menu** is a user-friendly interface to the program that lists all possible options. The user selects the number matching the option to be executed, and a particular procedure begins execution.

Let's look at a program that uses ON-GOSUBs and menus. The program below presents a primary menu with five possible choices. The user is prompted to enter an option, to which they respond with a number from 1 to 5. The program first verifies that the input value is a valid choice, and then will branch to the subroutine that matches the option specified and execute the desired task.

```
10 REM This program demonstrates the use of the ON-GOSUB command to aid in
20 REM the development of menus
30 REM
40 REM The primary menu offers 5 independent tasks, each of which is an
50 REM independent subroutine.
60 CLS
70 PRINT "              Primary Option Menu"
80 PRINT
90 PRINT "   1.  Calculate weekly paycheck"
100 PRINT "   2.  Calculate taxes to be deducted from pay"
110 PRINT "   3.  Print a paycheck"
120 PRINT "   4.  Print a mailing label"
130 PRINT "   5.  Calculate commission to be paid based on total sales"
140 PRINT
150 INPUT "   Select One ===> ",OPTION.CHOSEN
160 REM Make sure the option selected was a valid one before attempting to
170 REM to branch to a subroutine.
180 REM
```

```
190 IF (OPTION.CHOSEN >= 1) AND (OPTION.CHOSEN <= 5)
      THEN ON OPTION.CHOSEN GOSUB 210, 320, 480, 690, 940
      ELSE PRINT OPTION.CHOSEN;" is an invalid option. Program Aborting!"
200 END
210 REM Subroutine called by option 1 of the primary option menu.
220 REM This subroutine accepts as input the number of hours worked
230 REM and the pay rate per hour, and calculates the week's pay.
240 CLS
250 PRINT "Option 1 - Calculate weekly paycheck"
260 PRINT
270 INPUT "Enter hours worked, hourly rate ===> ",HOURS, RATE
280 IF HOURS <= 40
      THEN PAY = HOURS * RATE
      ELSE PAY = (40 * RATE) + ((HOURS - 40) * RATE * 1.5)
290 PRINT
300 PRINT "The weekly check for ";HOURS;" hours at ";RATE;" per hour is $";PAY
310 RETURN
320 REM Subroutine called by option 2 of the primary option menu.
330 REM This subroutine accepts as input the amount for the week's pay
340 REM and calculates the federal, state, and FICA taxes.
350 CLS
360 PRINT "Option 2 - Calculate taxes to be deducted"
370 PRINT
380 INPUT "Enter amount of weekly paycheck ===> ",PAY
390 IF PAY <= 300
      THEN FED.TAX = PAY * .2
      ELSE IF PAY <= 500
            THEN FED.TAX = PAY * .24
            ELSE FED.TAX = PAY * .28
400 IF PAY <= 300
      THEN STATE.TAX = PAY * .03
      ELSE IF PAY <= 500
            THEN STATE.TAX = PAY * .04
            ELSE STATE.TAX = PAY * .05
410 FICA.TAX = PAY * .075
420 PRINT
430 PRINT " For a paycheck of $";PAY
440 PRINT "     Federal tax is $";FED.TAX
450 PRINT "     State tax is $";STATE.TAX
460 PRINT "     FICA tax is $";FICA.TAX
470 RETURN
480 REM Subroutine called by option 3 of the primary option menu.
490 REM This subroutine accepts as input the name to which the check is to
500 REM be made out, and the amount of the check.
510 CLS
520 PRINT "Option 3 - Print a paycheck"
530 PRINT
540 INPUT "Enter name to make the check payable to: ",PAYABLE.TO$
550 INPUT "Enter the amount of the check: $",AMOUNT
560 PRINT
```

```
570  PRINT "*****************************************************************"
580  PRINT
590  PRINT "                                        ";DATE$
600  PRINT
610  PRINT "    Pay to the order of ";PAYABLE.TO$
620  PRINT "    The amount of ******************************$";AMOUNT
630  PRINT
640  PRINT "                                               "
650  PRINT "                      (authorized signature)"
660  PRINT
670  PRINT "*****************************************************************"
680  RETURN
690  REM Subroutine called by option 4 of the primary option menu.
700  REM This subroutine accepts as input a name, P.O. Box (optional),
710  REM apartment number (optional), street, city, state, and ZIP code and
720  REM prints out a mailing label.
730  CLS
740  PRINT "Option 4 - Print a mailing label"
750  PRINT
760  INPUT "Enter name: ",NAM$
770  INPUT "Enter P.O. Box number: ",P.O.BOX$
780  INPUT "Enter Apartment number: ",APART.NO$
790  INPUT "Enter Street address: ",STREET$
800  INPUT "Enter City: ",CITY$
810  INPUT "Enter State: ",STATE$
820  INPUT "Enter ZIP code: ",ZIP$
830  PRINT
840  PRINT "----------------------------------------------------------------"
850  PRINT
860  PRINT ,NAM$
870  IF P.O.BOX$ <> "" THEN PRINT ,"P.O. Box ";P.O.BOX$
880  IF APART.NO$ <> "" THEN PRINT ,"Apartment No. ";APART.NO$
890  PRINT  ,STREET$
900  PRINT ,CITY$;", ";STATE$;"      ";ZIP$
910  PRINT
920  PRINT "----------------------------------------------------------------"
930  RETURN
940  REM Subroutine called by option 5 of the primary option menu.
950  REM This subroutine accepts as input a Salesperson's name and the total
960  REM amount of the weeks sales, and calculates the appropriate commission.
970  CLS
980  PRINT "Option 5 - Calculate the commission based on total sales"
990  PRINT
1000 INPUT "Enter the total sales for the week's period: ",TOTAL.SALES
1010 PRINT
1020 IF TOTAL.SALES < 2000
     THEN COMMISSION = TOTAL.SALES * .1 ELSE IF TOTAL.SALES < 4000
     THEN COMMISSION = TOTAL.SALES * .15 ELSE COMMISSION = TOTAL.SALES  * .2
1030 PRINT
1040 PRINT "For a week's sales of $";TOTAL.SALES
```

```
1050 PRINT "the salesperson's commission is $";COMMISSION
1060 RETURN
1070 END
```

Running this program selecting option 3 results in the following output.

```
Primary Option Menu

1.    Calculate weekly paycheck
2.    Calculate taxes to be deducted from Pay
3.    Print a paycheck
4.    Print a mailing label
5.    Calculate commission to be paid based on total sales

Select One ===> 3
```

```
Option 3 - Print out a check

Enter name to make the check payable to : John J. Jones
Enter the amount of the check $2056.34

****************************************************************

                                           01-30-1989
Pay to the order of John J. Jones
The amount of ***************************$ 2056.34


                          _____
                               (authorized signature)


****************************************************************
Ok
```

This example shows how an ON-GOSUB is used, and the following box shows the structure of the ON-GOSUB command.

The ON-GOSUB Statement

Purpose   To branch to a given subroutine based on a specified variable

Format   ln ON <var> GOSUB <list of subroutine line numbers>
where *ln* is the line number of the BASIC statement, *<var>* is an integer from 1 to *n* (where *n* is the number of subroutines specified in <list of subroutines>), and *list of subroutine line numbers* is the line numbers at the beginning of the subroutines to be called depending on the value of *var*.

Examples   20 ON *a* GOSUB 100, 200, 300, 500, 1000

where *a* is a value from 1 to 5
If *a* = 1 then the program calls the subroutine starting at line 100
If *a* = 2 then the program calls the subroutine starting at line 200
If *a* = 3 then the program calls the subroutine starting at line 300
If *a* = 4 then the program calls the subroutine starting at line 500
If *a* = 5 then the program calls the subroutine starting at line 1000
If *a* is less than 1 or greater than 5, then an error occurs

Note   Upon completion of the subroutine (at the RETURN) the program returns control of the program to the line following the ON-GOSUB statement.

It is important to remember when using ON-GOSUB statements that the value of the variable specifying which subroutine to branch to should be positive and less than or equal to the number of subroutines in the list of line numbers. If a zero or a number greater than the limit (but less than 255) is specified, the program continues with the next statement in the normal sequence of the program. If the number specified is negative or greater than 255, the program returns the error message: "Illegal function call."

The ON-GOTO Statement

The ON-GOTO command is similar to ON-GOSUB, in that depending on the value of a variable, one of a number of possible branches is selected. Let's take a look at a program using ON-GOTOs.

```
10 REM Program to enter an employee's salary, and select a
20 REM performance code, and calculate the employee's raise.
30 CLS
40 INPUT "Enter Employee's Annual Salary: $",SALARY
50 PRINT
60 PRINT "            Performance Rating Codes"
70 PRINT "                1 - Unsatisfactory
80 PRINT "                2 - Below Average"
90 PRINT "                3 - Average"
100 PRINT "                4 - Above Average"
110 PRINT "                5 - Excellent"
120 INPUT "Enter the Employee's Performance Rating:",RATING
130 IF (RATING < 1) OR (RATING > 5) THEN 50
```

```
140 ON RATING GOTO 150,170,190,210,230
150 LET RAISE =  .03
160 GOTO 240
170 LET RAISE =  .04
180 GOTO 240
190 LET RAISE =  .05
200 GOTO 240 END
210 LET RAISE =  .06
220 GOTO 240
230 LET RAISE =  .07
240 REM Calculate the new salary
250 NEWSALARY = SALARY + (SALARY * RAISE)
260 PRINT
270 PRINT "The new salary is $";NEWSALARY
280 END
```

When run, the output will look like:

```
run
Enter Employee's Annual Salary:30000

              Performance Rating Codes
                 1 - Unsatisfactory
                 2 - Below Average
                 3 - Average
                 4 - Above Average
                 5 - Excellent
Enter the Employee's Performance Rating:2

The new salary is $ 31200
Ok
```

The features of ON-GOTO are summarized in the box on page 175. The ON-GOTO statement demands the same care as the GOTO statement. ON-GOTOs can make a program confusing and difficult to change at a later date. Care must also be taken to ensure that the value following the ON is in the correct range for the line numbers listed following the GOTO keyword. As with ON-GOSUB, if a zero value or a number greater than the number of line numbers specified in the ON-GOTO list is chosen (but less than 255) the program will continue with the next line in the normal program sequence. If a negative number or a number greater than 255 is specified, an "Illegal function call" message is displayed.

The ON-GOTO Statement

Purpose   To branch to a given line number based on a specified variable

Format   ln ON <var> GOTO <list of line numbers>
where *ln* is the line number of the BASIC statement, *<var>* is an integer from 1 to *n*
(where *n* is the number of line numbers specified in <list of line numbers>, and *list of line numbers* is the line numbers to be executed depending on the value of *var*

Examples   20 ON a GOTO 100, 200, 300, 500, 1000, 9999

Where *a* is a value from 1 to 6
If a = 1 then the program branches to line 100
If a = 2 then the program branches to line 200
If a = 3 then the program branches to line 300
If a = 4 then the program branches to line 500
If a = 5 then the program branches to line 1000
If a = 6 then the program branches to line 9999
If a is less than 1 or greater than 6, then an error occurs

Note   The same care should be taken with ON-GOTOs as with GOTOs. If they are not used carefully, they can make the program confusing and difficult to debug.

A Word on Programming Style

In this chapter, we have illustrated the fundamentals of structured programming. In structured programming, the program flows from the first line to the last line of code as efficiently as possible, without jumping all around within the program. It is often referred to as **top-down programming**.

The advantage of this top-down approach is that the program becomes easier to read and alter. Most changes that have to be made in the program will only affect the lines of code directly following the change. In contrast, a poorly written program that branches back and forth, skipping over sections of code and jumping back to the beginning, can be very difficult to edit. If a change had to be made, you would have to examine the entire program and trace all the possible ways to get to the changed section of code, as well as all the possible avenues the program could take after the changes.

The programming techniques necessary to write well-structured programs may seem trivial at this point, since up to now most of the programs you have seen have been simple, consisting of a page or two of code. This code is easy to view, so a branch or two doesn't seem to make the program that difficult to follow. In a longer program, however, it's a different story. The skills that you develop now in creating well-structured code will prove invaluable as you start writing more complex programs. The extra time spent writing a well-designed program is minimal compared to the time you would spend debugging and tracing problems.

Summary

- Subroutines make it possible for the same code to be executed from several places in a program. Upon completion of the subroutine, the program continues with the statement following the statement from which the subroutine was called.
- GOSUB causes a program to branch to a subroutine beginning at the line number specified following the GOSUB. RETURN causes the program to continue executing at the line number immediately following the GOSUB statement that called the subroutine.
- GOTO is the simplest BASIC statement to use but is also among the most difficult to use correctly. GOTOs should be avoided in favor of more organized structures such as GOSUB.
- ON-GOSUB allows for a number of subroutines to be executed depending on a given input (i.e., from a menu). ON-GOSUB is very similar to ON-GOTO, and should be used instead of ON-GOTO wherever possible to preserve a well-structured program.
- The same care should be taken with ON-GOTO as with GOTO. If an ON-GOTO is not used correctly, it can make the program confusing and prone to errors.

Exercises

True or False

_____ 1. An unconditional branch allows you to leave the normal flow of the program and terminates the program's execution immediately.

_____ 2. A subroutine is an independent group of statements that are located outside the logical sequence of execution of the main program and perform a separate, limited function.

_____ 3. A subroutine can be called from another subroutine.

_____ 4. The RETURN statement can be specified with a line number where the programmer wishes the program to continue executing upon completion of the subroutine.

_____ 5. There can only be one RETURN statement within a subroutine.

_____ 6. GOTO statements are similar to GOSUB statements except that for a GOTO statement the END command is used to signify the return back to the calling line number while a GOSUB uses a RETURN statement to accomplish this.

_____ 7. One of the most-criticized statements by programmers who use structured programming techniques is the GOTO statement.

_____ 8. ON-GOSUB statements prove to be very useful in the development of user-friendly menus.

_____ 9. ON-GOTOs provide a more structured means of accomplishing the same tasks as GOTOs.

_____   10. The two distinct programming techniques discussed in this chapter are structured
programming, in which GOTOs are not used, and top-down programming, in
which the use of GOTOs is encouraged.

Fill-In

1. Leaving the normal flow of a program to execute statements at another location in the program is
known as an _____.

2. The _____ command is used to branch the program to a designated subroutine.

3. The process of branching to a subroutine from the main section of code is known as
_____ a subroutine.

4. When a subroutine calls itself, it is known as _____.

5. Before the introduction of structured programming techniques, the _____ statement
was considered one of the most powerful and useful statements in BASIC.

6. A user-friendly list of all possible choices to be made within a program is known as a _____.

7. To call one of a list of subroutines based on the numeric value of a variable, the _____
statement can be used.

8. Each subroutine called from an ON-GOSUB statement must be terminated by a
_____ statement.

9. An even more potentially dangerous and unstructured command than the GOTO statement is the
_____ statement.

10. Another name for structured programming is _____ programming because of the
flow of the program from the first line to the last line without a lot of branching.

Short Answer

1. It may seem the GOTO and GOSUB commands perform the same function, that is, an unconditional
branch to another part of the program. Why, then, is the GOSUB recommended?

2. Why is it recommended to place the subroutines at the end of the program?

3. Can a subroutine call itself? If so, is it good programming style?

4. How are ON-GOSUB routines used to develop user-friendly menus?

5. How do structured programming techniques help create programs that can be modified easily and
efficiently?

Programming Problems

1. Write a BASIC program that prompts for the names of first, second, and third place winners and the amount they have won, and using a subroutine, print a letter of congratulations to each of the winners informing them which place they came in and how much they won.

2. Rewrite the program described on pages 176–177 using ON-GOSUBs instead of ON-GOTOs.

3. Write a program that displays a menu, of which the choices are the names of five customers. The program should use an ON-GOSUB statement to branch to each of the five subroutines, depending on the input from the menu, and print out a mailing label for the specified customer.

8

Looping

After reading this chapter you should understand:

- What a loop is and the most common ways to implement a loop in a BASIC program
- How to use FOR/NEXT to loop for a given number of iterations

- How and why to "nest" loops
- How to use WHILE/WEND to loop until a certain condition is met

Introduction

Computers are most noted for their ability to do repetitive tasks that would seem very tedious and boring to a human. One method of repetitive processing is handled by a BASIC program using a concept known as a **loop**. A loop is a means of controlling the repetition of a section of code so that it is repeated either a specified number of times or until a given condition is met. The use of looping provides a simple means to let your program do what it does best: repetitive processing.

Suppose for example you operate a small business that has an inventory consisting of 1000 various products. Suppose also you were undertaking a project to determine the dollar value of your entire inventory at the end of each week. To do this, you want a program into which you enter the quantity and the unit cost of each of the 1000 products in stock. Such a program would be relatively straightforward, as it could consist of INPUT statements using a variable which we call an **accumulator**. An accumulator is a variable that is used to store the running total when summing a list of numbers. The accumulator will be initially set equal to zero, which is called **initializing** a variable. We will then input the unit price and quantity, multiply the unit price by the quantity, and add this value to the accumulator for each of the 1000 different products. The program might look something like this:

```
10 REM Program to accept as input the quantity and unit
20 REM price for 1000 products, and print out the total
30 REM dollar value of the inventory
```

```
40 REM
50 REM Initialize total.value to zero
60 LET TOTAL.VALUE = 0
70 REM
80 REM Input quantity and unit price for 1st product.
90 REM "Enter quantity and Unit Price for product 1"
100 INPUT "===>",QUANTITY, UNIT.PRICE
110 TOTAL.VALUE = TOTAL.VALUE + (QUANTITY * UNIT.PRICE)
120 REM
130 REM Input quantity and unit price for 2nd product
140 PRINT "Enter quantity and unit price for Product 2"
150 INPUT "===>",QUANTITY, UNIT.PRICE
160 TOTAL.VALUE = TOTAL.VALUE + (QUANTITY * UNIT.PRICE)
170 REM
180 REM Input quantity and unit price for 3rd product
          .           .           .
          .           .           .
          .           .           .
             <repeat to the 999th product>
          .           .           .
          .           .           .
          .           .           .
50000 REM Input quantity and unit price for 1000th product
50010 PRINT "Enter quantity and unit price for product 1000"
50020 INPUT "===>",QUANTITY, UNIT.PRICE
50030 TOTAL.VALUE = TOTAL.VALUE + (QUANTITY * UNIT.PRICE)
50040 REM
50050 REM All the data have been entered, print out total
50060 PRINT "Total value of inventory is $";TOTAL.VALUE
50070 END
```

This program is rather simple in its logic. Two values (QUANTITY and UNIT.PRICE) are multiplied together and added to an accumulator (TOTAL.VALUE). This is performed 1000 times for all the parts, and then the total dollar value is printed out. REM statements are used to separate the repetitive sections of code for readability. This program does the same tasks a thousand times (input data, multiply, and sum). While the logic is simple, it requires keying in several thousand lines of code, and has to be modified if the number of parts changes. One way to simplify this program might be to use a subroutine. This would simplify keying in the program, but then the program would still need to use a thousand GOSUB statements.

Using the BASIC loop structure is a more efficient way of writing a program of this type. A loop performs a specified task (in this case input data, multiply, and sum) a specified number of times, or until a given condition is met. Each time the code within the loop is executed, it is called an **iteration**. To use a loop in the above program, lines 90, 100, and 110 would only have to be specified once within the program, yet the lines would be executed 1000 times. The most common loop in BASIC is the FOR/NEXT loop.

The FOR/NEXT Loop

Using the FOR/NEXT command, the sample program above would look as follows:

```
10   REM Program to accept as input the quantity and unit
20   REM price for 1000 products, and printing out the total
30   REM dollar value of the inventory.
40   REM
50   REM Initialize total.value to zero
60   LET TOTAL.VALUE = 0
70   REM
80   REM Input the quantity and unit price for each product
90   FOR I = 1 TO 1000
100      PRINT "Enter quantity and unit price for product";I
110      INPUT "===>",QUANTITY, UNIT.PRICE
120      TOTAL.VALUE = TOTAL.VALUE + (QUANTITY * UNIT.PRICE)
130 NEXT I
140 REM
150 REM All the data have been entered, print out total
160 PRINT "Total value of inventory is $";TOTAL.VALUE
170 END
```

This program accomplishes the same task as the earlier program except that by using a loop, the program is much more compact. The first time line 90 is executed, BASIC assigns I an initial value of 1 and marks this statement as the beginning of the loop. Then BASIC continues executing statements until the NEXT I statement (line 130) is reached, marking the end of the loop. At this point BASIC increments I by 1, making the value of I equal to 2. BASIC then transfers control back to the FOR statement (line 90) and compares the value of I (2) to the high-level value in the FOR statement, in this case 1000. If I is less than or equal to 1000, the program continues, executing line 100, 110, and 120. Once again, upon reaching the NEXT I statement (line 130), the value of I is incremented by 1, making I equal to 3. This continues until I is greater than 1000 (i.e., 1001), when the program continues executing at the line following the NEXT I statement, in this case line 140. The FOR statement is summarized in the box below.

The FOR Statement

Purpose   To mark the beginning of a loop by assigning a starting value, an ending value, and optionally an increment

Format   ln FOR <var> = <start> TO <finish> STEP <inc>
where *var* is a variable to represent the counter in the loop and is called the index, *start* is the starting value of *var*, *finish* is the maximum value of *var*, and *inc* is the increment by which *var* is increased each time the loop is repeated (default is 1)

Examples   10 REM Example of a FOR statement
        20 FOR I = 1 TO 10 STEP 2
        30   PRINT I
        40 NEXT I
        50 END

when this program is run, it would print the following:
        1
        3
        5
        7
        9

Notes   If the STEP parameter is omitted, the increment is 1. Negative values can also be used for STEP values (i.e., FOR J = 100 TO 10 STEP −10). STEP values are discussed in the next section. The parameter represented by *var* is often called the index.

The FOR statement marks the beginning of the loop. In the FOR statement, the beginning value for the index (see box) and the maximum possible value of the index are specified.

Optionally, a step value may be specified. The step value is the increment by which the index is to be increased (or decreased in the case of a negative step) each time the loop is processed. For every FOR statement, there must be a corresponding NEXT statement. The NEXT statement indicates where the last line in the loop is. When the program reaches the NEXT statement, the program increments the index and branches back up to the FOR statement. The NEXT statement is also used to indicate where the program will continue after the loop is complete. Upon completion of the loop, the program continues processing with the statement immediately following the NEXT statement. A summary of the NEXT statement is given in the box below.

The NEXT Statement

Purpose   To signal the end of a FOR loop. NEXT increments the index value by one step value and branches back to the beginning of the loop

Format   ln NEXT <var>
where *var* is a variable to represent the current iteration in the loop

Examples   10 REM Example of a NEXT statement
20 FOR J = 1 TO 5
30   PRINT J
40 NEXT J
50 END ∘

when this program is run, it would print the following:
1
2
3
4
5

Note   If there is no NEXT statement following a FOR, the error message, "FOR without NEXT" will be displayed.

The STEP Parameter

The program illustrating the use of the FOR/NEXT loop allows the entry of input on 1000 products, numbered 1 through 1000. Each time the loop is executed, the counter, I, is incremented by 1. However, there may be situations where you want to increment by a number other than 1. The STEP parameter allows you to specify that increment. For each NEXT statement, BASIC increments the variable by the number specified following the STEP keyword (using an increment of 1 if no STEP value is given) and compares the variable with the maximum specified. This keeps occurring until the variable is greater than the maximum. Let's examine the following example.

```
200 FOR K = 5 TO 15 STEP 3
210    PRINT "K is equal to:";K
220 NEXT K
230 END
```

In this example, K is initially assigned the value of 5 for the first pass through the loop, and the program will display "K is equal to: 5." At the NEXT statement on line 220, K is incremented by the STEP value, 3, making K equal to 8. The program then branches to the FOR statement, and compares K with the maximum value, 15. At this point K = 8, which is less than or equal to the maximum, 15, so the loop is entered again and prints "K is equal to: 8." The loop continues down to the NEXT statement, where K is incremented by 3, becoming 11. The program then goes back to the FOR statement, and compares K with 15. Since 11 is equal to or less than 15, the loop is entered again and prints "K is equal to: 11." The program proceeds to the NEXT statement, and again K is incremented by 3,

making it 14. The program branches back to the FOR statement, and compares
14 with 15. Since 14 is less than 15, the loop is entered again and prints "K is
equal to: 14." The program proceeds to the NEXT statement, and K is incremented by 3, making the value of K equal to 17. The program then jumps up to
the FOR statement, and K is compared with 15. K is greater than 15, and therefore nothing is printed and the program branches to the statement following the
NEXT statement, in this case the END statement. The output of our sample program looks like this:

```
run
K is equal to: 5
K is equal to: 8
K is equal to: 11
K is equal to: 14
Ok
```

Negative values can also be used as step values. To use a negative step value,
the iteration must go from a higher value to a lower one. For example:

```
200 FOR K = 15 TO 5 STEP -3
210    PRINT "K is equal to: ";K
220 NEXT K
230 END
```

This program would print the following run:

```
run
K is equal to: 15
K is equal to: 12
K is equal to: 9
K is equal to: 6
Ok
```

Variables can also be used for the start, maximum, and increment values. A
sample of this would be the following.

```
100 LET START = 4
110 LET MAXIMUM = 20
120 LET INCREMENT = 5
130 FOR L = START TO MAXIMUM STEP INCREMENT
140    PRINT "L is equal to ";L
150 NEXT L
160 END
```

This example assigns values to a variable, and that value is used as a specification
in the FOR/NEXT loop. If the ending value of the loop is specified within the program, in this case MAXIMUM = 20, the variable MAXIMUM can be used instead
of 20 in the FOR/NEXT loop. The START variable is given an initial value of 4,
and the INCREMENT variable is assigned the value of 5. The above example
would be the same as coding the statement directly with a start value of 4, a
maximum value of 20, and a step value of 5. (See the following program.)

```
100 FOR L = 4 TO 20 STEP 5
110 PRINT "L is equal to: ";L
120 NEXT L
130 END
```

When either of these programs is run, the results will be as follows:

```
run
L is equal to: 4
L is equal to: 9
L is equal to: 14
L is equal to: 19
Ok
```

Referring back to our example program that would read in 1000 parts and print the total dollar value, we can modify this to accept any number of parts, as shown below.

```
10 REM Program to accept as input the quantity and unit
20 REM price for N products, and printing the total
30 REM dollar value of the inventory.
40 REM
50 REM Initialize total.value to zero
60 LET TOTAL.VALUE = 0
70 REM
80 INPUT "Enter the number of parts to be entered:";PARTS
90 REM Input the quantity and unit price for each product
100 FOR I = 1 TO PARTS
110     PRINT "Enter quantity and unit price for product";I
120     INPUT "===>";QUANTITY, UNIT.PRICE
130     TOTAL.VALUE = TOTAL.VALUE + (QUANTITY * UNIT.PRICE)
140 NEXT I
150 REM
160 REM All the data have been entered, print out total
170 PRINT "Total value of inventory is $";TOTAL.VALUE
180 END
```

This version of the program has eliminated unnecessary looping when we don't have information for 1000 products. Line 80 has been added to allow the user to specify the number of parts that are going to be read in prior to starting to read in the data values. Line 100 has been modified to loop until the number of parts given has been reached.

Nested FOR/NEXT Loops

Let's complicate our inventory example a little more. Say instead of one location we have five different warehouses that keep separate running inventories. We wish to develop a program that will give a total dollar value for the combined inventories. Let's assume these warehouses buy parts from different suppliers and a shipping charge is added to the unit cost of a particular part, with the result that the unit price for the same item in a different warehouse varies. We must modify

our program to read in the five separate quantities and unit prices for each part.
One solution would be to change our program like this:

```
10 REM Program to accept as input the quantity and unit
20 REM price for N products, and printing out the total
30 REM dollar value of the inventory.
40 REM
50 REM Initialize total.value to zero
60 LET TOTAL.VALUE = 0
70 REM
80 INPUT "Enter the number of parts to be entered:";PARTS
90 REM Input the quantity and unit price for each product
100 FOR I = 1 TO PARTS
110     PRINT "For Warehouse #1"
120     PRINT "Enter quantity and unit price for product,I
130     INPUT "===>";QUANTITY, UNIT.PRICE
140     TOTAL.VALUE = TOTAL.VALUE + (QUANTITY * UNIT.PRICE)
150     PRINT "For Warehouse #2"
160     PRINT "Enter quantity and unit price for product",I
170     INPUT "===>",QUANTITY, UNIT.PRICE
180     TOTAL.VALUE = TOTAL.VALUE + (QUANTITY * UNIT.PRICE)
190     PRINT "For Warehouse #3"
200     PRINT "Enter quantity and unit price for product",I
210     INPUT "===>",QUANTITY, UNIT.PRICE
220     TOTAL.VALUE = TOTAL.VALUE + (QUANTITY * UNIT.PRICE)
230     PRINT "For Warehouse #4"
240     PRINT "Enter quantity and unit price for product",I
250     INPUT "===>",QUANTITY, UNIT.PRICE
260     TOTAL.VALUE = TOTAL.VALUE + (QUANTITY * UNIT.PRICE)
270     PRINT "For Warehouse #5"
280     PRINT "Enter quantity and unit price for product",I
290     INPUT "===>",QUANTITY, UNIT.PRICE
300     TOTAL.VALUE = TOTAL.VALUE + (QUANTITY * UNIT.PRICE)
310 NEXT I
320 REM
330 REM All the data have been entered, print out total
340 PRINT "Total value of inventory is $";TOTAL.VALUE
350 END
```

In each of the five different warehouses, the quantity and prices for each part are
requested. The program prompts the user to specify the number of parts that are
going to be input and this number is stored in the variable PARTS. The program
then enters the FOR/NEXT loop where I is initially assigned the value of 1. The
program then prompts for each of the five warehouses, adding these values to the
TOTAL.VALUE accumulator. I is incremented by 1 and is then checked to see if
its value is greater than PARTS. Since I now equals 2, the program enters the loop
again, prompting for all five warehouses and adding the values to TOTAL.VALUE.
This continues until I is greater than PARTS.

Now suppose the number of warehouses increases to ten, or perhaps to one
hundred. The program needs to be made more flexible. What we really need is a
loop within a loop, which is known as a **nested loop**. We could change our pro-

gram to use a nested FOR/NEXT loop: for every part, there would be a smaller loop that would accept input for each warehouse, and would look something like this:

```
10 REM Program to accept as input the quantity and unit
20 REM price for N products, and printing out the total
30 REM dollar value of the inventory.
40 REM
50 REM Initialize total.value to zero
60 LET TOTAL.VALUE = 0
70 REM
80 INPUT "Enter number of warehouses: ";WAREHOUSES
90 INPUT "Enter the number of parts to be entered:";PARTS
100 REM Input the quantity and unit price for each product
110 FOR I = 1 TO PARTS
120    FOR J = 1 TO WAREHOUSES
130       PRINT "For Warehouse #";J
140       PRINT "Enter quantity and unit price for product",I
150       INPUT "===>",QUANTITY, UNIT.PRICE
160       TOTAL.VALUE = TOTAL.VALUE + (QUANTITY * UNIT.PRICE)
170    NEXT J
180 NEXT I
190 REM All the data have been entered, print out total
200 PRINT "Total value of inventory is $";TOTAL.VALUE
210 END
```

In this program, the loop for the number of warehouses (also known as the inside loop), is nested, or embedded in the loop for the 1000 or so products (the outside loop). So for every iteration of I (each part), the program loops to read in the data for the number of different warehouses specified. Another example of nested FOR/NEXT loops is the following:

```
100 FOR I = 1 TO 5
110    FOR J = 1 TO I
120       PRINT "*";
130    NEXT J
140    PRINT
150 NEXT I
160 FOR I = 5 TO 1 STEP -1
170    FOR J = 1 TO I
180       PRINT "*";
190    NEXT J
200    PRINT
210 NEXT I
220 END
```

When this program is run, it would display the following:

```
run
*
**
***
****
*****
*****
****
***
**
*
Ok
```

Care should be taken that when a loop is nested within another loop, the inside loop is completely within the outside loop. If the loops overlap, they are called **cross loops** and will create an error. Consider the following cross loop:

```
10 FOR I = 1 TO 10
20    FOR J = 1 TO 5
30        PRINT I,J
40 NEXT I
50    NEXT J
60 END
```

Notice that the inside loop for J overlaps the outside loop for I. When this program is run the following error message will be displayed.

```
run
NEXT without FOR in 50
Ok
```

WHILE/WEND Loops

We have been developing our original inventory program into a more flexible and efficient program with FOR/NEXT loops throughout this chapter. It now looks like the following:

```
10 REM Program to accept as input the quantity and unit
20 REM price for N products, and printing out the total
30 REM dollar value of the inventory.
40 REM
50 REM Initialize total.value to zero
60 LET TOTAL.VALUE = 0
70 REM
80 INPUT "Enter number of warehouses: ",WAREHOUSES
90 INPUT "Enter number of parts to be entered:",PARTS
100 REM Input the quantity and unit price for each product
110 FOR I = 1 TO PARTS
120    FOR J = I TO WAREHOUSES
130        PRINT "For Warehouse #";J
140        PRINT "Enter quantity and unit price for product",I
```

```
150          INPUT "===>",QUANTITY, UNIT.PRICE
160          TOTAL.VALUE = TOTAL.VALUE + (QUANTITY * UNIT.PRICE)
170      NEXT J
180 NEXT I
190 REM
200 REM All the data has been entered, print out total
210 PRINT "Total value of inventory is $";TOTAL.VALUE
220 END
```

The FOR/NEXT Loops have greatly simplified the program, and have made it more flexible. In reality, we probably don't want to count all the parts in inventory prior to running this program. We would most likely receive a parts list with quantities and prices; note that the list might not have all parts listed for a particular warehouse. We would then wish to signal the program when we have finished entering data, and have the program write out the results. This can be implemented using the BASIC WHILE/WEND loop. If we further modify our inventory program to allow for this condition it would look like this:

```
10 REM Program to accept as input the quantity and unit
20 REM price for N products, and printing out the total
30 REM dollar value of the inventory.
40 REM
50 REM Initialize total.value to zero
60 LET TOTAL.VALUE = 0
70 REM
80 PRINT "For Warehouse #1"
90 PRINT "Enter quantity and unit price for product 1"
100 PRINT "(enter a negative quantity to signal end of data)"
110 INPUT "===>",QUANTITY, UNIT.PRICE
120 COUNT = 1
130 WHILE QUANTITY >= 0
140 LET TOTAL.VALUE = TOTAL.VALUE + (QUANTITY * UNIT.PRICE)
150     FOR J = 2 TO 5
160         PRINT "For Warehouse #";J
170         PRINT "Enter quantity and unit price for product",COUNT
180         INPUT "===>",QUANTITY, UNIT.PRICE
190         TOTAL.VALUE = TOTAL.VALUE + (QUANTITY * UNIT.PRICE)
200     NEXT J
210     COUNT = COUNT + 1
220     PRINT "For Warehouse #1"
230     PRINT "Enter quantity and unit price for product 1"
240     INPUT "===>";QUANTITY, UNIT.PRICE
250 WEND
260 REM
270 REM All the data have been entered, print out total
280 PRINT "Total value of inventory is $";TOTAL.VALUE
290 END
```

In this program, we've had to change our logic a little. The WHILE/WEND loop is set up to test if a condition (in this case quantity >= 0) is met. If the condition is met, the statements following the WHILE statement are executed until the WEND statement is reached, then this transfers control to the WHILE statement to see if the condition is still met (See boxes below for summaries of WHILE and WEND.) In our program, we want to loop until a certain value for QUANTITY is reached, indicating that data entry is complete. The range of possible valid quantities includes any positive integer or zero. By entering a negative number (something less than zero), we signal that we are through entering data. When a negative number is entered for the quantity of the part from Warehouse #1, the condition (QUANTITY >= 0) specified in the WHILE statement is false, and BASIC continues executing from the statement following the WEND statement.

The WHILE Statement

Purpose   To signify the beginning of a loop and to define the condition that must remain true to stay in the loop

Format   ln WHILE <condition>
where *condition* is a valid BASIC conditional clause made up of relational and logical operators that check the status of a variable which is changed within the loop

Example   10 REM Example of WHILE statement
20 I = 1
30 WHILE I <= 5
40   PRINT I
50   I = I + 1
60 WEND
70 END

When run, this program would print the following:
1
2
3
4
5

Note   The condition that is being tested in the WHILE statement must change and eventually prove false or the program will loop forever, which is known as an *infinite loop*.

The WHILE statement signifies the beginning of a loop and defines a condition that must be true for the loop to continue. Once the condition becomes false, the program continues executing at the line following the last line of the loop. The last line of a WHILE loop is a WEND statement. This statement does what the NEXT statement does for the FOR loop. The WEND statement signifies the end of the loop. When the WEND statement is reached, the program branches back to the WHILE statement, and determines if the condition is still true. If the condition is still true, the loop is processed again. If the condition has become false, the program continues execution at the first line following the WEND statement.

The WEND Statement

Purpose   To mark the last line of code that is part of the WHILE loop

Format   ln WEND

Example   10 REM Example of a WEND statement
20 I = 10
30 WHILE I > 5
40   PRINT I
50   I = I − 1
60 WEND
70 END

When run, this program would print the following:
10
9
8
7
6

Note   Only one WEND is allowed for each WHILE statement and for every WHILE statement there must be a corresponding WEND statement.

The conditions specified in the WHILE statement can be fairly complex, provided they follow the rules of relational and logical operators defined in Chapter 6. Such an example is shown below:

```
100 LET A = 20
110 LET B = 5
120 WHILE ((A < 100) AND (B >= 0))
130     PRINT A,B,A + B
140     A = A + A
150     B = B - 1
160 WEND
170 END
```

When run, the output of this program would be:

```
run
20              5              25
40              4              44
80              3              83
Ok
```

Tracing through this example, the third iteration assigns the value of 160 to A, which makes the condition

```
((A < 100) AND (B >= 0))
```

false, thus ending the loop.

The WHILE/WEND loop evaluates the condition specified at the WHILE statement prior to entering the loop. The condition must be true for the program to ever enter the loop, and the condition must eventually become false for the program to exit the loop. If the condition never becomes false, the program will continue looping indefinitely. This is known as an **endless**, or **infinite loop**. In the case of an infinite loop, the user must terminate the program by forcing the program to have an **abnormal ending**. At this point, steps must be taken to determine and correct the problem prior to rerunning the program. After a program has terminated, the validity of any output should be questioned. A Ctrl-Break or Ctrl-C is necessary to generate the ABEND which will terminate the infinite loop and terminate the program. An example of a program that would cause an infinite loop would be as follows.

```
100 LET K = 5
110 LET SUM = 10
120 WHILE SUM > K
130     PRINT K, SUM
140     SUM = SUM + K
150 WEND
160 END
```

In this example, the condition (SUM > K) is true the first time the loop is entered. On each pass through the loop, SUM is incremented by K, so that at no time will SUM ever be less than or equal to K. In this case, the condition (SUM > K) would never become false, so the loop would never terminate, causing an infinite loop.

A Word on Programming Style

Just as it was important to follow structured programming techniques when using nested IF statements, it is as important when using loops. Quite often, you will find yourself coding multiple nested loops or multiple loops within a loop. Proper indentation ensures optimum readability. In addition to readability, there are several other important ideas to keep in mind when using loops.

The first concerns FOR/NEXT loops. When using FOR/NEXT loops, it is important that you don't attempt to change the value of the counter variable (or index) while within the loop. If you have a loop that looks like this:

```
10  FOR I = 1 TO 10
20      PRINT I
30      I = I - 1
40  NEXT I
```

your program can produce strange results. Similar problems can occur if you change the variable representing the starting value, the maximum value, or the step value. Good programming style strongly recommends that you don't alter the value of any of the variables that represent parameters specified in a FOR statement from within the loop.

Another concern arises when using WHILE/WEND loops. Consider the following program:

```
10 COUNTER = 1
20 WHILE COUNTER < 10
30    SUM = COUNTER + 10
40 WEND
50 PRINT SUM
60 END
```

There is no way to satisfy the condition that allows this program to leave the WHILE/WEND loop. Since COUNTER is never changed within the loop, there is no way to exit the loop and the program goes into an infinite loop and will have to be terminated.

One final point to remember with loops is that while they allow you to perform multiple tasks easily and efficiently, if the loop is incorrectly coded, your program can perform multiple errors just as quickly and easily.

Summary

- Loops are used to repeat a series of statements for a specified number of times, or until a given condition becomes false.
- FOR/NEXT loops are used when the number of iterations that will occur within the loop is known.
- When a loop occurs within another loop, it is known as a nested loop. Either FOR/NEXT or WHILE/WEND structures, or a combination of the two, can be nested.
- The WHILE/WEND loop is used when you don't know how many iterations will be necessary, but rather want to loop until a given condition becomes false.
- Care must be taken when using a WHILE/WEND loop to make sure that there is a way out of the loop. If the condition never becomes false, the program will enter an infinite loop and will never end, unless terminated abnormally by the user by pressing Ctrl-Break or Ctrl-C.

Exercises

True or False

_____ 1. When a subroutine is called multiple times, it is known as looping.

_____ 2. A FOR/NEXT loop allows the program to execute a section of code for a specified number of iterations.

_____ 3. The STEP parameter in the FOR/NEXT loop specifies how many iterations the loop will make.

_____ 4. If a NEXT statement is not used to terminate the FOR loop, only the statement immediately following the FOR statement is executed for the number of iterations designated by the FOR statement.

_____ 5. It is possible to have a FOR/NEXT loop within another FOR/NEXT loop and this is known as a nested loop.

_____ 6. WHILE/WEND loops continue looping until a condition made up of relational and logical expressions is no longer satisfied.

_____ 7. A WHILE loop will keep looping until the first WEND statement is reached, at which time the loop will terminate.

_____ 8. Care should be taken not to branch into the middle of a WHILE/WEND loop since unpredictable results can occur.

_____ 9. When using a WHILE/WEND loop, the condition evaluated following the WHILE must be true prior to trying to enter the loop or the loop will never be entered.

_____ 10. When a WHILE/WEND loop becomes an infinite loop, the Ctrl-Break or Ctrl-C keys will generate an interrupt and the program will continue processing at the line following the WEND statement.

Fill-In

1. An _____ is a variable that is used to keep a running sum while in a loop.

2. If you want to execute a section of code until a condition is no longer true, you should use a _____ loop.

3. The _____ statement is used to signify the end of a FOR loop.

4. A loop within another loop is known as a _____ loop.

5. The _____ parameter is used to determine by how much the index value is incremented each time the loop repeats and has a default value of 1.

6. The condition that must remain true to remain in a WHILE/WEND loop can be made up of _____ and _____ operators.

7. When a WHILE/WEND loop is entered, but there is never any way for the WHILE condition to become false, the program is said to be in an _____ or _____ loop.

8. When a program is in an endless loop, Ctrl-Break or Ctrl-C must be used to force the program to _____ .

9. In a FOR/NEXT loop, the starting value and the maximum value in the FOR statement are separated by a _____ .

10. A pair of loops that overlap yet are not nested are known as _____ loops and will produce an error.

Short Answer

1. What is the purpose of a loop?

2. What is the fundamental difference between a FOR/NEXT loop and a WHILE/WEND loop?

3. What is essential to prevent a WHILE/WEND loop from becoming an infinite loop?

4. What is a nested loop?

5. Why is changing the START, MAXIMUM, or STEP values within the FOR/NEXT loop discouraged?

Programming Problems

1. Using a pair of nested FOR/NEXT loops, write a program to print the following output:

```
*
**
***
****
*****
******
*******
********
*********
**********
```

2. Write a program that uses a FOR/NEXT loop to prompt the user to key in ten numbers and then prints out the average.

3. Write the program described in Problem 2, except use a WHILE/WEND loop and have the program accept any number of values, until a zero is entered. When a zero is entered the program should print out the average up to but not including the zero.

4. Write a problem that uses a WHILE/WEND loop to input an employee number and pay rate. The program then uses a nested FOR/NEXT loop to read in the number of hours worked each day for the week (7 days). For days over 8 hours, the employee is paid time and a half for the additional hours. The WHILE/WEND loops until a value of 0,0 is input for the employee number–pay rate pair, at which time the program prints out the total amount paid out and terminates.

5. Write a program that uses a pair of nested FOR/NEXT loops to print out the following results:

I is equal to	20	J is equal to	5
I is equal to	20	J is equal to	8
I is equal to	20	J is equal to	11
I is equal to	20	J is equal to	14
I is equal to	15	J is equal to	5
I is equal to	15	J is equal to	8
I is equal to	15	J is equal to	11
I is equal to	15	J is equal to	14

I is equal to	10	J is equal to	5
I is equal to	10	J is equal to	8
I is equal to	10	J is equal to	11
I is equal to	10	J is equal to	14
I is equal to	5	J is equal to	5
I is equal to	5	J is equal to	8
I is equal to	5	J is equal to	11
I is equal to	5	J is equal to	14

9

Advanced I/O

Learning Objectives

After reading this chapter you should understand:

- How to use the READ and DATA statements
- How to create and use end-of-data markers in DATA statements
- How to use the RESTORE command to read data more than once
- How to use the TAB and SPC functions

- How to use the PRINT USING command to format output
- How to specify special characters in a PRINT USING statement to format output
- How to send formatted output to an attached printer

Introduction

This chapter presents more advanced techniques of input and output (I/O). In previous chapters, the programs we presented dealt with relatively small amounts of data keyed into the program via the INPUT command or through assignment statements. For programs using small amounts of data this method is fine. However, for large applications requiring lots of data, BASIC provides another method of data entry, the READ and DATA commands. These allow a program to access multiple data items without any intervention from the user. More advanced ways of controlling output, including the use of the PRINT command to create visually stimulating and easy-to-use displays and menus, will also be discussed, with particular emphasis on the PRINT USING and LPRINT statements. We will also show you how to use description fields and symbols to position numeric and character output.

Input via READ and DATA Statements

The INPUT command introduced in Chapter 5 is used to prompt the user for data. Using the READ and DATA statements in your program eliminates the need to input all data manually.

The DATA Statement

The DATA statement is used to put individual items or large volumes of data directly into a program. You can have multiple DATA statements anywhere within a program. For the sake of readability, sample programs in this book follow the convention of placing all DATA statements together at the end of the program. The elements of the DATA statement are summarized in the box below.

The DATA Statement

Purpose   To specify numeric or string information to be assigned to variables within a program using the READ statement

Format   ln DATA item1 <,item2,item3, ... item*n* >
where *ln* is a valid line number, and *item1* through *item*n are either string constants enclosed in double quotes or numbers

Examples   3000 DATA 45
3001 DATA 3,4.5,4,5,7,8,12234,9
3020 DATA "John Doe"
3030 DATA "Jane Doe","123-45-6789",40

Notes   Place all DATA statements together at the end of your program. Commas must be used to separate items in each DATA statement.

Values that follow the DATA statement are kept in memory, during program execution, in a **list format**. A list format in BASIC means that the first item of the first DATA statement is the first item in the list, followed by the second item of the first DATA statement, and so on. When the data is referenced by the program, the first item in the list is used, followed by the second item, and so on.

For instance, let's assume that we have a program with multiple DATA statements containing numeric values. The data consist of employee number, hourly wage, and year of service with the company (three data items per employee). We could specify the data:

```
1960 'Data for salary program is below.  The data for a
1970 'single employee is specified on each line.
1980 'The items specified on each line are:
1990 'Employee number, hourly wage, years of service
2000 DATA 23456 , 4.55 , 4
2010 DATA 23457 , 4.55 , 3
2020 DATA 11345 , 8.44 , 7
2030 DATA 00001 , 24.01 , 11
```

Specification of the data in this format is meaningful, in that the data for each employee is specified on a separate line. However, we can also specify the same data in the following format:

```
1980 'Employee data for program.  The information
1990 'for two employees is specified on each line.
2000 DATA 23456, 4.55, 4 ,23457 , 4.55 , 3
2010 DATA 11345, 8.44 , 7 , 00001, 24.01 , 11
```

or

```
2000 DATA 23456,4.55,4,23457,4.55,3,11345,8.44,7,00001,24.01
2010 DATA 11
```

BASIC will interpret all of these DATA statements the same way. More important than the way the data are spread out over multiple lines is the **order** in which the data appear in the program. The order that the data items will appear in memory, and the order that they will be read via the READ statement, is shown below:

```
23456
4.55
4
23457
4.55
3
11345
8.44
7
00001
24.01
11
```

The comma is used to separate or *delimit* items in the DATA statement. String constants in DATA statements do not need to be surrounded by quotation marks unless the constant contains commas, colons, or significant leading or trailing blanks. Table 9.1 shows some examples of valid and invalid DATA statements.

Table 9.1   Examples of Valid and Invalid DATA Statements

DATA Statement	Valid/Invalid	Explanation
10 DATA 3,4,"G"	Valid	
20 DATA "Test,6,5	Invalid	string must be enclosed in double quotes
30 DATA "Test,6",5,56	Valid	
40 DATA 88888,99999,44444	Valid	
50 DATA 67,34.5667,TELEPHONE$	Invalid	strings must be enclosed in double quotes
60 DATA 23,456.00	Valid	items are 23 and 456.0
60 DATA 23456.00	Valid	
99 DATA 89 87 "Paper clips"	Invalid	multiple items must be delimited by commas
99 DATA 89,,,79,,4	Valid	BASIC will assign a 0 or "" to numeric or string variables respectively when values are not specified in a DATA statement

The READ Statement

The READ statement works in much the same fashion as the INPUT command, except that no prompt is displayed on the computer screen. The READ command gets data from DATA statements, instead of asking the user for data. For every variable specified in a READ statement, one data item is read from the list of data items specified in DATA statements. The READ statement is summarized in the box below.

The READ Statement

Purpose   To assign values to variables using information contained in DATA statements

Format   ln READ item1 <,item2, ... itemn>
where *ln* is a valid line number, and *item1* through *itemn* are the valid names of numeric or string variables

Examples   20 READ SALARY
             45 READ FIRST.NAM$,MIDDLE.NAM$,LAST.NAM$
             50 READ WAGE,TITLE$,EMPLOYEE.NUM,LOCATION$

Notes   The variables specified in the READ command must be separated by commas. The types of variables must match the types of values specified by the corresponding DATA statements.

Assume that we want to create a BASIC program, with DATA and READ statements, to read in ten checkbook entries and determine the amount of money spent, including the amounts of the largest and smallest checks. Such a program could take the following format (see Figure 9.1 for the flowchart and pseudocode used in planning this program).

Figure 9.1

```
Program: Checks
Clear screen and turn key display off
Execute subroutine initialize
Execute subroutine READDATA
Execute subroutine report
Turn key display on
END: Checks

Subroutine: Initialize
Set Number.Of.Checks to 10
Set Total.Amount to 0
Set Smallest.Check, Largest.Check to 0
Set Smallest.Amount to 99999.99
Set Largest.Amount to 0
END: Initialize

Subroutine: READDATA
Do check = 1 to Number.Of.Checks
  READ Check.Number,Check.Amount
  IF Check.Amount greater than Largest.Amount
    THEN execute subroutine Set.Largest
  IF Check.Amount less than Smallest.Amount
    THEN execute subroutine Set.Smallest
  Set Total.Amount to sum of Total.Amount and Check.Amount
END: Do
END: READDATA

Subroutine: Set.Largest
Set Largest.Number to Check.Number
Set Largest.Amount to Check.Amount
END: Set.Largest

Subroutine: Set.Smallest
Set Smallest.Number to Check.Number
Set Smallest.Amount to Check.Amount
END: Set.Smallest

Subroutine: Report
Display Total.Amount
Display Largest.Number, Largest.Amount
Display Smallest.Number, Smallest.Amount
Display end of program
END: Report
```

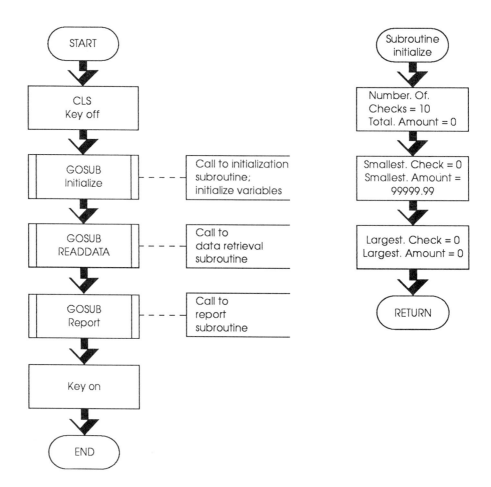

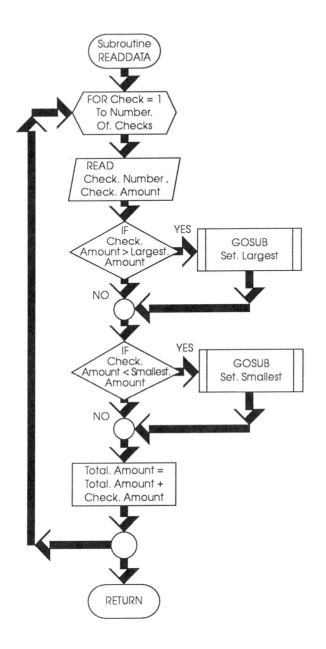

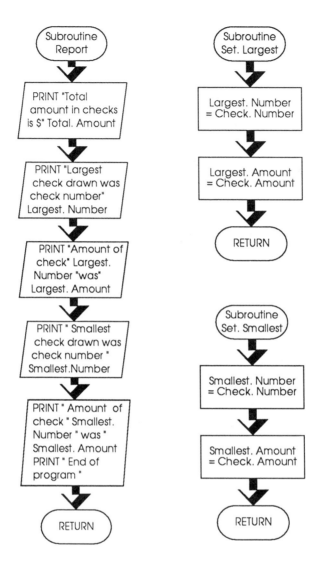

```
1000 'Sample check program - read in information about 10 checks,
1010 'and then display various statistics about the checks.
1020 '
1030 'Main procedure:
1040 '
1050 CLS : KEY OFF
1060 GOSUB 2000
1070 GOSUB 3000
1080 GOSUB 6000
1090 KEY ON
1100 END
2000 '
2010 'Initialization subroutine: Initialize counters and constants
2020 '
2030 NUMBER.OF.CHECKS = 10
2040 TOTAL.AMOUNT = 0
2050 SMALLEST.CHECK = 0
2060 SMALLEST.AMOUNT = 99999.99
2070 LARGEST.CHECK = 0
2080 LARGEST.AMOUNT = 0
2090 RETURN
3000 '
3010 'Data retrieval subroutine: Read in data
3020 '
3030 FOR CHECK = 1 TO NUMBER.OF.CHECKS
3040  READ CHECK.NUMBER,CHECK.AMOUNT
3050  IF CHECK.AMOUNT > LARGEST.AMOUNT
        THEN GOSUB 4000
3060  IF CHECK.AMOUNT < SMALLEST.AMOUNT
        THEN GOSUB 5000
3070  TOTAL.AMOUNT = TOTAL.AMOUNT + CHECK.AMOUNT
3080 NEXT CHECK
3090 RETURN
4000 '
4010 'Subroutine to update largest.number, largest.amount variables
4020 '
4030 LARGEST.NUMBER = CHECK.NUMBER
4040 LARGEST.AMOUNT = CHECK.AMOUNT
4050 RETURN
5000 '
5010 'Subroutine to update smallest.number, smallest.amount
5020 'variables
5030 SMALLEST.NUMBER = CHECK.NUMBER
5040 SMALLEST.AMOUNT = CHECK.AMOUNT
5050 RETURN
6000 '
6010 'Report subroutine: Display statistics
6020 '
6030 PRINT "Total amount in checks is $"TOTAL.AMOUNT
6040 PRINT
```

```
6050 PRINT "Largest check drawn was check number "LARGEST.NUMBER
6060 PRINT "  Amount of check "LARGEST.NUMBER" was $"LARGEST.AMOUNT
6070 PRINT
6080 PRINT "Smallest check drawn was check number "SMALLEST.NUMBER
6090 PRINT "  Amount of check "SMALLEST.NUMBER" was $"SMALLEST.AMOUNT
6100 PRINT
6110 PRINT "End of program."
6120 RETURN
7000 '
7010 'Data for program: the check number and amount for two checks
7020 'is specified on each line.
7030 '
7040 DATA 200,143.47,201,154.02
7050 DATA 203,650.00,204,46.73
7060 DATA 205,500.00,206,9.09
7070 DATA 207,102.69,208,41.07
7080 DATA 209,39.82,213,43.86
7090 'End of program.
```

This program demonstrates several good programming techniques that we've discussed in previous chapters. First, we've used descriptive variables. Second, we've broken up the program into several small subroutines, each of which is easy to understand. Third, we've added comments throughout, to make the program easier to read and understand.

The main part of the program consists of the CLS and KEY commands, three subroutine calls, a KEY command, and the END command. The program will perform three different functions. The first subroutine initializes constants that will be used in the program. The variable NUMBER.OF.CHECKS sets the number of checks to be read to 10. We could have left this variable out of the program, but its inclusion makes the FOR-NEXT loop a little easier to understand. Since we'll never read in a check with a number equal to 0, the variables SMALLEST.CHECK and LARGEST.CHECK will be set to 0. These variables will hold the check number of the smallest and largest checks drawn. We set SMALLEST.AMOUNT to a very large number and LARGEST.AMOUNT to a very small number so that when the program reads in the first check amount, SMALLEST.AMOUNT and LARGEST.AMOUNT will be set to this amount.

The second subroutine reads in data, using a FOR-NEXT clause. For every check number and amount that is read, comparisons are made to see if the amount is either the largest or smallest amount encountered so far. If an amount is determined to be the largest or smallest amount, another subroutine is called to set the LARGEST.AMOUNT or SMALLEST.AMOUNT variables. The third subroutine displays the statistics that have been generated by the program.

The READ statement in the second subroutine has two variables specified, CHECK.NUMBER and CHECK.AMOUNT. Every time the READ statement is executed, two items will be read from the list. After reading, the two items will not be read again; BASIC keeps an **address** or **pointer** to remember which items in the list have not yet been read. This pointer initially points to the top of the list, to the first data item from the first DATA statement.

If we had one more data item specified in the last DATA statement, nothing adverse would happen to the program; the extra data item would not be read by the program. If we did not have enough data specified in the DATA statement, BASIC would display an error message when a READ statement attempted to grab more data, "Out of DATA in ln," (where *ln* refers to the line number of program where the READ command was issued.)

The program above will read two data items at a time, ten times, and then display the total amount of money drawn on checks, plus the largest and smallest checks drawn. The program will work fine for only ten checks. The output for this sample check program would be as follows:

```
Total amount in checks is $ 1730.75

Largest check drawn was check number  203
   Amount of check  203 was $ 650

Smallest check drawn was check number  206
   Amount of check  206 was $ 9.09

End of program.
Ok
```

This program is limited by the fact that if more or fewer checks were to be examined, not only would more or fewer DATA statements have to be added to or subtracted from the program, but the constant NUMBER.OF.CHECKS would have to be changed to the correct number of checks.

Specifying End-of-Data Markers

To allow the check program above to read in any number of checks, we could use a **trailer record** or an **end-of-data** marker. An end-of-data marker marks the end of a data list and aids the program in determining when all valid data have been processed. Without specifying an end-of-data record, the program would have no way of determining when all data items had been read and processed.

An end-of-data marker is merely the last of a set of DATA lines, but one of the data items contains a unique value, one you would never expect a particular variable to have, to show that it marks the end of the data. It is important that the end-of-data marker contain enough data items to satisfy the READ statement. For example, if the READ statement contains two variable names, then the end-of-data marker must contain two data items of the same data type (numeric or character) as the corresponding variables. Instead of using a FOR/NEXT loop to read through the data, we will use a WHILE/WEND clause in this example.

```
1000 'Sample check program - read in information about any number
1010 'of checks, and then display various statistics about the checks.
1020 'An end-of-data marker must be specified as the last data item
1030 '
1040 'Main procedure:
1050 '
1060 CLS : KEY OFF
1070 GOSUB 1120
1080 GOSUB 1210
1090 GOSUB 1450
```

```
1100 KEY ON
1110 END
1120 '
1130 'Initialization subroutine: Initialize counters and constants
1140 '
1150 TOTAL.AMOUNT = 0
1160 SMALLEST.CHECK = 0
1170 SMALLEST.AMOUNT = 99999.99
1180 LARGEST.CHECK = 0
1190 LARGEST.AMOUNT = 0
1200 RETURN
1210 '
1220 'Data retrieval subroutine: Read in data
1230 '
1240 READ CHECK.NUMBER, CHECK.AMOUNT
1250 WHILE CHECK.NUMBER <>0
1260   IF CHECK.AMOUNT > LARGEST.AMOUNT
          THEN GOSUB 1320
1270   IF CHECK.AMOUNT < SMALLEST.AMOUNT
          THEN GOSUB 1380
1280   TOTAL.AMOUNT = TOTAL.AMOUNT + CHECK.AMOUNT
1290 READ CHECK.NUMBER,CHECK.AMOUNT
1300 WEND
1310 RETURN
1320 '
1330 'Subroutine to update largest.number, largest.amount variables
1340 '
1350 LARGEST.NUMBER = CHECK.NUMBER
1360 LARGEST.AMOUNT = CHECK.AMOUNT
1370 RETURN
1380 '
1390 'Subroutine to update smallest.number, smallest.amount variables
1400 '
1410 SMALLEST.NUMBER = CHECK.NUMBER
1420 SMALLEST.AMOUNT = CHECK.AMOUNT
1430 RETURN
1440 '
1450 'Report subroutine: Display statistics
1460 '
1470 PRINT "Total amount in checks is $"TOTAL.AMOUNT
1480 PRINT
1490 PRINT "Largest check drawn was check number "LARGEST.NUMBER
1500 PRINT "  Amount of check "LARGEST.NUMBER" was $"LARGEST.AMOUNT
1510 PRINT
1520 PRINT "Smallest check drawn was check number "SMALLEST.NUMBER
1530 PRINT "  Amount of check "SMALLEST.NUMBER" was $"SMALLEST.AMOUNT
1540 PRINT
1550 PRINT "End of program."
1560 RETURN
1570 '
```

```
1580 'Data for program: the check number and amount for two checks is
1590 'specified on each line.
1600 '
1610 DATA 200,143,47,201,154.02
1620 DATA 203,650.00,204,46.73
1630 DATA 205,500.00,206,9.09
1640 DATA 207,102.69,208,41.07
1650 DATA 209,39.82,213,43.86
1660 DATA 0,0
1670 'End of program.
```

With relatively few changes to the program, we can now read and examine any number of checks, as long as the end-of-data marker is specified as the last DATA statement. Examination of the first subroutine shows that the variable NUMBER.OF.CHECKS is no longer needed. Examination of the second subroutine shows the WHILE/WEND clause that manages the reading of the check data. Instead of entering the loop and reading, we must have another READ statement before the WHILE statement, so that the loop will be entered. If we did not read a value into CHECK.NUMBER, the comparison CHECK.NUMBER < > 0 would be false. Also notice how the second READ statement has been placed at the bottom of the loop, just before the WEND statement. Only after we've examined a check amount do we read another check number and amount.

The very last DATA statement contains the values 0,0. The program uses the fact that no valid check would ever have a check number of 0. The READ command will execute the same way as before, except that now, when the last group of data items is read in, the WHILE statement will cause the program to leave the WHILE/WEND clause. If the program were reading character data instead of numeric data, an end-of-data marker could also be used, provided that the marker is a unique string, such as "EOD" (for End of Data) or "EOF" (for End of File).

The RESTORE Command

The check program above reads through the data items only once. To read through the data items a second time without respecifying the data, you must instruct the program to reposition the pointer to the first item in the data list. The RESTORE command does just that, as shown in the box below.

The RESTORE command, which may be used repeatedly within a program, tells BASIC to reset the pointer to the beginning of a particular DATA statement. If the program executes a RESTORE command with no line number specified, the next READ statement will read data items starting at the first DATA statement in the program. If the program executes a RESTORE command with a line number specified, the next READ statement will read data items starting at the DATA statement on the line specified by the RESTORE command.

The RESTORE Command

Purpose   To reset the BASIC pointer in the list of data items in memory to the beginning of a particular DATA statement

Format   ln RESTORE <ln1>
where *ln* is a valid line number, and *ln1*, if specified, is the line number of a DATA statement within the program

Examples   20 RESTORE
                55 RESTORE 90   ' Reset pointer to DATA on line 90

Notes   If RESTORE is specified without a line number after the command, then the BASIC pointer is reset to the first item of the first DATA statement within the program. If a line number is specified, the BASIC pointer will be reset to the first item of the DATA statement on the line specified.

To see how RESTORE works, let's look at the following program.

```
 10 'Trivial program to demonstrate use of RESTORE command
 20 '
 30 'This program reads in 3 numbers, then calculates and displays
 40 'the sum of these numbers.
 50 READ A, B, C
 60 SUM = A + B + C
 70 PRINT "The sum of "A", "B", "C" is "SUM
 80 READ A, B, C
 90 SUM = A + B + C
100 PRINT "The sum of "A", "B", "C" is "SUM
110 RESTORE
120 READ A, B, C
130 SUM = A + B + C
140 PRINT "The sum of "A", "B", "C" is "SUM
150 END
160 DATA 88, 99, 100
170 DATA 2, 3, 4
180 DATA 56, 78, 9, 3.6
```

The READ command on line 50 will assign the values 88, 99, and 100 to the variables A, B, and C, respectively. The READ command on line 80 will assign the values 2, 3, and 4 to variables A, B, and C. The RESTORE command on line 110 will reposition the pointer back to the first DATA statement, so that the READ command on line 120 will again assign the values 88, 99 and 100 to the variables A, B, and C. The output of this sample summing program is as follows:

```
run
The sum of  88 ,  99 ,  100  is  287
The sum of  2 ,  3 ,  4  is  9
The sum of  88, 99 ,  100  is  287
Ok
```

If the RESTORE statement on line 110 above is changed to specify line number 170, then the READ command on line 120 would assign the values 2, 3, and 4 to A, B, and C, resulting in the following output.

```
run
The sum of  88 ,  99 ,  100   is  287
The sum of  2 ,  3 ,  4  is  9
The sum of  2 ,  3 ,  4  is  9
Ok
```

If you use the RESTORE command in a program, you will want to ensure that the constants you specify on DATA statements are grouped together corresponding to the READ commands that reference the data. For instance, consider the following program:

```
 10 'Trivial program to demonstrate use of RESTORE command
 20 '
 30 'This program reads in 3 numbers, then calculates and displays
 40 'the sum of those numbers.
 50 READ A, B, C
 60 SUM = A + B + C
 70 PRINT "The sum of "A", "B", "C", is "SUM
 80 READ A, B, C
 90 SUM = A + B + C
100 PRINT "The sum of "A", "B", "C", is "SUM
110 RESTORE 170
120 READ A, B, C
130 SUM = A + B + C
140 PRINT "The sum of "A", "B", "C" is "SUM
150 END
160 DATA 88, 99
170 DATA 100, 2, 3, 4, 56.78
180 DATA 9, 3.6
```

This program is exactly the same as the earlier program with the exception of a change to line 110 (RESTORE 170) and the reordering of the data items in lines 160 through 180. Notice that the data items have not been rearranged; the order of the data items, in list format, has not changed. Since RESTORE is based on line numbers and not on positions within the data list kept in memory, when the program is run, it will display different output as follows:

```
run
The sum of  88 ,  99 ,  100   is  287
The sum of  2 ,  3 ,  4  is  9
The sum of  100 ,  2 ,  3  is  105
Ok
```

In this run, the first READ statement assigns the values of 88, 99, and 100 to A, B, and C, then assigns the values 2, 3, and 4 to A, B, and C. After the RESTORE statement is executed, the next READ statement assigns the values *100, 2,* and *3* to A, B, and C. If you use RESTORE with a line number, pay careful attention to the order of items in DATA statements.

More on the PRINT Statement

It is essential that the output of a program be in a usable form that is pertinent for the end user. The format of the information displayed on a PC screen has a major impact on its usefulness. Information displayed by a program should be easy to read and uncluttered. This section will show you different ways that you can control the format of information on the screen so that it is easily read and understood.

In Chapter 5, we learned how the comma can be used to separate items in a PRINT statement to automatically generate tabular reports. However, use of the comma alone is insufficient for most reports; remember that commas cause items to be printed separately within print zones, and that there are only five print zones per line.

We also saw that while the use of semicolons as delimiters allowed us to print more than five items per line, the information was no longer in tabular form. Items separated by semicolons are printed with a single space between each item.

The TAB Function

In order to print an item starting in a particular position without regard to print zones, the TAB function is specified immediately before the item in the PRINT command. (*Functions* are BASIC utilities that will be described in greater detail in the next chapter.)

The TAB Function

Purpose   Function used to specify in which position the next item is to be printed in a PRINT command

Format   TAB (position)
where *position* is a number between 1 and 255 corresponding to a position in the output.

Examples   20 PRINT TAB (10); "Salaries now being analyzed"
30 PRINT "Name";TAB(20);"Title";TAB(50);"Salary"

Notes   You can specify a numeric variable within the parentheses of the TAB function so long as the variable has been assigned a number between 1 and 255. You cannot have any spaces between the keyword TAB and the left parenthesis.

Thus, if we had the following PRINT command in a program,

```
300 PRINT "Name";TAB(10);"Title";TAB(20);"Salary"
```

when the program is executed BASIC would display a screen like this:

```
Name          Title          Salary
```

When it executes line 300 above, BASIC first prints out the character string "Name," starting at position 1. The TAB function then instructs BASIC to "skip" to position 10. The next character string, "Title" is then printed. The next TAB function instructs BASIC to skip to position 20. The final item in the PRINT command, "Salary," is then printed.

Notice how semicolons are used as separators between PRINT items. If we used commas instead of semicolons, BASIC would skip to the next print zone before interpreting the TAB function. Note that the TAB function does not permit backspacing; if instead of printing "Name" we printed "Corporation" (more than 10 characters long) in line 300 above, when the TAB(10) function was interpreted, BASIC would skip a line, skip to position 10 of the new line, and begin printing remaining items:

```
Corporation
          Title          Salary
```

The SPC Function

If we did not care at which position items were to be printed but we wanted a certain number of spaces between items, we would use the SPC function. When you use the SPC function, BASIC will display the number of spaces you specify. Thus, if we had the following PRINT command in a program,

```
300 PRINT "Name";SPC(10);"Title";SPC(10);"Salary"
```

BASIC would display the following when the program is executed.

```
Name          Title          Salary
```

The SPC Function

Purpose   Function used to display spaces

Format   SPC (number)
where *number* is the number of spaces you wish to have inserted from the beginning of the line

Examples   20 PRINT SPC(10); "Salaries now being analyzed"
30 PRINT "Name";SPC(20);"Title";SPC(50);"Salary"

Note   Spaces are always counted from the beginning of the line or column (not from the previous SPC function).

The PRINT USING Statement

The next time you take a close look at a paycheck or any printed bill, you'll notice that names and amounts are printed in boxes or specific locations. You can use the PRINT USING command to tell BASIC exactly how you want output formatted. PRINT USING allows you to overcome the restrictions of commas and print zones, and is summarized in the box below.

The PRINT USING Statement

Purpose   To allow complete control of the format of output for items to be printed

Format   ln PRINT USING <string expression>; <item1, . . . itemn>
where *ln* is a valid line number, *string expression* is either a string constant or string variable containing the format template to be used, and *item1* through *itemn* are the valid names of string or numeric expressions to be printed

Examples   300 PRINT USING "Salary is #####";WEEKLY.SALARY
300 PRTFORM.SALARY$ = "Salary is #####"
310 PRINT USING PRTFORM.SALARY$;WEEKLY.SALARY

The PRINT USING command uses a template that describes where and how data will be printed. A **template** is a character string containing **descriptor fields**. Descriptor fields are special symbols that dictate how information will be formatted. Consider a template as an empty form, with empty locations where information will be inserted. A template can be included as part of the PRINT USING command, or can be referred to separately when it is previously assigned to a string variable.

```
300 EMPLOYEE.NUMBER = 12345
310 PRINT USING "Employee number is #####"; EMPLOYEE.NUMBER
```

or

```
540 EMPLOYEE.NUMBER = 12345
550 PRTFORM.EMPNO$ = "Employee number is #####"
560 PRINT USING PRTFORM.EMPNO$; EMPLOYEE.NUMBER
```

will both cause BASIC to display "Employee number is 12345" on the PC screen.

In the above program, we see the template specified directly as a character string constant in the PRINT USING command on line 310. Lines 550 and 560 demonstrate another method of specifying the template: line 550 sets the string variable PRTFORM.EMPNO$ to the template, and line 560 specifies the string variable name instead of the string constant itself.

To determine which format of the PRINT USING command you should use, you should consider how many times in your program you'll be using a particular template. If you'll use the template again later in the program, define the template as a string variable, and refer to the variable in the PRINT USING command, as in the second format shown above.

Descriptor Fields

The template in the program above contains characters to be printed ("Employee number is "), and also includes special format characters, in this case, a group of number signs (#####). The group of number signs is a numeric descriptor field, which is used to describe the placement and format of values within the template. Descriptor fields can be either numeric or character. When the PRINT USING command is executed, BASIC will determine the value of the variables specified after the template (in this case, EMPLOYEE.NUMBER is 12345) and replace the descriptor fields with the variables' determined values (in this case, ##### gets replaced with 12345).

Since there are five number signs in the example above, BASIC will format correctly a number up to five digits in length. The "#" character tells BASIC to replace the special characters with a numeric value in integer form.

A template can have several descriptor fields, and likewise, several variables or constants can be specified after the template in the PRINT USING command. The order of the variables after the template dictates which variables will replace which descriptor fields; the value of the first variable will replace the first descriptor field, the value of the second variable will replace the second descriptor field, and so on.

Special Characters Used in Formatting Numbers

The following section describes various symbols to format numbers in a template in a PRINT USING command. These symbols are shown in Table 9.2.

Table 9.2   Format Symbols Used with PRINT USING Commands

Symbol	Use
#	One or more number signs define a numeric field and will cause an integer to be displayed
.	Used with number signs, the period designates where the decimal point will be displayed
,	Used anywhere within a group of number signs to the right of a period to cause automatic display of commas
$	Used with number signs, a single dollar sign will cause a dollar sign to be displayed in that location
$$	Used with number signs, two dollar signs will cause a dollar sign to be displayed immediately to the left of a number
**	Specified on the left of a group of number signs, two asterisks will cause any nonused symbols within a numeric expression to be replaced by asterisks
+	A plus sign specified to the left or right of a group of number signs will cause a "+" to be displayed in that position
−	A minus sign specified to the left or right of a group of number signs will cause a "−" to be displayed in that position

The # Symbol Displaying Numbers

The "#" character, as we have seen, is used to display integers. The number of number signs you specify determines the number of digits that will be displayed. Numbers that have fewer digits than the number of number signs specified will be right-justified, with the remaining number signs converted into spaces. Numbers that have more than the specified number of number signs will be displayed in their entirety, with a percent sign (%) appended to the left-hand sign of the number. Examples are given in Table 9.3.

Table 9.3   Examples of the # Descriptor Symbol

Descriptor Field	Data	Result
####	12	12
####	13456	%13456
####	34.67	35
####	−2	−2
#####	1	1

The . Symbol for Displaying Numbers

You can place a period anywhere within or around a group of number ("#") signs to indicate where the decimal point will be placed. Without specifying a period, values get rounded to the next highest integer; this is sometimes useful when you want to ignore any digits to the right of the decimal point in a real number. Table 9.4 shows some example of the use of the "." descriptor.

Table 9.4   Examples of the . Descriptor Symbol

Descriptor Field	Data	Result
##.##	23	23.00
##.##	5.678	5.68
##.##	.3	0.30
##.##	−2	−2.00
####.#	5.678	5.7
##.###	3456.234	%3456.234

The , Symbol for Displaying Numbers

Placing a comma anywhere to the left of a period in a numeric descriptor field causes BASIC to print a comma to the left of every third number to the left of the decimal point. The comma comes in handy when printing numbers larger than 999. The comma needs to be specified only once to activate this feature, as shown in Table 9.5.

Table 9.5   Examples of the , Descriptor Symbol

Descriptor Field	Data	Result
#,###	2345	2,345
##,##	2345	2,345
#,####	5	5
####,.##	12567.456	12,567.46

The $ and $$ Symbols for Displaying Numbers

Specifying a single dollar sign to the left of a numeric descriptor field will cause BASIC to display a dollar sign in that print location. If you specify two dollar signs (with no spaces between them) to the left of a numeric descriptor field, BASIC will display a dollar sign immediately to the left of the number. Specifying two dollar signs informs BASIC to print a *floating* dollar sign; BASIC will determine where to place the dollar sign based on the size of the number. The use of the dollar sign symbol is illustrated in Table 9.6.

Table 9.6   Examples of the $ and $$ Descriptor Symbols

Descriptor Field	Data	Result
$##.##	23.45	$23.45
$##.##	.67	$ 0.67
$#,###	234	$ 234
$#,###	1235.5	$1,236
$##,###.##	1235.5	$ 1,235.50
$$##.##	23.45	$23.45
$$##.##	.67	$0.67
$$####,.##	3.45	$3.45
$$####,.##	5656.09	$ 5,656.09
$$####,.##	11234.44	$11,234.44

The ** Symbol for Displaying Numbers

Specifying two asterisks to the left of a numeric descriptor field instructs BASIC to fill all unfilled "#" descriptors with an asterisk. The output using this descriptor is sometimes used when printing out checks, to prevent someone from altering the value printed in otherwise empty spaces. Its use is shown in Table 9.7.

Table 9.7   Examples of the ** Descriptor Symbol

Descriptor Field	Data	Result
**####	45	****45
**####	.67	*****1
**##.#	.67	***0.7
**$##,###.##	1235.53	***$1,235.53
**$##,###.##	99.95	******$99.95

The + and − Symbols for Displaying Numbers

In some instances, you may want to emphasize the fact that a number is positive or negative in a display of information. For instance, if you are displaying profit/loss information, you will probably want to display a minus sign alongside all figures that indicate a loss, and display a plus sign alongside all profit figures. A plus sign specified at the beginning or end of a numeric descriptor field instructs BASIC to display a plus sign in that position, if the numeric descriptor field is replaced with a positive number. If the number is negative, a minus sign will be displayed instead of the plus sign.

Plus signs specified on the left-hand side of a numeric descriptor field will cause a *floating* plus sign to be displayed immediately to the left of the first digit of the formatted positive number. If the formatted number is negative, a minus sign will be displayed to the left of the first digit of the negative number.

If you specify a minus sign at the end of a numeric descriptor field, negative numbers will be displayed with a trailing minus sign and positive numbers will be displayed with a trailing space. Table 9.8 gives examples of various uses of the plus and minus signs.

Table 9.8　Examples of the + and − Descriptor Symbols

Descriptor Field	Data	Result
#####.##+	23456.47	23456.47+
#####.##−	−3455.91	3455.91−
####.##−	34.67	34.67
####.##+	−452.70	452.70−
+#####.##	78.54	+78.54
+#####.##	123876.21	%+123876.21
+###.##	−0.24	−0.24
+###.##	−63.34	−63.34

Special Characters Used in Formatting Character Strings

Just as you need to format numerical data, character data should also be formatted neatly. BASIC provides several descriptor symbols to allow the formatting of character information, shown in Table 9.9.

Table 9.9　Character Format Symbols Used with PRINT USING Commands

Symbol	Use
&	An ampersand will cause the display of a string value to be justified to the left
\\	Two backslashes with any number of spaces in between the slashes will cause the display of a string value of length 2 plus the number of spaces in between the slashes. The string value will be justified to the left
!	An exclamation point will cause the display of the first character of a string expression
_	An underscore will cause the display of the next character. Used to display format symbols within a PRINT USING template

The & Symbol for Displaying Characters

The ampersand ("&") character, used for displaying strings within a PRINT USING statement is similar to the "#" character used for displaying numbers. An ampersand within a PRINT USING template identifies the left-most position where a character string should be placed; note that you only need to specify a single ampersand. The ampersand will be replaced by the first character of the string; all other characters in the string will be placed on the right side of the ampersand. Let's look at an easy example.

```
10 'Simple program to demonstrate use of & symbol for
20 'displaying characters.
30 PRTFORM.TITLE$ = "& works in department ### as a &"
40 READ EMP.NAM$,EMP.DEPT,EMP.TITLE$
50 WHILE EMP.DEPT<>0
60   PRINT USING PRTFORM.TITLE$; EMP.NAM$,EMP.DEPT,EMP.TITLE$
70   READ EMP.NAM$,EMP.DEPT,EMP.TITLE$
80 WEND
90 END
100 ' Data for program: One employee per DATA statement
110 DATA "John Doe",302,"Draftsman"
120 DATA "Jane Doe",234,"Assistant Manager"
130 DATA "Jim Smith",589,"Senior Engineer"
140 DATA "Helen Jones",342,"Receptionist"
150 DATA "",0,""
```

The template for PRINT USING specified in the variable on line 30 above demonstrates the use of the "&" descriptor. With EMP.NAM$,EMP.DEPT, and EMP.TITLE$ assigned values via the READ statement, the program will display the following when executed:

```
run
John Doe works in department 302 as a Draftsman
Jane Doe works in department 234 as a Assistant Manager
Jim Smith works in department 589 as a Senior Engineer
Helen Jones works in department 342 as a Receptionist
Ok
```

Each ampersand character in the PRINT USING statement identifies where the beginning of each character string will be displayed, and BASIC automatically aligns each character string with regard to the rest of the template and other character strings. Notice in the sample program above that each line of output is spaced the same way a sentence is spaced, with one space between words. No matter how long the names are that are read into EMP.NAM$, each line of output is spaced in the same manner. The use of the "&" symbol within a template helps alleviate text-formatting problems. Table 9.10 gives some examples of the use of the ampersand symbol.

Table 9.10   Examples of the & Descriptor Symbol

Descriptor Field	Data	Result
&	Word	Word
&	Word	Word
name &	Sellers	name Sellers

The \\ Symbol for Displaying Characters

Suppose you were assigned the task of creating a program that displayed, in column format, information about employees of a company. Also assume that since there is so much information about each employee, you are limited to the number of characters of the employee's last name that you can display, for instance the first five characters of the last name. BASIC provides such a function.

The use of two backslashes within a template will limit the number of characters within a string to be displayed. The first backslash tells BASIC where to begin displaying a character string, and the second backslash marks the last position within the template where characters of the string can be displayed. If the character string does not fit in the area defined by the backslashes, the string gets truncated in the display. If the character string is too small to fit in the area defined by the backslashes, spaces are added to the right of the string to fill the rest of the area. Spaces inserted between the two backslashes indicate that more than two characters are to be displayed. Table 9.11 gives examples.

Table 9.11   Examples of the \\ Descriptor Symbols

Descriptor Field	Data	Result
\\	Magic	Ma
\ \	Magic	Mag
\ \	Magic	Magi
\ \	Magic	Magic
\ \ahead	Go	Go ahead

The ! Symbol for Displaying Characters

While the use of backslashes can limit the number of characters displayed from a string down to two characters, use of the exclamation point will display only the first character of a string. The "!" character comes in handy if you want to display the first initial of a name stored in a string variable, as shown in Table 9.12.

Table 9.12   Examples of the ! Descriptor Symbol

Descriptor Field	Data	Result
!	ethereal	e
!	Jonathan	J

The _ Symbol for Displaying Characters

If you want to specify a number sign, an ampersand, or any of the other special descriptor symbols themselves within a template, the underscore character "_" is used to tell BASIC not to interpret the following character for formatting but to display it literally. Table 9.13 shows some examples of this.

Table 9.13   Examples of the _ Descriptor Symbol

Descriptor Field	Data	Result
Curly _& &	Larry	Curly & Larry
& _!	Help	Help !
Ext _# ####	5555	Ext # 5555
Only $#.## _!_!	9.95	Only $9.95 !!

LPRINT and LPRINT USING

The PRINT command displays information on the PC screen. If you want to send output to a printer attached to your PC, use the LPRINT and LPRINT USING commands in place of PRINT and PRINT USING, respectively. The rules for LPRINT and LPRINT USING are the same as those for PRINT and PRINT USING, including the use of character and numeric field descriptors and symbols.

Page Ejecting

To display several lines of output and avoid screen clutter, we learned in Chapter 5 how to use the BASIC CLS command. It is also important that printouts generated by programs do not look cluttered; the information on a page generated by a program should all be related, with different information located on a separate page. For instance, a program that generates listings of all parts in inventory for each of ten warehouses might want to keep the information for each warehouse separate from that for other warehouses by listing each on a separate page.

For printed output, page ejection (bringing the printhead to the top of a new page) is performed using the LPRINT command. If you want to start printing on a new page, then you would include the following command in your program, just before any LPRINT commands:

```
2000 LPRINT CHR$(12);        'Page eject
```

Line 2000 above uses the CHR$ function to print a special print control character, which tells the printer to eject a page, so that the next LPRINT command will print output to the first line of a new page. The CHR$ functions, as well as functions in general, will be described in detail in the next chapter.

Summary

- The READ and DATA statements are used in a BASIC program so that you can assign values to variables without using the INPUT command.
- DATA statements can be located anywhere in a BASIC program, but it is a good idea to group all DATA statements together at the end of the program.
- The READ statement assigns values from DATA statements to variables specified by the READ statement. Each DATA item must be the same type as each variable specified by the READ command (numeric values with numeric variables, string values with string variables).
- An end-of-data marker is a string or numeric value, specified in the last DATA statement, which is used to trigger the program into a "no more data" condition. An end-of-data marker should be a unique value, one the data values would not normally contain.
- The RESTORE command is used to reset the BASIC pointer in the list of data items in memory. RESTORE allows you to READ values in DATA statements more than once.
- When using the RESTORE command, you should group all values together in one DATA statement that would be read by one READ command.
- The PRINT command is used to display information to the PC screen.
- The PRINT USING command gives you complete control over the way program output is displayed on the PC screen.
- Special characters, called descriptor symbols, are used with the PRINT USING command to control output.
- The LPRINT and LPRINT USING commands are used to direct program output to a printer, as opposed to the PC screen. LPRINT and LPRINT USING function in the same manner as the PRINT and PRINT USING commands, and use the same descriptor symbols for formatting.
- Including the command LPRINT CHR$(12) in a program will cause the printer to eject a page, so that the next LPRINT command will print output at the top of a new page.

Exercises

True or False

_____ 1. The INPUT command gathers information from DATA statements.

_____ 2. You can only use commas as separators between items in a DATA statement.

_____ 3. You do not need to place double quotes around a character string in a DATA statement.

_____ 4. The READ command never displays a prompt; it just gets information from DATA statements.

_____ 5. If there are not enough items in a DATA statement to satisfy a READ command, the program will end abnormally, with an error message.

_____   6. BASIC deletes data items from memory after they are read, preventing any reuse of the data.

_____   7. The "," and "." are format symbols you can use within a template for character string formatting.

_____   8. The "&" symbol specifies the left-most position where a character string will be displayed.

_____   9. If a number does not fit within a numeric descriptor field, it will not be displayed.

10. To display a formatting symbol with the PRINT USING command, you must precede the symbol with an underscore ("_").

Fill-In

1. During program execution, BASIC keeps items from DATA statements in _____.

2. The comma is the only _____ or _____ you can specify between items in a DATA statement.

3. A _____ or _____ is used by BASIC to keep track of which items in a data list have not yet been read.

4. An _____ record is used in a DATA statement to signify that there are no more items to be read.

5. The _____ command allows you to read items in DATA statements more than once.

6. If you want to begin displaying information at a specific position, you can use the _____.

7. The PRINT USING command relies on _____ to describe where and how information will be displayed.

8. _____ will display a floating dollar sign to the left of a number.

9. To display just the first character of a character string, you can use the _____ descriptor symbol.

10. When printing output on a printer, it is a good idea to use _____ in the program to put output on a new page.

Short Answer

1. We saw how a program can use end-of-data markers to overcome the restriction of hard-coding a variable with the number of values to be read in. Without using either a variable with the number of data values or end-of-data markers, describe a method of limiting the number of values read in by a program. Is this method better than end-of-data markers? Why?

2. Why must end-of-data markers be unique?

3. Why should special care be taken when using the RESTORE command with a line number?

4. Each of the following statements below is invalid. Explain why.
   (a) 1000 DATA 89 55 43
   (b) 2010 DATA CANADA,BERMUDA,AUSTRALIA
   (c) 3300 DATA 5;"Joe Doe";"Jane Doe"
   (d) 1020 DATA 'CANADA','BERMUDA','AUSTRALIA'
   (e) 400 READ CUSTOMER$;STOCKNUM;VALUE
   (f) 30 RESTORE START
   (g) 2010 PRINT "Total amount in checks is $,TOTAL.CHECK.AMT
   (h) 90 PRINT TAB(100);"Name";TAB(200);"Dept";TAB(300);"Address"

5. Create a PRINT USING command to create the desired output below, assuming the following variables have been assigned:

   FIRSTNAM$ = "Janet"   LASTNAM$ = "Jones"   COMMISSION = 11234.00
   STREETAD$ = "101 Main Street"   TOWN$ = "Anywhere"   PHONE$ = "(111) 555-5432"

   (a) J. Jones's phone number is (111) 555-5432
   (b) Janet lives in Anywhere on 101 Main Street
   (c) Janet lives in Anywhere on 101 Main St
   (d) Janet lives somewhere in Anywhere
   (e) J. Jones made $11,234.00 in commission last year.

6. What will each of the commands below display, assuming the following variables have been assigned?

   CUSTOMER$ = "John H. Smith"   REFUND = 7342.45   ACCTNO = 33030
   ADDRESS$ = "1515 Chestnut Road, Anytown, ZZ, 99999"
   CUST.FIRST$ = "John"   CUST.MIDDLE$ = "Herbert"
   CUST.LAST$ = "Smith"   SOCSEC$ = "765-43-2100"
   EMP.TITLE$ = "Entertainer"   EMP.SALARY = 55673.99
   PART.TYP$ = "Left-handed widget"   PART.QUANT = 456
   PART.PRICE=6.39   COMPANY.1 = "Acme Inc."   COMPANY.2 = "ZZ Co."
   PROFIT.1 = 23432.00   PROFIT.2 = 3423.93

   (a) TMP$ = "Pay to the order of &   **######,.##"
       PRINT USING TMP$;CUSTOMER$,REFUND
   (b) TMP$ = "&_,! & & $$###,###.##"
       PRINT USING TMP$;CUST.LAST$,CUST.FIRST$,SOCSEC$,EMP.TITLE$,EMP.SALARY
   (c) TMP$ = "&   #####   ##.## $#####,.##"
       PRINT USING TMP$;PART.TYP$,PART.QUANT,PART.PRICE,PART.QUANT*PART.PRICE
   (d) PRINT USING "Profit for & was $$#####.##+";COMPANY.1,PROFIT.1
   (e) PRINT USING "Profit for & was $$#####.##+";COMPANY.2,PROFIT.2
   (f) TMP$ = "&_,/   / ##### $$####.##"
       PRINT USING TMP$;CUSTOMER$,ADDRESS$,ACCTNO,REFUND
   (g) TMP$ = "!_. !_.&"
       PRINT USING TMP$;CUST.FIRST$,CUTS.MIDDLE$,CUST.LAST$
   (h) TMP$ = "Pay to the order of & $$####.##"
       PRINT USING TMP$;CUSTOMER$,EMP.SALARY

Programming Problems

1. Assume you've been given the task of calculating the total amount of checks withdrawn for each customer of a bank. You must report the total amount for each customer, including the customer's name and account number. Assuming that the DATA statements below reflect one day's worth of data, write a program to solve this task. Note: the DATA statements are grouped so that the name, account number, and social security number of each customer are on the first line, followed by check number and check amount information. The end-of-data marker for a customer's check information is 0,0. The end-of-data marker for the program is "+++",0,"+++".

```
DATA "Joe Smith",23455,"012-34-5678"
DATA 100,34.56,101,123.78,102,4.56,103,65.29
DATA 104,78.01,105,98.01,0,0
DATA "Jane Doe",12345,"001-02-0987"
DATA 345,45.09,346,67.90,347,345.02,346,7.89
DATA 347,90.02,348,12.56,349,23.76,0,0
DATA "John Doe",12346,"345-67-8901"
DATA 900,12.67,901,9.89,902,7.89,903,90.02
DATA 904,1234.56,905,345.67,906,9.00,0,0
DATA "+++",0,"+++"
```

2. Write a program to display how much can be saved in various savings accounts, earning simple interest at various rates, for each year in a ten-year period. Assume that the rates are 3.4%, 5.6%, 7.5%, 8.8%, 9.2%, and 11.1%. The program should display a tabular chart. Assume that the amount, input by the user, is invested in each account at the same time, for the full ten-year period, and that all interest in the account is "rolled over" in the account.

3. Change the multiplication table program on page 114 so that it displays a table up to 9 in tabular format.

4. Write a program that looks up phone numbers. Assume that the DATA for your program looks like the following:

```
2000 DATA "JOHN","555-6666"
```

The program should prompt for the first name of the person whose phone number is desired, and display a message if the phone number exists or does not exist "on file." The program should also prompt the user to enter another name, to avoid having to rerun the program, and should provide a way of stopping the program.

10

Functions

Learning Objectives

After reading this chapter you should understand:

- What functions are and why they are used
- How to use BASIC numeric functions
- How to use BASIC string functions
- How to create and use a user-defined function

Introduction

With the programming tools and techniques you've learned so far, it is difficult to examine and manipulate character strings easily, for example, to search for one string within another string. Or sometimes you just need to do a calculation, or to extract only part of a character string. This chapter will introduce you to BASIC- and user-defined functions, which meet these and other programming needs.

What Is a Function?

A **function** is like a subroutine in that it is an independent piece of a program, located outside of the main program. Functions, however, only calculate a value based on certain variables, and return this value to the program. A call to a function can be placed anywhere within any numeric or string expression. In other words, while a subroutine can perform many tasks such as initializing groups of variables or gathering information from a user, a function calculates and returns a single value, which is used in the expression in place of the function call.

With a function call, you can calculate a numeric value, examine character data like the first three characters of a name, or manipulate data in many other ways. BASIC provides functions that perform various calculations, eliminating the need to code an algorithm to generate the square root of a number, for instance. BASIC also provides several string-oriented functions, which aid in the manipulation and creation of string data.

All BASIC functions fall into one of three categories.

1. BASIC-supplied functions that handle mathematical calculations and manipulate numbers.
2. BASIC-supplied functions that allow the manipulation of string data.
3. User-defined functions: functions you can write to solve a particular need that is not provided by any BASIC-supplied function.

Functions are also similar to system variables since both return values to a program. Functions operate like system variables because they are replaced with a value when the program is run.

Why Use Functions?

Certain tasks cannot be performed easily using the BASIC commands covered to this point. For instance, suppose you were asked to write a program that displays the whole dollar figure of an amount keyed in by a user. If the user keys in 23.95, the program displays 23. One version of this program might look like the following:

```
100 REM Sample program to display whole dollar figure of
110 REM any amount keyed in.
120 REM
130 INPUT "Enter the sale price of part type widget: ",PRICE
140 DOLLAR = 0
150 WHILE DOLLAR <= PRICE
160   DOLLAR = DOLLAR + 1
170 WEND
180 DOLLAR = DOLLAR - 1
190 PRINT "Whole dollar amount of ";PRICE;" is ";DOLLAR
200 END
```

Because we have no way of knowing whether the price input is an integer (34 or 897) or a real number (23.45 or 10023.01), the program above uses a whole-number counter (DOLLAR) to determine the next-highest integer over the value of PRICE. The program counts from 0 upward until DOLLAR surpasses the value of PRICE. The program then subtracts one from DOLLAR to obtain the integer value of PRICE.

While this program solves a simple problem, it suffers from poor design. If a very large amount is keyed in, the program must count from 0 to the amount and, depending on the amount, could take a long time to run. All we really want the program to do is display the integer value of the amount.

BASIC provides the INT numeric function which returns the largest integer that is less than or equal to the number passed to it. If we rewrite the program above to use the INT function, it would look like the following:

```
100 REM Sample program which uses INT function to display
110 REM whole dollar figure.
120 INPUT "Enter the sale price of part type widget: ",PRICE
130 DOLLAR = INT(PRICE)
140 PRINT "Whole dollar amount of ";PRICE;" is ";DOLLAR
150 END
```

We can see immediately that the size of the program has been reduced dramatically; a single line now assigns the value of DOLLAR. In line 130 of the second program, the INT function is *called* with the variable PRICE. We say that PRICE is *passed* to the function. When BASIC interprets line 130, BASIC determines the value of PRICE, determines the integer value of PRICE, and then *returns* the greatest integer value. The function call, INT(PRICE) is replaced by the integer value, which is then assigned to the variable DOLLAR.

As shown in this example, we use BASIC functions because they allow us to perform calculations and manipulate strings easily and efficiently.

How Functions Work

When a function is called, BASIC calculates a value dependent on the variables passed to the function. The values that are passed to a function are commonly known as **arguments**. Arguments provide a function with enough information to allow a value to be calculated. The parentheses that immediately follow the function name enclose all arguments to the function.

After a value is calculated, it is returned to the expression in place of the function call. Let's examine how functions work using the sample program displayed below.

```
100 REM Sample program to demonstrate how functions work.
110 AMOUNT = 25.95
120 DOLLAR = INT(AMOUNT)
130 PRINT "Whole dollar amount of ";AMOUNT;" is ";DOLLAR
140 END
```

The program above is simple in form. Besides line 120, the program assigns a value, 25.95, to the variable AMOUNT and issues a PRINT command to display results. Line 120 contains the *function call* to the BASIC function INT. The INT function expects one numeric value as input. When we specify AMOUNT within parentheses immediately after the function name, we are passing an argument to the function. Note that the value of AMOUNT does not change; we are merely providing information to the function. Therefore, when INT(AMOUNT) is first interpreted, BASIC sees the function call as INT(25.95). BASIC then executes its INT function, and determines what the largest integer that is less than or equal to 25.95 is, in this case 25. BASIC then returns the value (25) to the program. Therefore, when INT(25.95) is evaluated, it becomes 25, and the value 25 is then assigned to DOLLAR. When the program is run, it will display as follows:

```
Whole dollar amount of  25.95  is  25
```

The box below describes the general format of a BASIC function call. The name of the function (INT,MID$,etc.) determines the type of result the function will return. If the function name ends with a dollar sign, the function will return a string value, which can be used wherever a string value can be specified. If the function name does not end with a dollar sign, the function will return a numeric value.

A BASIC Function Call

Format   <var> = Function (<item1>,...<itemn>)

where *var* is a numeric or string variable, and *item1* through *item*n are numeric or string expressions called arguments. The number and types of items that need to be specified vary for each function

Examples   30 BASE.SALARY = INT(SALARY)
                 70 MIDDLE.NAME4$ = MID$(NAM$,8,3)

Notes   The function name determines whether the returned value will be a number or a string. If the function name ends with a $, the function will return a string result, otherwise the function will return a numeric result. The type of a variable that is assigned a value through a function call must match the type of function.

A function call can be placed anywhere a variable or expression can be placed. In the program above, instead of assigning DOLLAR the value of the function call INT(AMOUNT), we can replace DOLLAR in the PRINT command on line 130 with INT(AMOUNT) and remove line 120. This program will display the same information as the earlier version.

```
100 REM Sample program to demonstrate how functions work.
110 AMOUNT = 25.95
130 PRINT "Whole dollar amount of ";AMOUNT;" is ";INT(AMOUNT)
140 END
```

When calling a function, whether it be a BASIC-supplied or a user-defined function, you must ensure that the minimum number of necessary arguments are specified in the function call. Failure to supply enough arguments will cause BASIC to display the error message "Syntax error in ln," and BASIC will stop interpretation of the program.

BASIC Numeric Functions

BASIC supplies several numeric functions to aid in the manipulation of numbers. Table 10.1 describes some of the general numeric functions that BASIC provides. For a more complete list, consult your DOS BASIC reference manual.

Table 10.1   General Numeric Functions

Function Name	Purpose
INT(number)	Returns the greatest whole number less than or equal to the number specified
ABS(number)	Returns the absolute value of the number specified
FIX(number)	Returns the integer part of the number specified

The INT Function

The INT function is used to return the largest integer that is less than or equal to the number passed as an argument (see box below). As described earlier in this chapter, INT is handy when you want to return the dollar amount of a number. Suppose we have a program that works with sales information. If we wanted to calculate refunds based on the whole dollar amount of the sales price of a product, we could use INT to extract this information. For example, if the variable SALES is assigned the value 123.45, then the following command,

```
40 SALES.DOLLARS = INT(SALES)
```

assigns the integer 123 to the variable SALES.DOLLARS.

The INT Function

Purpose   Returns the greatest whole number less than or equal to the number specified

Format   INT(num)
where *num* is a numeric expression

Examples   30 LET BASERATE = INT(23.4)
　　　　　　40 SALES = INT(CHARGES) + RATE.ADJUST

There may be times that you want to extract the integer part of a number, whether positive or negative. If you use the INT function, you may not necessarily get the integer part of a negative number. Since INT determines the largest integer that is less than or equal to the passed argument, if you specify INT(−9.3), INT won't return −9, but −10.

The ABS Function

Suppose you had to write a program that dealt with the net change in profit over several years for a company. For some years, the company may have earned large amounts of income, indicated by large positive values for profit. Depending on the economy and health of the company, great losses may have been reported as well, indicated by negative values of profit. Therefore, you might want to examine the absolute or positive value of profit, from year to year.

The ABS Function

Purpose   Returns the absolute or positive value of the number specified

Format   ABS(num)
where *num* is a numeric expression

Examples   60 LET NETCHANGE = ABS(-4589.22)
　　　　　　90 TOTAL.LOSS = ABS(PROFIT.YR1) + ABS(PROFIT.YR7)

The FIX Function

Purpose   Returns the integer part of any number

Format   FIX(num)
where *num* is a numeric expression

Examples   100 CASH = FIX(MONEY)
210 CHANGE = PRICE - FIX(PRICE)

The ABS function returns the absolute value, or positive value, of the number passed as an argument (see box). If the variable PROFIT is assigned the value 18123.45, then the line below,

```
30 NET.AMOUNT = ABS(PROFIT)
```

causes BASIC to assign the value 18123.45 to the variable NET.AMOUNT. If the variable PROFIT were assigned the value −3489.23, then the command below,

```
30 NET.AMOUNT = ABS(PROFIT)
```

causes BASIC to assign the value 3489.23 to NET.AMOUNT.

The FIX Function

The FIX function works in exactly the same manner as the INT function, except when a negative value is passed as an argument (see box below). For any number, FIX will return the integer part of the number passed as an argument. With negative numbers, FIX returns the integer part of the negative number, while INT returns the integer that is less than or equal to the negative number. For example, when −9.3 is passed to the FIX function, it will return the value −9.

Table 10.2 shows some examples of BASIC numeric function calls with the results that they would return.

Table 10.2   Examples of BASIC Numeric Function Calls

Expression	Result
INT(.34)	0
INT(45.6)	45
INT(−3.2)	−4
ABS(4)	4
ABS(2−6)	4
INT(ABS(−56.67))	56
FIX(34.5)	34
FIX(1234)	1234
FIX(−3.2)	−3

Notice in Table 10.2 that function calls can be *nested*, as in INT(ABS(−56.67)). When multiple functions are specified in a nested manner, the innermost function gets evaluated first, followed by the next innermost function, etc. When BASIC interprets INT(ABS(−56.67)), it first evaluates ABS(−56.67), which becomes 56.67. Then, BASIC interprets INT(56.67), which becomes 56.

BASIC String Functions

Suppose you wanted to write a billing program to generate billing statements. A return address is printed on a statement based on the first three characters of the customer's last name. With the BASIC commands covered to this point in the text, it is very difficult to examine or manipulate a portion of a string.

BASIC provides several functions that allow you to examine and manipulate strings within a program. Table 10.3 illustrates some important string functions that will be described in the following sections. For other string functions, consult your DOS BASIC reference manual.

The LEFT$, RIGHT$, and MID$ Functions

The LEFT$, RIGHT$, and MID$ string functions all perform similar string manipulation operations. These functions create **substrings** from strings that are passed as arguments. (A portion or part of a string is commonly referred to as a substring.)

Table 10.3   General String Functions

Function Name	Purpose
LEFT$(string,n)	Extracts the first *n* characters of the string specified. Left-most character is in position 1
RIGHT$(string,n)	Extracts the *n* characters of the string specified from the right-most side
MID$(string,p,n)	Extracts *n* characters of the string specified starting at position *p*
LEN(string)	Returns the length of the string specified
INSTR(p,string1,string2)	Returns the beginning position of string2 in string1. The string search begins at position *p*
STRING$(n,string)	Returns *n* copies of the first character in the string specified
SPACE$(n)	Returns *n* spaces
CHR$(n)	Returns the single character that is equal in ASCII code to *n*
ASC(string)	Returns the three-digit ASCII code for the first character of the string specified
STR$(n)	Returns the string equivalent of *n*
VAL(string)	Returns the numeric equivalent of the string specified

A substring can be a single character or a group of words. Think of a substring as a smaller group of characters within a large string. For instance, suppose we have a string variable that contains the name of an employee, perhaps "John James Doe." Valid substrings of this string are:

"John James Doe"	"John"	"James"
"Joh"	"Doe"	"D"

The LEFT\$, RIGHT\$, and MID\$ functions create a substring of a larger string, based on specified character positions within the larger string. The leftmost character in a string is in position 1, with the character positions counted upward toward the right. In the string "John James Doe", for example , the name "John" occupies character positions 1 through 4 of the string.

LEFT\$ creates a substring starting at the left-hand side of the specified character string; LEFT\$ takes two arguments, the first argument a string variable, the second argument the length of the desired substring. Thus, with EMP.NAM\$ = "John James Doe", specifying LEFT\$(EMP.NAM\$,4) will return "John". Specifying LEFT\$(EMP.NAM\$,2) will return "Jo". Note that a comma must be used to delimit the string variable name from the length parameter. (See the box below.)

The LEFT\$ Function

Purpose   Extracts the first *n* characters of the string specified

Format   LEFT\$(string,n)
where *string* is a string expression, and *n* is an integer representing the number of characters to be extracted

Example   1100 FIRST.NAM\$ = LEFT\$(EMPLOYEE.NAM\$,5)

Notes   If the number of characters to be extracted is less than 0 or greater than 255, then the function call is illegal. If the number specified is 0, a null string is returned. If the number specified is greater than the length of the string, the entire string is returned.

RIGHT\$ works similarly to the LEFT\$ function, except that the substring is created starting from the right-most side of the specified character string. With EMP.NAM\$ = "John James Doe", specifying RIGHT\$(EMP.NAM\$,3) will return "Doe".

If a length of zero (0) is specified by either the RIGHT\$ or LEFT\$ function, a substring of length zero is requested. BASIC in this case will return a null string. If a length is specified that is greater than the length of the string from which substrings are to be created, the entire string will be returned as the substring. For example, if COMPOSER\$ = "Wolfgang Amadeus Mozart", then LEFT\$(COMPOSER\$,99) would return "Wolfgang Amadeus Mozart" and RIGHT\$(COMPOSER\$,99) would also return "Wolfgang Amadeus Mozart".

The RIGHT$ Function

Purpose   Extracts the right-most *n* characters of the string specified

Format   RIGHT$(string,n)
where *string* is a string expression, and *n* is an integer representing the number of characters to be extracted

Example   1200 LAST.NAM$ = RIGHT$(EMPLOYEE.NAM$,LASTPOS)

Notes   If the number of characters to be extracted is less than 0 or greater than 255, then the function call is illegal. If the number specified is 0, a null string is returned. If the number specified is greater than the length of the string, the entire string is returned.

While LEFT$ and RIGHT$ can be used to create substrings of varying length from either side of a larger character string, the MID$ function is used to create substrings starting anywhere within a character string. MID$ takes three arguments: the first argument is the string variable name, the second argument is the string starting position within the character string from which the substring will be created, and the third argument is the length of the desired substring. The third argument is optional; if it is not specified, MID$ will create a substring starting at the character position specified and including the rest of the string (see box below).

The MID$ Function

Purpose   Extracts *n* characters of the string specified starting at the position specified

Format   MID$(string,p,n)
where *string* is a string expression, and *p* is the starting position within string where the next *n* characters will be extracted

Examples   1100 MIDDLE.NAM$ = MID$(EMPLOYEE.NAM$,START,POSITION)
    2000 ID.NO = MID$(EMPLOYEE.NAM$,15,5)

Notes   If the number of characters to be extracted is less than 0 or greater than 255, then the function call is illegal. If the number specified is 0, a null string is returned. If the number specified is greater than the remaining length of the string, the rest of the string starting from position *p* through the remaining portion of the string is extracted.

For example, in the string EMP.NAM$ = "John James Doe", specifying MID$(EMP.NAM$,6,5) would result in "James" being returned. If MID$(EMP.NAM$,6) were specified without a length argument, the substring "James Doe" would be returned.

Table 10.4 shows examples of the LEFT$, RIGHT$, and MID$ functions. Assume the following string variables have been assigned: NAM$ = "John E. Doe"; PART.NAM$ = "Right-handed widget"; CHECK.AMT$ = "Thirty-five thousand fourteen".

Table 10.4   Examples of Calls to the LEFT\$, RIGHT\$, and MID\$ Functions

Expression	Valid/Invalid	Result
LEFT\$(NAM\$,4)	Valid	"John"
RIGHT\$(NAM\$,3)	Valid	"Doe"
LEFT\$(45,4)	Invalid	Must specify a string expression
RIGHT\$(PART.NAM\$ 4)	Invalid	Must specify a comma between items on function call
MID\$(CHECK.AMT\$,8,4)	Valid	"five"
MID\$(CHECK.AMT\$,8,543)	Invalid	Length specified must be in range 0 through 255

Table 10.4, MID\$(CHECK.AMT\$,8,543) is listed as invalid. If this were specified within a program, BASIC would display the error message, "Illegal function call." The string functions LEFT\$, RIGHT\$, and MID\$ will generate that message whenever a position or length greater than 255 or less than 0 is specified as one of the arguments. Since a character string can only have 255 characters, specifying a string position or length greater than 255 is invalid. Similarly, since a character string cannot have a length of less than 0, specifying a string position or length less than 0 is invalid.

The LEN and INSTR Functions

BASIC also provides string functions that can extract information about the contents of a string. These functions can be very handy. For instance, if you had to write a program that created business cards, you would be concerned with the length of various character strings to be printed on the card, such as a person's name, title, company name, address, etc. Likewise, if you were writing a program that performed keyword searches on information stored in DATA statements, you would need a way of performing string searches within other strings.

The LEN function (see summary in box below) is used to count the number of characters in a string. LEN takes one argument, a string variable name. If a string variable COMPANY\$ is assigned the value "Canada", then LEN(COUNTRY\$) would return 6. If COUNTRY\$ is assigned the value "New Zealand", then LEN(COUNTRY\$) would return 11.

The LEN Function

Purpose   Returns the length of the string specified

Format   LEN(string)
where *string* is a string expression

Example   1200 SIZE.OF.NAM = LEN(FIRSTNAM\$) + LEN(LASTNAM\$)

The LEN function, combined with use of the TAB function, can be used to center output very easily. If we wanted to display a title on the PC screen, such as "Acme Payroll Menu," we can use LEN to determine the length of the string, divide the length by 2, and then subtract this amount from half of the width of the PC screen to come up with the starting position on the screen where the text should be positioned for centering, as shown in the program below.

```
10 TITLE.TEXT$ = "Acme Payroll Menu"
20 TITLE.LENGTH = LEN(TITLE.TEXT$)
30 PRINT TAB((80/2)-(TITLE.LENGTH/2));TITLE.TEXT$
40 END
```

Running the sample program above will display the string "Acme Payroll Menu" centered on a line of a PC screen that is 80 characters wide.

The INSTR function is used to determine the existence of a substring within another string (see box below). Similar to the LEN function, INSTR returns the character position in a string where a substring begins. If the substring does not exist in the string, INSTR will return a value of 0. For example, if the string ASSEMBLY$ were assigned "PLASTIC,TITANIUM,GREASE,WIDGETS" and the string PART$ were assigned "WIDGET", then INSTR(ASSEMBLY$,PART$) would return the number 25. If the string PART$ were assigned "WHEEL", then INSTR(ASSEMBLY$,PART$) would return 0.

The INSTR Function

Purpose   Returns the beginning position of a second string within the first string

Format   INSTR(position,string1,string2)
where *string1* and *string2* are string expressions, and *position* is the position within the first string where searching should start. The position argument can be omitted

Example   100 IF (INSTR(1,ASSEMBLY$,PART$)
             THEN PRINT "Part type ";PART$;" required."

Note   If position is not specified, the search starts at the first character of the first string specified.

To better understand how INSTR function works, let's consider the following BASIC program (see Figure 10.1 for the flowchart and pseudocode).

Figure 10.1

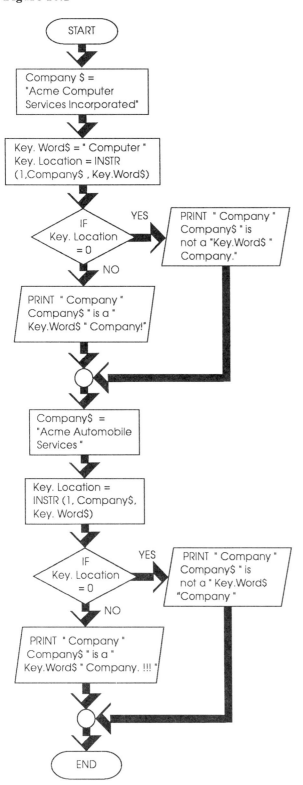

Program: Sample of INSTR
Set company to Acme Computer Services
    Incorporated
Set Key.Word to computer
Set Key.Location to position of Key.Word in
    company
IF Key.Location is equal to 0
    THEN display company is not a Key.Word
        company
    ELSE display company is a Key.Word
        company
Set company to Acme Automobile Services
Set Key.Location to position of Key.Word in
    company
IF Key.Location is equal to 0
    THEN display company is not a Key.Word
        company
    ELSE display company is a Key.Word
        company
END: Sample of INSTR

```
10 ' Sample program to demonstrate the use of the INSTR function
20 '
30 COMPANY$ = "Acme Computer Services Incorporated"
40 KEYWORD$ = "Computer"
50 KEYLOCATION = INSTR(1,COMPANY$,KEYWORD$)
60 IF KEYLOCATION = 0
      THEN PRINT "Company "COMPANY$" is not a "KEYWORD$" company."
      ELSE PRINT "Company "COMPANY$" is a "KEYWORD$" company!!!"
70 COMPANY$ = "Acme Automobile Services"
80 KEYLOCATION = INSTR(1,COMPANY$,KEYWORD$)
90 IF KEYLOCATION = 0
      THEN PRINT "Company "COMPANY$" is not a "KEYWORD$" company."
      ELSE PRINT "Company "COMPANY$" is a "KEYWORD$" company!!!"
100 END
```

When this program is run, the INSTR function is called twice, in lines 50 and 80, to determine the existence of the substring KEYWORD$ (in this case, "Computer") in the string COMPANY$. When COMPANY$ is set to "Acme Computer Services Incorporated," line 50 will assign the value of 6 to KEYLOCATION; 6 is the character position within "Acme Computer Services Incorporated" where "Computer" exists. When COMPANY$ is set to "Acme Automobile Services," line 80 assigns 0 to variable KEYLOCATION, since "Computer" is nowhere in the string. When run, this program will display:

```
Company Acme Computer Services Incorporated is a Computer company!!!
Company Acme Automobile Services is not a Computer company.
```

The number 1, specified as the first argument to INSTR in the program above, tells BASIC to look for the occurrence of the substring KEYWORD$ starting at the first character position in COMPANY$. Since we want to start the search at the first character position, we really didn't have to specify 1 as the first argument; if no number is specified as the first argument to INSTR, the substring search is started at the first character position.

Table 10.5 gives various examples of the LEN and INSTR functions. Assume the following string variables have been assigned: TITLE$ = "Introduction to the XYZ System Service"; KEYWD$ = "XYZ"; COUNTRY$ = "Commonwealth of Utopia"; and KEYWD2$ = "ABC".

Table 10.5 Examples of Calls to the LEN and INSTR Functions

Expression	Result
LEN(TITLE$)	38
LEN(KEYWD$) + LEN(KEYWD2$)	6
LEN(COUNTRY$) - 6	16
INSTR(TITLE$,KEYWD$)	21
INSTR(TITLE$,KEYWD2$)	0
INSTR(22,TITLE$,KEYWD$)	0
LEN(TITLE$) - INSTR(TITLE$,KEYWD$)	17

Creating Strings with STRING$ and SPACE$

When a program has to display several pieces of information at once on the PC screen, it is good programming practice to make the screen as easy to read as possible. An easy way to make several items of information look less intimidating and confusing is to break up the screen by dividing it with a solid line of asterisks or dashes. To duplicate particular characters or strings easily, BASIC provides the STRING$ and SPACE$ functions. Both functions return strings that can be used to create or concatenate other strings.

STRING$ takes two arguments, the number of copies to be made, and a string expression. BASIC will take the first character of the string expression and duplicate it as many times as specified. For instance, if you wanted to assign 55 asterisks to a variable named ASTERISKS$, then you could include in your program:

```
230 ASTERISK$ = "*"
240 ASTERISK$ = STRING$(55,ASTERISK$)
```

You could also specify a string constant, as in the following:

```
240 ASTERISKS$ = STRINGS$(55,"*")
```

You could also specify:

```
240 ASTERISKS$ = STRING$(55,42)
```

where 42 represents the ASCII code for an asterisk. Refer to the ASCII Character Code table in Appendix C for a list of ASCII codes for all characters.

The STRING$ Function

Purpose   Returns a string containing a specified number of copies of the first character in the string specified

Format   STRING$(number,string)
where *number* is a number from 1 to 255 indicating the number of copies, and *string* is a string expression

Example   200 BRK.LIN$=STRING$(75,"*")

Note   The first character of the string specified is used to create the new string.

Note that if ASTERISK$ had been mistakenly set to "*&%", the result would still be the same, since the STRING$ function only duplicates the first character of the string specified as the second argument.

SPACE$ takes only one numeric argument, and is actually a special instance of the STRING$ function. SPACE$, as you can probably tell by its name, duplicates spaces. To assign 50 spaces to a string variable ADDRESS$, you would specify:

```
30 ADDRESS$ = SPACE$(50)
```

Translating and Converting Characters

It is sometimes important to know the exact order of characters and numbers for instance, when sorting a list of addresses. If you wanted to compare the address "Chestnut Road" to "11 East 67th Street," you would need to be able to compare the characters of each string and determine which is first or last in order.

The BASIC function CHR$ and ASC perform character conversion between characters and ASCII code. ASCII code, as described in Chapter 4, is a special code that is used to store characters on many different kinds of computer systems. Every character that is displayable on a PC has a corresponding ASCII code. When a character or number is assigned to a variable, the corresponding ASCII code sequence is actually stored in memory. For example, when assigning a string variable with the value "computer," the ASCII sequence that gets stored in memory is 09911110911211711610114.

The ASC function converts the first character of the string passed to it as an argument to the corresponding ASCII code. Thus, ASC("computer") would result in a value of 099. Note that only the first character of the string is converted to ASCII code.

CHR$ is used to perform the opposite operation that ASC performs. With a numeric argument, CHR$ returns a single character that is equivalent to the ASCII code specified. The BASIC statement

```
20 LANGUAGE$ = CHR$(66) + CHR$(65) + CHR$(83) + CHR$(73) + CHR$(67)
```

would assign the strings "B", "A", "S", "I", and "C", ultimately assigning the word "BASIC " to LANGUAGE$.

Table 10.6 gives examples of the use of the ASC and CHR$ functions. Assume the following string variables have been assigned: CUSTOMER1$ = "Mary Doe"; CUSTOMER2$="John Smith".

Concatenating Strings and Numbers

In Chapter 3 we learned how to concatenate character strings to create a larger string. However, if you attempt to concatenate a numeric expression and a string

Table 10.6   Examples of Calls to the ASC and CHR$ Functions

Expression	Result
ASC(CUSTOMER1$)	77
ASC(CUSTOMER2$)	74
ASC(RIGHT$ (CUSTOMER1$,3))	44
ASC(RIGHT$ (CUSTOMER2$,5))	53
CHR$(65)	A
CHR$(12)	Nondisplayable; causes page eject when printed
CHR$(07)	Nondisplayable; causes PC to beep when printed
CHR$(ASC(CUSTOMER1$))	M

expression, BASIC will display the error message "Type mismatch on *ln*," and will cease interpretation of your program.

When you write programs, you may want to concatenate numeric and string expressions, for instance, a dollar sign (a character string) with a salary (a number). BASIC provides the STR$ and VAL functions to perform character-to-number and number-to-character translation.

The STR$ Function

Purpose   Returns the string equivalent of the number specified

Format   STR$(number)
where *number* is any numeric expression

Example   340 AMOUNT$ = "$" + STR$(CASH.ON.HAND)

Note   The resulting string created by STR$ cannot be used in a numeric expression, even though it appears as a number.

Let's look at the following BASIC statements to understand how the STR$ function works.

```
2340 WAGE = 11.90
2350 HRS.WORKED = 45
2360 SALARY = WAGE * HRS.WORKED
2370 COMPENSATION$ = "$" + STR$(SALARY)
```

STR$ takes a numeric argument and returns a string containing the number. This is not the same as merely assigning the number to the string variable. The result of STR$(SALARY) and SALARY are not the same, even though they look the same when both values are displayed. While SALARY could be used in another numeric expression, STR$(SALARY) is a string (text), and can only be used in string expressions. On line 2370 in the sample program above, BASIC would interpret STR$(SALARY) by taking the value of SALARY, 535.5, and making a string equal to "535.5". COMPENSATION$ would then be assigned "$" concatenated with the string "535.5", resulting in "$535.5".

The VAL function performs character-to-number translation (see box). To understand how the VAL function works, let's assume that the last four digits of a social security number determine where the number was initially distributed. We want to create a program that would prompt for a social security number and display a message stating where the number was initially distributed.

The VAL Function

Purpose   Converts an alphanumeric sequence of the string specified to a numeric equivalent

Format   VAL (string)
where string is any string expression

Example   340 NUMB1 = VAL ("123")
300 AREA.CODE = VAL (Mid$(PHONE$,1,2,3,))

Note   The resulting number created by VAL can only be used in a numeric expression.

```
1000 REM Simple program to demonstrate VAL function
1010 INPUT "Enter your social security number: ",SSN$
1020 SSN.SUFFIX = VAL(RIGHT$(SSN$,4))
1030 IF (SSN.SUFFIX > 3000) and (SSN.SUFFIX < 7999)
       THEN PRINT "Social security number from West Coast"
       ELSE PRINT "Social security number from East Coast"
1040 END
```

When the BASIC statements are executed, the input prompt "Enter your social security number:" is displayed. Let's assume the user enters 555-66-3456. With the value in SSN$, no comparisons or calculations can be easily done. However, using the VAL function in conjunction with the RIGHT$ function, we can extract the last four digits of the social security number, convert the string value to a numeric value, and assign this number (3456) to SSN.SUFFIX. Evaluation of the last four digits of the social security number can now be easily performed, using numeric expressions. With SSN.SUFFIX equal to 3456, the program would display "Social security number from the West Coast." If SSN.SUFFIX evaluated to 3000 or less, or 7999 or more, the program would display "Social security number from the East Coast."

User-Defined Functions

Programs should be well documented and easy to read. At times, however, it can be difficult to create easily read and understood code. An algorithm or formula may be copied into a program several times, making the program larger and difficult to follow.

When you create a user-defined function, formulas or equations only have to be described once within a program. This makes programs shorter and easier to read. User-defined functions, like subroutines, may be called repeatedly in a program.

BASIC allows you to define numeric or string functions that it doesn't otherwise provide. The following sections discuss how to write and use a user-defined function.

User-defined functions are created using the DEF FN statement (see box below). The DEF FN statement tells BASIC to execute a specific BASIC expression every time that the function name appears. As with system-supplied functions, the function name determines the type of information the function will return: if the function name ends with a $, the result will be a string expression; otherwise the result will be a numeric expression. User-defined function names follow the same rules as variable names, except that the first two characters of the function name must be "FN." Unlike subroutines, which are located toward the end of your program, user-defined functions should be defined at the beginning of your program so that they may be used at any time in the program. (A function must be defined before it can be used.)

The DEF FN Statement

Purpose   To define a function

Format   ln DEF FNvar(pl,p2, . . . p*n*) = expression
where *ln* is a valid line number, *var* is a variable name, *p1, p2*, through *pn* are variables, and *expression* is any valid expression

Examples   1010 DEF FNAVERAGE(A,B,C,D,E) = (A + B + C + D + E)/5
1020 DEF FNINITIAL$(NAM$) = LEFT$(NAM$,1)

Notes   The name of the function must agree in type with the expression specified; i.e., if the function name ends with a $, the expression specified must be a string expression. The variables specified within the parentheses describe the arguments that the function needs. A user-defined function always has a name that begins with the characters "FN."

Suppose we have a program that generates a printout of year-end salaries for a company's employees. If, for instance, certain benefits were based on the employee's weekly salary, we could define a function that would return the weekly salary when the yearly salary is passed as an argument to the function, as shown in the following program.

```
100 'Sample program to demonstrate user defined functions.
110 '
120 'FNWEEKLY takes yearly salary and returns weekly salary
130 '
140 TMPL$ = "Benefits for ##### are $$####.##"
150 DEF FNWEEKLY(SAL) = SAL / 52
160 READ EMPLOYEE.NAM$, EMPLOYEE.NUMBER, EMPLOYEE.SALARY
170 WHILE EMPLOYEE.NUMBER <> 0
180   IF FNWEEKLY(EMPLOYEE.SALARY) > 200
        THEN EMPLOYEE.BENEFITS = 300
        ELSE EMPLOYEE.BENEFITS = FNWEEKLY(EMPLOYEE.SALARY) * .5
190 PRINT USING TMPL$;EMPLOYEE.NUMBER, EMPLOYEE.BENEFITS
200 READ EMPLOYEE.NAM$, EMPLOYEE.NUMBER, EMPLOYEE.SALARY
210 WEND
```

```
220 END
230 REM Data for program
240 DATA "Joseph Smith", 23234, 15000.00
250 DATA "Jane Doe", 44445, 10000.00
260 DATA "John Anyman", 12345, 23010.50
270 DATA "+++", 0, 0
```

Line 150 of the program defines a function called FNWEEKLY, which takes as an argument a number, SAL. The variable SAL is a variable used only within the function; SAL does not need to have a value assigned to it, it is merely a place-holder within the function. When the function FNWEEKLY gets called, the value of the argument passed to the function replaces every occurrence of SAL on the right-hand side of the equals sign.

When run, the program will first read in the name, number, and yearly salary of Joseph Smith, assigning 15000.00 to EMPLOYEE.SALARY. FNWEEKLY(EMPLOYEE.SALARY), which is on line 180, will then evaluate to 15000.00/52 or 288.46. Since 288.46 is greater than 200, EMPLOYEE.BENEFITS would be assigned 300. Notice that user-defined functions follow the same rules as system-supplied functions: a numeric function may be used anywhere a numeric variable or constant would be used.

Also notice in the program above how much easier the program is to read: instead of copying the formula throughout the program, it appears only once. The program is also easier to understand because of the descriptive function name FNWEEKLY. If the calculation of weekly salary were to change (because, for instance, monthly salary is now read in by the program), we would only have to change the function definition rather than changing several lines throughout the program.

User-defined string functions are defined in the same way as user-defined numeric functions. Again, the only difference in the naming of a string function is that the last character of the function name must be a dollar sign ($).

To understand how user-defined string functions work, let's write a program that will read in customer names and generate a character code based on certain letters of each name. Such a code might be used by a business to identify a customer but obscure the name. Therefore, we need to create a string function that returns certain letters of the first and last name concatenated as a string. Our program might look like the following.

```
100 REM Sample program to demonstrate user-defined string
110 REM functions.
120 REM
130 REM Define function that will create code based on
140 REM the first three characters of the last name,
150 REM followed by the first two characters of the first
160 REM name
170 REM
180 DEF FNCODE$(FIRST$,LAST$) = LEFT$(LAST$,3) + LEFT$(FIRST$,2)
190 REM
200 INPUT "Enter the first name of the customer: ",C.FIRST$
210 INPUT "Enter the last name of the customer: ",C.LAST$
220 PRINT "Character code is ";FNCODE$(C.FIRST$,C.LAST$)
230 END
```

Notice that the string expression on the right side of the equals sign can contain other function calls, as seen in line 180 of the program above. If we ran the program and keyed in a first name of "Howard" and a last name of "Hughes", the FNCODE\$ function call would return "HugHo".

User-defined functions can be passed to more than one argument. The number of allowable arguments is defined by the number of dummy variables enclosed within parentheses in the function definition. If we wanted to define a function to generate and return the average of three numbers, we could use the following BASIC statement:

```
20 DEF FNAVG(NUM1,NUM2,NUM3) = (NUM1 + NUM2 + NUM3)/3
```

Therefore, if we specify FNAVG(3,4,5) within a program, the function would return the result of 4.

When calling a function, whether it be a BASIC-supplied function or a user-defined function, you must ensure that the minimum number of necessary arguments is specified on the function call. Failure to supply enough arguments will cause BASIC to display the error message "Syntax error in *ln*," and BASIC will stop interpretation of your program.

A Word on Programming Style

The use of BASIC-supplied and user-defined functions can make your program much easier to understand, not to mention much smaller. For some tasks, such as character manipulation, concatenation, and examination, functions are indispensable. For any numeric formula, such as sales tax calculation, user-defined functions make your program much easier to read and enhance. To make your program as structured and efficient as possible, take advantage of the power and flexibility of BASIC functions.

Summary

- A function is like a subroutine. It is an independent piece of a program, located outside of the logical sequence of statements of the main program. Functions are also similar to system variables, as both return values to a program.
- BASIC provides string and numeric functions. BASIC also allows you to define your own functions, called user-defined functions.
- The function name determines whether the function will return string or numeric data. The function name also determines whether the function is a system-supplied function or a user-defined function.
- The items that you specify on a call to a function are called arguments. For every function, the number and types of arguments will vary.
- The INT function returns the greatest whole number less than or equal to the number specified.
- The ABS function returns the positive value of the number specified.
- The FIX function returns the integer part of the number specified.

■ The LEFT\$, RIGHT\$, and MID\$ functions are used to extract characters from the left side, from the right side, or from anywhere within a string. These string functions are very handy when you want to create a substring from a string.

■ The LEN function returns the length of the string specified.

■ The INSTR function returns the beginning position of one string in another string. INSTR is useful for testing the occurrence of a string within another string.

■ The STRING\$ function returns a string containing multiple copies of the character specified. The SPACE\$ function returns a string containing multiple copies of a space.

■ The CHR\$ and ASC functions are used to convert characters into ASCII code and vice versa.

■ The STR\$ and VAL functions are used to convert strings to numbers and vice versa.

■ User-defined functions are identified by the first two characters of the function name, which must always be "FN." You can create both numeric and string functions.

Exercises

True or False

_____   1. Once you use a function within a program, you cannot use that function again.

_____   2. A function call can be placed anywhere a variable or expression can be placed.

_____   3. Arguments for BASIC-supplied numeric functions can only be variables.

_____   4. When BASIC evaluates nested function calls, functions are evaluated from left to right.

_____   5. The LEFT\$, RIGHT\$, and MID\$ functions can be used to create substrings.

_____   6. If you specify a length of 0 with the the LEFT\$ and RIGHT\$ functions, a null string is returned.

_____   7. BASIC functions allow you to manipulate strings in many ways, but there is no way to allow a search for one string inside another string.

_____   8. BASIC functions allow you to convert characters to their corresponding ASCII code and back again.

_____   9. You should code all functions at the bottom of your program, just as you code all subroutines at the bottom.

_____   10. A user-defined function name must begin with the characters "FN".

Fill-In

1. When you call a function, it _____ a value.

2. The variables or expressions you pass to a function are called _____.

3. When you want to get the integer part of any positive or negative number, use the _____ function, instead of the INT function.

4. The _____ function is used to get the positive value of any number.

5. If you want to create a substring from anywhere within a string, use the _____ function.

6. To obtain the length of a string, use the _____ function.

7. If you don't specify a starting position on the INSTR function, the starting position is the _____.

8. Use the _____ and _____ functions when you need to concatenate strings and numbers together.

9. The _____ statement defines a user-defined function.

10. You must specify a _____ at the end of a user-defined string function.

Short Answer

1. Each of the following lines are invalid. State why.
    (a) 30 BASE.SALARY$ = INT(SALARY)
    (b) 100 MIDDLE.NAM$ = MID$(POSITION,NAM$)
    (c) 3330 MYSTRING$ = RIGHT$(TEMP$,−3)
    (d) 1010 DEF MYFUNC(A,B) = ((A * B)/2) + 100
    (e) 1100 COMPANY$ = MID$(ADDRESS,1,15)
    (f) 1200 MIDDLE.INITIAL$ = LEFT$(INSTR(NAM$,NAM2$),4)
    (g) 5050 IF(INSTR(EMP.TITLE$,KEYWD$) = "Found"
             THEN PRINT "Keyword found in title"
             ELSE PRINT "Title is invalid"

2. Assuming that EMPTITLE$ = "Vice-President of Operations", what will be the evaluation of the following expressions?
    (a) LEFT$(EMPTITLE$,2)
    (b) RIGHT$(EMPTITLE$,9)
    (c) RIGHT$(EMPTITLE$,65)
    (d) MID$(EMPTITLES,16,2)
    (e) MID$(LEFT$(EMPTITLES,20),6,9)
    (f) MID$(EMPTITLE$,6,9) + RIGHT$(EMPTITLE$,14)
    (g) LEN(EMPTITLE$)
    (h) LEN(EMPTITLE$) − INSTR(EMPTITLE$,"rat")

3. Assume that CASH\$ = "\$199,355.42". What will be the following evaluation of the following expressions?
   (a) VAL(RIGHT\$(CASH\$,6))
   (b) CASH\$ + STR\$(LEN(CASH\$))
   (c) STRING\$(LEN(CASH\$),MID\$(CASH\$,5,2))
   (d) CHR\$(66) + CHR\$(114) + CHR\$(97) + CHR\$(118) + CHR\$(111) + CHR\$(33)
   (e) SPACE\$(15)

4. What is the difference between a subroutine and a function?

5. Describe some of the reasons to use functions.

Programming Problems

1. Write a program that will prompt for the user's full name and print out each part of the name on its own line.

2. The local library needs a program to allow librarians to quickly identify all books that have a keyword in their title. Write a program to read book titles and book numbers from DATA statements, and display all books whose titles contain a keyword input by the user. The program should allow multiple runs without having to exit the program and restart it.

3. Write a program to prompt for a number, and then display the number in English form, digit-for-digit. For instance, if the user keys in 43.2, the program will display "four three point two." The program should be able to run multiple times without having to exit the program and restart it.

4. You've been assigned the project of determining the year-end bonuses for all salespeople of Company XYZ. You've also been assigned to determine the raises for all salespeople for the next year. Write a program that solves both of these problems. Assume that DATA statements contain employee name, employee number, base salary for the year, number of years of service, and total sales for the year. You should use user-defined functions for all bonus and raise calculations.

   Assume that bonuses are calculated by the following: If total sales are less than 5% of the base salary, then the bonus is .4% of the base salary. If sales are between 5% to 10% of the base salary, then the bonus is .5% of the base salary plus 20% of the total sales over 5% of the base salary. If sales are between 11% to 25% of the base salary, then the bonus is 1.5% of the base salary plus 40% of the total sales over 11% of the base salary. If sales are between 26% to 35% of the base salary, then the bonus is 6% of the base salary plus 60% of the total sales over 26% of the base salary. If sales are between 36% to 50% of the base salary, then the bonus is 11.5% of the base salary plus 70% of the total sales over 36% of the base salary. If sales are over 51% of the base salary, then the bonus is 22% of the base salary plus 75% of the total sales over 51% of the base salary.

   Assume that raises are calculated by the following: If the number of years of service is less than 5, then the raise is 3% of the base salary. If the number of years is between 5 to 10, then the raise is 5% of the base salary. If the number of years is between 11 to 15, then the raise is 6% of the base salary. If the number of years is between 16 to 20, then the raise is 6.5% of the base salary. If the number of years is between 21 to 25, then the raise is 7% of the base salary. If the number of years is greater than 26, then the raise is 7.5% of the base salary.

11

Arrays

After reading this chapter you should understand:

- What an array is and the benefits of using arrays to manipulate large amounts of data
- How to define, populate, and use a one-dimensional array
- How to define, populate, and use a two-dimensional array
- How to define, populate, and use a multidimensional array

- How to use multiple arrays to store string and numeric variables
- How to search through an array
- How to sort an array
- The use of the SWAP command

Introduction

We have demonstrated in previous chapters how loops can perform repetitive tasks effectively, such as reading in and summing large quantities of data. If all that is needed from a program is a total value upon completion of a loop, then an accumulator can be used as demonstrated in Chapter 8. However, what if later you want to use the individual values that created that total in another section of the program? For example, suppose you need a program that would read in the quantity of ten products that you currently have in inventory, then read in the projected sales for these same products for the next month. You would like the output to be a report that shows the current inventory, the projected quantity sold, and the negative or positive balance of these products if these projected sales were met. This would allow you to order more of a particular item if the quantity projected to be sold were greater than the quantity currently in inventory. Since all the data are going to be printed out at the end, a loop using a single variable to hold the data could not be used because it would overwrite the previous value at each iteration. Your program would have to look something like this:

```
100 REM Program to read in the quantity of 10 parts
110 REM currently in inventory, the quantity of these
120 REM same 10 parts projected to be sold, and a
130 REM negative or positive balance if all these parts
140 REM were sold.
150 REM
160 REM Read in the quantity currently in inventory:
170 INPUT "ENTER QUANTITY IN INVENTORY FOR PART 1: ";IN1
180 INPUT "ENTER QUANTITY IN INVENTORY FOR PART 2: ";IN2
190 INPUT "ENTER QUANTITY IN INVENTORY FOR PART 3: ";IN3
200 INPUT "ENTER QUANTITY IN INVENTORY FOR PART 4: ";IN4
210 INPUT "ENTER QUANTITY IN INVENTORY FOR PART 5: ";IN5
220 INPUT "ENTER QUANTITY IN INVENTORY FOR PART 6: ";IN6
230 INPUT "ENTER QUANTITY IN INVENTORY FOR PART 7: ";IN7
240 INPUT "ENTER QUANTITY IN INVENTORY FOR PART 8: ";IN8
250 INPUT "ENTER QUANTITY IN INVENTORY FOR PART 9: ";IN9
260 INPUT "ENTER QUANTITY IN INVENTORY FOR PART 10: ";IN10
270 REM
280 REM Read in quantity of projected parts.
290 INPUT "ENTER QUANTITY PROJECTED FOR PART 1: ";PR1
300 INPUT "ENTER QUANTITY PROJECTED FOR PART 2: ";PR2
310 INPUT "ENTER QUANTITY PROJECTED FOR PART 3: ";PR3
320 INPUT "ENTER QUANTITY PROJECTED FOR PART 4: ";PR4
330 INPUT "ENTER QUANTITY PROJECTED FOR PART 5: ";PR5
340 INPUT "ENTER QUANTITY PROJECTED FOR PART 6: ";PR6
350 INPUT "ENTER QUANTITY PROJECTED FOR PART 7: ";PR7
360 INPUT "ENTER QUANTITY PROJECTED FOR PART 8: ";PR8
370 INPUT "ENTER QUANTITY PROJECTED FOR PART 9: ";PR9
380 INPUT "ENTER QUANTITY PROJECTED FOR PART 10: ";PR10
390 REM
400 REM Print out headings for report.
410 PRINT "QUANTITY ", " PROJECTED ", " QUANTITY"
420 PRINT "  IN    ", " QUANTITY ", "  AFTER   "
430 PRINT " STOCK   ", "   SOLD   ", "  SALE"
440 PRINT "----------","----------","----------"
450 REM Print out the report.
460 PRINT IN1, PR1, PR1 - IN1
470 PRINT IN2, PR2, PR2 - IN2
480 PRINT IN3, PR3, PR3 - IN3
490 PRINT IN4, PR4, PR4 - IN4
500 PRINT IN5, PR5, PR5 - IN5
510 PRINT IN6, PR6, PR6 - IN6
520 PRINT IN7, PR7, PR7 - IN7
530 PRINT IN8, PR8, PR8 - IN8
540 PRINT IN9, PR9, PR9 - IN9
550 PRINT IN10, PR10, PR10 - IN10
560 END
```

This program presents a problem that is very similar to the problem we had when
we were defining loops in Chapter 8. We are doing very similar tasks repetitively

and have little flexibility to specify the number of parts we are going to carry (if the number of parts increases or decreases, we have to make many changes to the program). Such a program is unnecessarily long. We also have an additional problem, one that makes the use of a loop to read in and print out data difficult. We would like to preserve the values of each variable until the end of the program instead of reading a value into a single variable and overwriting it on each iteration of the loop.

The solution to these problems is the use of an **array**. An array is a list or table of values. Arrays in their simplest form are just a list of values stored under one variable name and referenced in sequence. That is, the first location in the array is referenced as 1, the second as 2, etc. In the program above, you need ten variables to represent the quantity in inventory (IN1, IN2, IN3, ..., IN10) and ten variables to represent the quantity projected to be sold (PR1, PR2, PR3, ..., PR10). These variables would look something like Figure 11.1 in memory. These values could be stored equally well in two arrays, IN and PR, with ten elements each. Figure 11.2 is a diagram of how the same number of memory locations can be defined using two arrays.

Figure 11.1

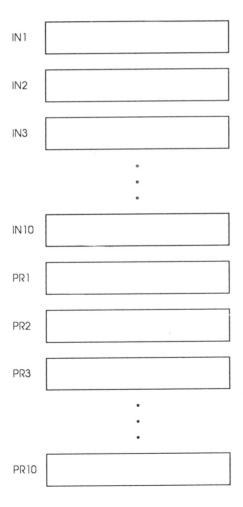

Figure 11.2

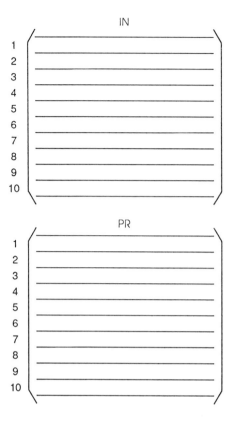

Using arrays, the program on page 256 would look like the following. The flowchart and pseudocode used for planning this program are seen in Figure 11.3.

Figure 11.3

Program: Inventory balance
INPUT number of inventory items
Do FOR I equal to 1 to number of inventory items
     Display input prompt
     Input inventory(I)
END-Do
Do FOR J equal to 1 to number of inventory items
     Display input prompt
     Input projected (J)
END-Do
Display headings
Do FOR K equal to number of inventory items
     Display inventory (K), projected (K), and projected (K) minus
          inventory (K)
END-Do
END: Inventory balance

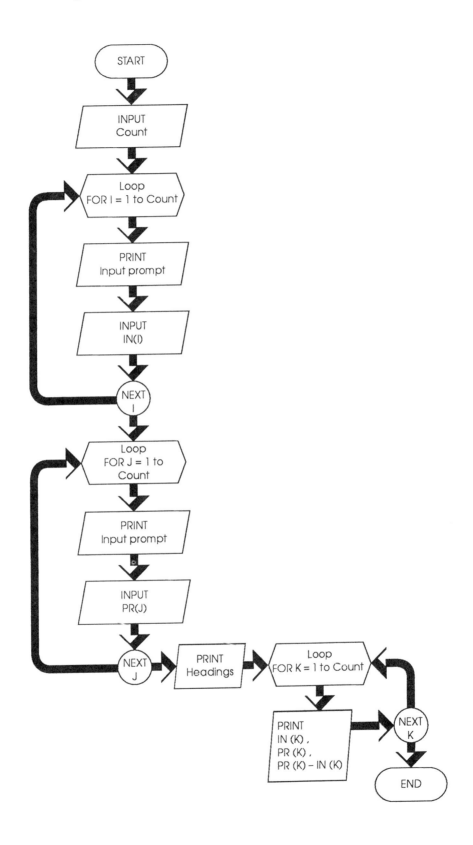

```
100 REM Program to read in the quantity of N parts
110 REM currently in inventory, the quantity of these
120 REM same N parts projected to be sold, and a
130 REM negative or positive balance if all these parts
140 REM were sold.
150 REM
160 REM Read in the number of parts.
170 INPUT "Enter the number of different parts ===>",COUNT
180 REM Dimension the two arrays.
190 DIM IN(COUNT), PR(COUNT)
200 REM
210 REM Read in the quantity currently in inventory:
220 FOR I = 1 TO COUNT
230    PRINT "ENTER QUANTITY IN INVENTORY FOR PART "I
240    INPUT IN(I)
250 NEXT I
260 REM
270 REM Read in quantity of projected parts.
280 FOR J = 1 TO COUNT
290    PRINT "ENTER QUANTITY PROJECTED FOR PART "J
300    INPUT PR(J)
310 NEXT J
320 REM
330 REM Print out headings for report.
340 PRINT "QUANTITY ", " PROJECTED ", " QUANTITY"
350 PRINT "  IN    ", "  QUANTITY ", " AFTER   "
360 PRINT " STOCK   ", "   SOLD    ", "  SALE"
370 PRINT "---------", "----------", "----------"
380 REM Print out the report.
390 FOR K = 1 TO COUNT
400    PRINT IN(K), PR(K), PR(K) - IN(K)
410 NEXT K
420 END
```

This program uses two arrays, IN and PR, each of which can be a list of whatever length is specified for COUNT. In the first FOR/NEXT loop, I goes from 1 to COUNT. IN(I) represents a particular location within IN where a value can be stored. If I equals 3, the data location is the third location of I, and is represented by IN(3). If COUNT is equal to 10, then there would be ten values that can be stored in IN, and ten values that can be stored in PR. By using IN, PR, and COUNT = 10, we define twenty possible variable locations.

Dimensioning Arrays

The first step in using an array is to define the size of the array, which is known as **dimensioning**. This is done with the DIM statement, shown in line 190 of the above program. The DIM statement allocates space in memory for a specified number of **elements**. An element is the particular location in memory where a data value is stored. The numeric value that points to a particular element is known as an **index**. In the example:

```
200 LET PRICE(7) = 5445
```

PRICE(7) is the element and 7 is the index to that element.

The format of the DIM statement is as shown in the following box.

The DIM Statement

Purpose   To declare the number of elements for each array to be defined

Format   ln DIM array(size)[, array(size), . . .]
where *array* is the numeric or string variable representing the array and *size* is the number of elements in the array

Examples   100 DIM PARTS(100)
200 DIM COST(50),NAMES$(50),EMP.NUMB(1000)
300 DIM STUDENTS$(30),EXAMS(30,5),FINAL(30)

Notes   The default dimension for an array is 10 if the array is not specified in a DIM statement. The array name designates whether the data type of the elements within the array will be numeric or character strings by using the same variable-naming conventions as any BASIC variable ($ for strings).

The DIM statement allocates contiguous locations in memory to store the specified number of elements. This reserves these locations so that all of the elements are stored together, sequentially, enabling the computer to access the information more quickly. For example:

```
100 DIM N(100),C(20,30),R$(40),S$(10,10)
```

allocates 100 memory locations for array N, 600 (20 rows by 30 columns) memory locations for array C, 40 memory locations for array R$, and 100 (10 rows by 10 columns) memory locations for array S$. Normally, a BASIC variable points to a location in memory and the value of the variable is stored in that location. For arrays, the variable name of the array (such as N, C, R$, and S$ for our arrays defined above) points to the starting location of the list of elements. So if we use the statement 10 DIM PART(20), 20 locations in memory are reserved for the 20 elements in PART. The variable PART points to the first location reserved for PART, so PART(15) would point to the fifteenth location in the PART array. This does not say that the variable PART is equivalent to the variable PART(1) initially, but rather that there is a pointer to the first element of the array PART.

One-Dimensional Arrays

One-dimensional arrays are the simplest form of array. A one-dimensional array is simply a list of related values stored under one variable name. For example, say you had a program to read in the total monthly sales for a year. You might have statements like the following to read in the sales data:

```
200 READ JAN,FEB,MAR,APR,MAY,JUN,JUL,AUG,SEP,OCT,NOV,DEC
300 DATA 100,300,50,75,125,90,200,200,225,175,100,300
```

The same lines of code can be written using an array with twelve elements, each representing one month.

```
100 DIM MONTHS(12)
200 FOR K = 1 TO 12
210    READ MONTHS(K)
220 NEXT K
300 DATA 100,300,50,75,125,90,200,200,225,175,100,300
```

Now let's try using arrays in a complete program. This program is going to read seven names into an array called DWARFS$ using a FOR/NEXT loop, and use another FOR/NEXT loop to print out the array:

```
100 DIM DWARFS$(7)
110 FOR I = 1 TO 7
120    READ DWARFS$(I)
130 NEXT I
140 PRINT " # |  Dwarf"
150 PRINT "--------------------"
160 FOR J = 1 TO 7
170    PRINT J;" |   ";DWARFS$(J)
180 NEXT J
190 DATA "Dopey", "Sneezy", "Happy", "Grumpy", "Bashful"
200 DATA "Doc", "Sleepy"
210 END
```

The program first dimensions the array DWARFS$. Since the number of elements in DWARFS$ is ten or less, the DIM statement is not necessary; however, it is usually a good practice to include it anyway, for readability. The second step is a FOR/NEXT loop from 1 to 7, and variable I represents the current element of the array as all seven values are read in. Next, we use a couple of PRINT statements to print out headings for our output. We then have another FOR/NEXT loop to print out all seven elements of the array. Finally we have the data statements for the values to be read into the array. When run, the output will look like this:

```
run
 # |  Dwarf
--------------------
 1 | Dopey
 2 | Sneezy
 3 | Happy
 4 | Grumpy
 5 | Bashful
 6 | Doc
 7 | Sleepy
Ok
```

Populating an Array

Arrays are often **populated** using FOR/NEXT or WHILE/WEND loops. Populating an array simply means entering values into each element of the array. This isn't to say that these values cannot be changed (repopulated) later in the program. Elements in an array can be treated like any other BASIC variable. They can be compared, printed, assigned, or used in any BASIC expression.

Two-Dimensional Arrays

While a one-dimensional array is like a list, a two-dimensional array is more like a table with rows and columns. For example, consider the following:

```
100 DIM TABLE(10,5)
110 FOR I = 1 TO 10
120   FOR J = 1 TO 5
130     TABLE(I,J) = I + J
140   NEXT J
150 NEXT I
160 REM Print out TABLE
170 PRINT "TABLE"
180 FOR I = 1 TO 10
190   FOR J = 1 TO 5
200       PRINT TABLE(I,J),
210   NEXT J
220   PRINT
230 NEXT I
240 END
```

This program defines an array called TABLE which has ten rows and five columns. The variable I is assigned to represent the row number, and the variable J is assigned to represent the column number. The first nested FOR/NEXT loop begins with I equal to 1 in the outside loop and J equal to 1 in the inside loop. During the first pass through the loop, TABLE(1,1) is assigned the value of I + J, which is 2. J is then incremented to 2. The inside loop is performed a second time, assigning TABLE(1,2) a value of I + J, which is now 3. The inside loop continues until J is greater than 5. At that point the outside loop increments I to 2 and the loop is entered again. J is initialized to 1 and the inside loop begins for 1 to 5 again. This continues until both loops are complete, and the program prints a heading: TABLE.

A nested FOR/NEXT loop is then used to print the values of TABLE. The second PRINT statement prints the elements of TABLE similar to the first FOR/NEXT loop, and is followed by a comma to suppress the carriage return, which prints the elements on the same line. After the inside loop, there is a PRINT statement with nothing following it. This PRINT statement simply provides a carriage return, so the next row of data will print on the next line. When run, the program would print out the following:

```
run
TABLE
 2              3              4              5              6
 3              4              5              6              7
 4              5              6              7              8
 5              6              7              8              9
 6              7              8              9             10
 7              8              9             10             11
 8              9             10             11             12
 9             10             11             12             13
10             11             12             13             14
11             12             13             14             15
Ok
```

The values are accessed by (row,column) so the value of TABLE(3,5) would be the value of 3 plus 5 which would be 8, the value of TABLE(9,4) would be 9 plus 4 or 13, etc.

Combinations of one- and two-dimensional arrays can be used to store groups of data. Say, for example, you have a list of ten students whose names you want to store in a one-dimensional string array called STUDENT$. For each of those ten students, you will have five test scores, so you will store them in a 10-by-5 array called GRADES. Your program is going to first read in the names and exam scores for all ten students, and write into another array the average for the five exams. The final output will be a list of the ten students, their test scores, and their averages. The program would look something like this:

```
100 DIM STUDENT$(10), GRADES(10,5), AVERAGE(10)
110 FOR I = 1 TO 10
120    READ STUDENT$(I)
130    SUM = 0
140    FOR J = 1 TO 5
150      READ GRADES(I,J)
160      SUM = SUM + GRADES(I,J)
170    NEXT J
180    AVERAGE(I) = SUM/5
190 NEXT I
200 REM Print out the names, grades and averages
210 PRINT "NAME",,"GRADES",,"AVERAGE"
220 FOR I = 1 TO 10
230    PRINT STUDENT$(I),"    ";
240    FOR J = 1 TO 5
250      PRINT GRADES(I,J);"    ";
260    NEXT J
270    PRINT ,AVERAGE(I)
280 NEXT I
290 DATA "Jones",79,80,65,98,88
300 DATA "Doe",87,88,92,75,80
310 DATA "Smith",99,92,87,99,100
320 DATA "Leahy",78,88,76,90,89
330 DATA "Cleary",65,67,76,70,56
340 DATA "Johnson",87,98,87,90,92
```

```
350 DATA "White",88,78,84,92,83
360 DATA "Brown",75,72,75,81,69
370 DATA "Doherty",87,96,86,73,85
380 DATA "Murphy",86,87,97,99,87
390 END
```

In this example, three arrays are used. The first array is STUDENT$, a one-dimensional array of character strings. The second array, GRADES, is a two-dimensional array. The two-dimensional array is defined to be (10,5) in the DIM statement. The first value (10) is the number of rows in the array, and the second number (5) is the number of columns. The GRADES array is a table with ten rows and five columns of numeric data. The final array, AVERAGE, is a one-dimensional array of ten numeric elements.

When this program is run, the output would look like this:

```
run
NAME                          GRADES                    AVERAGE
Jones            79   80   65   98   88      82
Doe              87   88   92   75   80      84.4
Smith            99   92   87   99  100      95.4
Leahy            78   88   76   90   89      84.2
Cleary           65   67   76   70   56      66.8
Johnson          87   98   87   90   92      90.8
White            88   78   84   92   83      85
Brown            75   72   75   81   69      74.4
Doherty          87   96   86   73   85      85.4
Murphy           86   87   97   99   87      91.2
Ok
```

Three-Dimensional Arrays

There are some situations where the use of a one-dimensional or two-dimensional array may be awkward. For instance, suppose that in our student grading program we wish to change the program so that it will read information about student grades from several classes; instead of just using grading information about each student in a particular class, we want the program to use grading information about different students in different classes.

With an additional item of information to include (which class contains which student's grades), we could continue to use two-dimensional arrays, setting up a two-dimensional array to hold all grades for each class. However, if we want the program to generate a grade report for all classes, the use of many two-dimensional arrays would make the program very large. To enter information from each class, a separate set of nested loops would have to be included for each class. And, for every additional group of grades for another class, additional program statements would have to be included. While the program's logic would remain fairly simple, it would contain duplicate lines of code that all performed the same function.

It would be easier to use a three-dimensional array to solve this problem. Rather than hold each class's grades in a separate array, we can define a three-dimensional array to hold all grading information. The concepts covered for one-dimensional and two-dimensional arrays still hold true for three-dimensional arrays, with the exception that three-dimensional arrays require an additional numeric value in the DIM statement. In order to change the student grading program listed above so that it uses a three-dimensional array, the DIM statement could be changed so that the GRADES array is listed as GRADES(4,10,5); this array would be able to hold 4 classes of grading information, each class containing 10 students, each student having 5 grades.

Whereas DIM statements for one-dimensional arrays contain a single number and two numbers for two-dimensional arrays, DIM statements for three-dimensional arrays contain three numbers, designating the number of rows and columns, as well as the "depth" of the table. You can visualize a three-dimensional array as a layered cube, a collection of two-dimensional arrays (tables) stacked on top of one another. The advantage of using a three-dimensional array is evident when we populate and manipulate the array. To populate the three-dimensional GRADES array, we would only have to include another FOR/NEXT loop around the nested FOR/NEXT loops, so that we populate one "layer" of the GRADES array for each class. The actual implementation of three-dimensional arrays in the student grading program is left as Programming Problem 6 at the end of this chapter.

Multidimensional Arrays

Based on the concepts of one-, two-, and three-dimensional arrays, we can define multidimensional arrays to solve complex problems. For instance, suppose that we wanted to change our student grading program further, so that it would read grading information for several different students, in several different classes, at several different colleges. Instead of using a collection of three-dimensional arrays, we could define and use a four-dimensional array to hold all of the grading information.

The DIM statement allows you to define arrays with up to 255 dimensions. Again, the main things to consider when using multidimensional arrays are the definition of the array by the DIM statement and the method that is used to populate and manipulate the array. Usually, the number of dimensions of the array dictates the number of nested FOR/NEXT loops.

Searching Through an Array

Arrays provide the means to store large lists of data with a single variable name, but that doesn't imply that all of that data are going to be necessary each time the array is used. Often, only a single data element within an array needs to be accessed for a given application. We need a means to search through an array and select a given element of that array based on certain criteria. While elements of an array can be accessed directly by specifying the row number in a one-dimensional array, or by specifying the row and column numbers in a two-dimensional array, elements in an array are most likely to be processed sequentially, starting from the first row (or first row, first column for two-dimensional arrays) and ending with the last row (or last row, last column for two-dimensional arrays), processing each element in sequence. This is the most common way to search through a list or table that is in no particular order. In the case of a two-dimensional array, the table could be searched either row by row or column by column. Since data in a two-dimensional array are stored row by column, it is most efficient to search the two-dimensional array row by row, to minimize the amount of times the PC has to read the data from memory.

To search an array, it is important to define the path of the search, and to set criteria against which each element is checked. For example, in the previous program, say we would like to modify the code to print out the highest and the lowest grades. To do this we would assign the first value read as both the highest and the lowest. We would then process the array from the second value to the end, and if the current value is higher or lower than what is stored as the high or low value, that value is replaced with the current value. The flowchart and pseudocode would look like Figure 11.4, and the program would look something like this.

Figure 11.4

```
Program: Grade average
Do FOR I equal to 1 to 10
        READ student (I)
        Set sum to 0
        Do FOR J equal to 1 to 5
                READ grades(I,J)
                Set sum to sum plus grade(I,J)
        END-Do
        Set average(I) to sum divided by 5
END-Do
Display headings
Do FOR I equal to 1 to 10
        Display student(I)
        Do FOR J equal to 1 to 5
                Display grade(I,J)
        END-Do
        Display average
END-Do
Set highest to 1
Set lowest to 1
Do FOR I equal to 2 to 10
        IF average(I) greater than average(highest)
            THEN set highest to I
        END-IF
        IF average(I) less than average(lowest)
            THEN set lowest to I
        END-IF
END-Do
Display student(highest), average(highest)
Display student(lowest), average(lowest)
END: Grade average
```

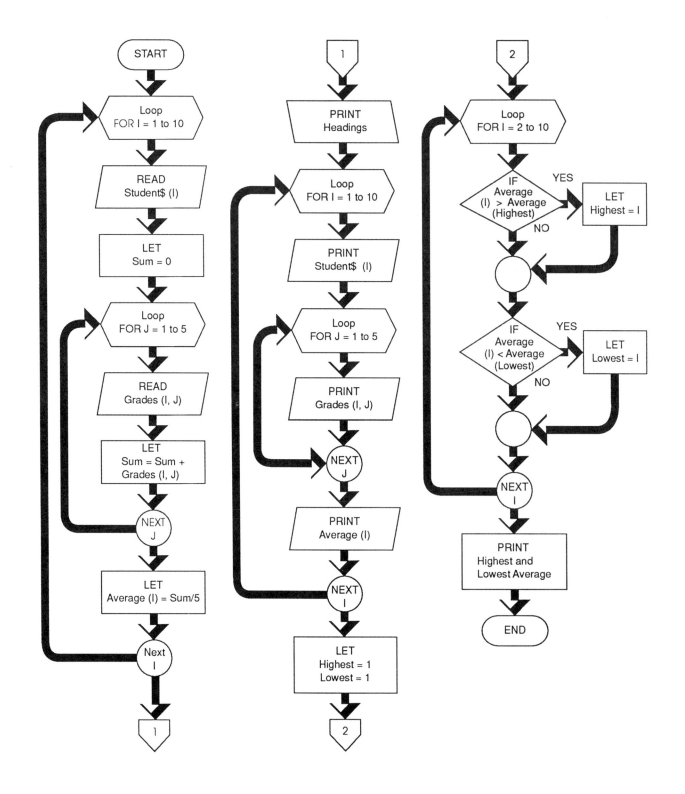

```
100  DIM STUDENT$(10), GRADES(10,5), AVERAGE(10)
110  FOR I = 1 TO 10
120     READ STUDENT$(I)
130     SUM = 0
140     FOR J = 1 TO 5
150        READ GRADES(I,J)
160        SUM = SUM + GRADES(I,J)
170     NEXT J
180     AVERAGE(I) = SUM/5
190  NEXT I
200 REM Print out the names, grades and averages
210 PRINT "NAME",,"GRADES",,"AVERAGE"
220 FOR I = 1 TO 10
230    PRINT STUDENT$(I),"      ";
240    FOR J = 1 TO 5
250       PRINT GRADES(I,J);"   ";
260    NEXT J
270    PRINT ,AVERAGE(I)
280 NEXT I
290 REM Print out the names and averages of the students with the
300 REM highest and lowest averages.
310 REM
320 REM Start by assuming the first student has both the highest and
330 REM the lowest average.
340 PRINT
350 HIGHEST = 1
360 LOWEST = 1
370 REM Loop through the remaining 9 students, if an average is higher
380 REM or lower than the value in average(highest) or average(lowest)
390 REM then make the current iteration the highest or lowest.
400 FOR I = 2 TO 10
410    IF AVERAGE(I) > AVERAGE(HIGHEST) THEN HIGHEST = I
420    IF AVERAGE(I) < AVERAGE(LOWEST) THEN LOWEST = I
430 NEXT I
440 PRINT "The highest average belongs to ";STUDENT$(HIGHEST);
450 PRINT "with an average of";AVERAGE(HIGHEST)
460 PRINT "The lowest average belongs to ";STUDENT$(LOWEST);
470 PRINT " with an average of";AVERAGE(LOWEST)
480 DATA "Jones",79,80,65,98,88
490 DATA "Doe",87,88,92,75,80
500 DATA "Smith",99,92,87,99,100
510 DATA "Leahy",78,88,76,90,89
520 DATA "Cleary",65,67,76,70,56
530 DATA "Johnson",87,98,87,90,92
540 DATA "White",88,78,84,92,83
550 DATA "Brown",75,72,75,81,69
560 DATA "Doherty",87,96,86,73,85
570 DATA "Murphy",86,87,97,99,87
580 END
```

After running this program, the output would be:

```
run
NAME                              GRADES                      AVERAGE
Jones          79    80    65    98    88       82
Doe            87    88    92    75    80       84.4
Smith          99    92    87    99    100      95.4
Leahy          78    88    76    90    89       84.2
Cleary         65    67    76    70    56       66.8
Johnson        87    98    87    90    92       90.8
White          88    78    84    92    83       85
Brown          75    72    75    81    69       74.4
Doherty        87    96    86    73    85       85.4
Murphy         86    87    97    99    87       91.2

The highest average belongs to Smith with an average of 95.4
The lowest average belongs to Cleary with an average of 66.8
Ok
```

Sorting an Array

Sorting large amounts of data is a tedious and very repetitive task, making it a perfect application for a BASIC program. While there are many techniques for sorting an array of data, one of the simplest and most common is the **bubble sort**. The bubble sort can be explained most easily with an example. We will assume that we have a one-dimensional string array with five elements containing the values "A", "B", "C", "D", "E". We will sort this array alphabetically, and we will assume a worst-case scenario in which the array is completely out of order and looks like this: E D C B A where A$(1) is "E", A$(2) is "D", A$(3) = "C", A$(4) = "B", and A$(5) = "A", shown below.

Element	Current Value	Sorted Value
A$(1)	E	A
A$(2)	D	B
A$(3)	C	C
A$(4)	B	D
A$(5)	A	E

The bubble sort compares the ASCII values of the first two characters A$(1) and A$(2). If A$(1) is greater than A$(2), then the two values are swapped. Then A$(2) and A$(3) are compared. If A$(2) is greater than A$(3) then those two are swapped. A$(3) and A$(4) are compared and swapped if A$(3) is greater than A$(4). Finally A$(4) and A$(5) are compared and swapped if necessary. This completes the first pass through the array, and this pass has left the highest value in the last location, A$(5). The second pass does the same thing from the first location (A$(1)) to the second-from-last location (A$(4)), swapping in the same manner. Upon completion of the second pass, the last two variables are where they belong: A$(4),A$(5). This continues until all of the variables are in order. Let's trace through a bubble sort of A$ in Figure 11.5.

Figure 11.5   BUBBLE SORT

```
START       E D C B A
            D E C B A
            D C E B A
            D C B E A
            D C B A E      (end of first pass, E is in position)
            C D B A E
            C B D A E
            C B A D E      (end of second pass, D and E in position)
            B C A D E
            B A C D E      (end of third pass, C, D, and E in position)
            A B C D E      (end of fourth pass, A, B, C, D, and E in position)
```

Note: For a bubble sort sorting n elements, $n - 1$ passes will be made. For instance, with the five elements above, the program would have to make four passes through the data to complete the bubble sort.

To perform a bubble sort in a BASIC program, a pair of nested FOR/NEXT loops can be used. The outside loop increments I from 1 to one less than the number of elements in an array (N − 1). The inside loop increments J from 1 to (N − I). If A$(J) is greater than A$(J + 1), then these values are swapped. This continues until both loops are processed. The example below uses this method.

```
 10 DIM A$(5)
 20 REM Initialize the array A$
 30 READ A$(1), A$(2), A$(3), A$(4), A$(5)
 40 PRINT "   ";A$(1);A$(2);A$(3);A$(4);A$(5)
 50 REM Let N = the size of the array
 60 N = 5
 70 REM Enter the nested loop
 80 FOR I = 1 TO N - 1
 90     FOR J = 1 TO N - I
100         IF A$(J) > A$(J+1) THEN GOSUB 160
110         PRINT "    ";A$(1);A$(2);A$(3);A$(4);A$(5)
120 NEXT J
130 NEXT I
140     DATA "E", "D", "C", "B", "A"
150     END
160     REM Subroutine to swap A$(J) and A$(J+1)
170     TEMP$ = A$(J+1)
180     A$(J+1) = A$(J)
190     A$(J) = TEMP$
200     RETURN
210 END
```

When this program is run, the contents of the array are displayed after each swap of elements. The results would look like this:

```
run
     EDCBA
     DECBA
     DCEBA
     DCBEA
     DCBAE
     CDBAE
     CBDAE
     CBADE
     BCADE
     BACDE
     ABCDE
Ok
```

Let's try adding a bubble sort to our student exam score program. We want to sort the list of students alphabetically by name. When we swap the name elements, we must also remember to switch the averages at the same time. We will assume that the data for the individual grades will no longer be printed or sorted.

```
10   DIM STUDENT$(10), GRADES(10,5), AVERAGE(10)
20   FOR I = 1 TO 10
30      READ STUDENT$(I)
40      SUM = 0
50      FOR J = 1 TO 5
60        READ GRADES(I,J)
70        SUM = SUM + GRADES(I,J)
80      NEXT J
90      AVERAGE(I) = SUM/5
100    NEXT I
110 REM Sort the array by name.
120 FOR I = 1 TO 9
130    FOR J = 1 TO 10-I
140      IF STUDENT$(J) > = STUDENT$(J+1) THEN GOSUB 600
150    NEXT J
160 NEXT I
170   REM Print out the names and averages
180   PRINT "NAME","AVERAGE"
190   FOR I = 1 TO 10
200      PRINT STUDENT$(I),AVERAGE(I)
210   NEXT I
220 REM Print out the names and averages of the students with the
230 REM highest and lowest averages.
240 REM
250 REM Start by assuming the first student has both the highest and
260 REM the lowest average.
270 PRINT
280 HIGHEST = 1
290 LOWEST = 1
300 REM Loop through the remaining 9 students. If an average is higher
310 REM or lower than the value in average(highest) or average(lowest)
320 REM then make the current iteration the highest or lowest.
```

```
330   FOR I = 2 TO 10
340      IF AVERAGE(I) > AVERAGE(HIGHEST) THEN HIGHEST = I
350      IF AVERAGE(I) < AVERAGE(LOWEST) THEN LOWEST = I
360   NEXT I
370   PRINT "The highest average belongs to ";STUDENT$(HIGHEST);
380   PRINT " with an average of";AVERAGE(HIGHEST)
390   PRINT "The lowest average belongs to ";STUDENT$(LOWEST);
400   PRINT " with an average of";AVERAGE(LOWEST)
410   DATA "Jones",79,80,65,98,88
420   DATA "Doe",87,88,92,75,80
430   DATA "Smith",99,92,87,99,100
440   DATA "Leahy",78,88,76,90,89
450   DATA "Cleary",65,67,76,70,56
460   DATA "Johnson",87,98,87,90,92
470   DATA "White",88,78,84,92,83
480   DATA "Brown",75,72,75,81,69
490   DATA "Doherty",87,96,86,73,85
500   DATA "Murphy",86,87,97,99,87
510   END
600   REM Subroutine to swap name and average during sort.
610   TEMP.NAME$ = STUDENT$(J+1)
620   STUDENT$(J+1) = STUDENT$(J)
630   STUDENT$(J) = TEMP.NAME$
640   TEMP.AVG = AVERAGE(J+1)
650   AVERAGE(J+1) = AVERAGE(J)
660   AVERAGE(J) = TEMP.AVG
670   RETURN
680   END
```

Upon running this program the results would be:

```
run
```

NAME	AVERAGE
Brown	74.4
Cleary	66.8
Doe	84.4
Doherty	85.4
Johnson	90.8
Jones	82
Leahy	84.2
Murphy	91.2
Smith	95.4
White	85

```
The highest average belongs to Smith with an average of 95.4
The lowest average belongs to Cleary with an average of 66.8
Ok
```

We could also rewrite the program to sort in order of averages. This could be done by STUDENT$(J) and STUDENT$(J + 1) IN LINE 140 with AVERAGE(J) and AVERAGE(J + 1), respectively.

The SWAP Statement

The bubble sort, as well as other sorts, compares the entire array two elements at a time, and if the first number is greater than the second (or vice versa if sorting largest value to smallest), the values of the two elements are exchanged. We have accomplished this bubble sort in the previous examples by using a temporary variable, as illustrated in the following lines of code:

```
300 LET TEMP = A(3)
310 LET A(3) = A(4)
320 LET A(4) = A(3)
```

These three lines of code can be replaced with a single BASIC statement that accomplishes the same function, the SWAP statement. The format of the SWAP statement is shown in the box below.

The SWAP Statement

Purpose   To exchange the values of two variables

Format   SWAP var1, var2
where *var1* is a variable or array element, and *var2* is a second variable or array

Examples   100 SWAP X,Y
200 SWAP A(3),TEMP
300 SWAP $NAME,$EMP
400 SWAP V(I),V(I + 1)

Using the SWAP command, you can replace the three lines of code above with this single line of code:

```
300 SWAP A(3),A(4)
```

The following example demonstrates the use of the SWAP command:

```
10 REM Program to demonstrate the SWAP statement.
20 LET X = 50
30 LET Y = 100
40 PRINT "Before the SWAP: X = ";X;" and Y =";Y
50 SWAP X,Y
60 PRINT "After the SWAP: X =";X;" and Y =";Y
70 END
```

The result would be as follows:

```
run
Before the SWAP: X = 50 and Y = 100
After the SWAP: X = 100 and Y = 50
```

Now let's try rewriting our bubble sort example using the SWAP statement.

```
 10 DIM STUDENT$(10), GRADES(10,5), AVERAGE(10)
 20 FOR I = 1 TO 10
 30     READ STUDENT$(I)
 40     SUM = 0
 50     FOR J = 1 TO 5
 60       READ GRADES(I,J)
 70       SUM = SUM + GRADES(I,J)
 80     NEXT J
 90     AVERAGE(I) = SUM/5
100 NEXT I
110 REM Sort the array by name.
120 FOR I = 1 TO 9
130     FOR J = 1 TO 10 - I
140       IF STUDENT$(J) >= STUDENT$(J+1) THEN GOSUB 520
150     NEXT J
160 NEXT I
170  REM Print out the names and averages
180  PRINT "NAME","AVERAGE"
190  FOR I = 1 TO 10
200     PRINT STUDENT$(I),AVERAGE(I)
210  NEXT I
220 REM Print out the names and averages of the students with the
230 REM highest and lowest averages.
240 REM
250 REM Start by assuming the first student has both the highest and
260 REM the lowest average.
270 PRINT
280 HIGHEST = 1
290 LOWEST = 1
300 REM Loop through the remaining 9 students, if an average is higher
310 REM or lower than the value in average(highest) or average(lowest)
320 REM then make the current iteration the highest or lowest.
330 FOR I = 2 TO 10
340    IF AVERAGE(I) > AVERAGE(HIGHEST) THEN HIGHEST = I
350    IF AVERAGE(I) < AVERAGE(LOWEST) THEN LOWEST = I
360 NEXT I
370 PRINT "The highest average belongs to ";STUDENT$(HIGHEST);
380 PRINT " with an average of";AVERAGE(HIGHEST)
390 PRINT "The lowest average belongs to ";STUDENT$(LOWEST);
400 PRINT " with an average of";AVERAGE(LOWEST)
410 DATA "Jones",79,80,65,98,88
420 DATA "Doe",87,88,92,75,80
430 DATA "Smith",99,92,87,99,100
440 DATA "Leahy",78,88,76,90,89
450 DATA "Cleary",65,67,76,70,56
460 DATA "Johnson",87,98,87,90,92
470 DATA "White",88,78,84,92,83
480 DATA "Brown",75,72,75,81,69
```

```
490  DATA "Doherty",87,96,86,73,85
500  DATA "Murphy",86,87,97,99,87
510  END
520 REM Subroutine to swap name and average during sort.
530 SWAP STUDENT$(J), STUDENT$(J+1)
540 SWAP AVERAGE(J), AVERAGE(J+1)
550 RETURN
560 END
```

Upon running this program, the results would be:

```
run
NAME                    AVERAGE
Brown                   74.4
Cleary                  66.8
Doe                     84.4
Doherty                 85.4
Johnson                 90.8
Jones                   82
Leahy                   84.2
Murphy                  91.2
Smith                   95.4
White                   85

The highest average belongs to Smith with an average of 95.4
The lowest average belongs to Cleary with an average of 66.8
Ok
```

Summary

- Arrays are used to store large amounts of associated data as a group of elements under one variable name. This prevents the need for many different variables and allows the program to process data by looping.
- The DIM statement is used to define and preallocate the locations in memory where the data in an array will be stored. The default allows for ten locations in memory, but even smaller arrays should be dimensioned to maintain good programming practices.
- A one-dimensional array is similar to a list of data. One index is used to represent where the item of data is located.
- A two-dimensional array is similar to a table of data. Data are stored in row and column format, and two indexes are used to specify a data element.
- A three-dimensional array is similar to a cube of data, or a collection of layered, two-dimensional arrays. Three indexes are used to specify data elements within the array.
- Multidimensional arrays can be defined using the DIM statement to accommodate complex problems. The maximum number of dimensions an array can have is 255.

- The bubble sort is a simple and commonly used sorting technique in BASIC. The bubble sort moves the higher-valued elements (or lower-valued for a descending sort) to the end one by one, until the array is in order from lowest to highest or vice versa.
- The SWAP statement is used to exchange the values of two variables.

Exercises

True or False

_____ 1. An array is an ordered list of related data values.

_____ 2. Dimensioning an array is necessary to preallocate contiguous memory locations for the elements within the array.

_____ 3. A one-dimensional array is an array that has been defined in a DIM statement to have an index value of one.

_____ 4. Loading data elements into an array is known as populating the array.

_____ 5. A two-dimensional array is defined in a DIM statement such as DIM PARTS(5,20) where 5 is the number of columns and 20 is the number of rows.

_____ 6. A FOR/NEXT loop is often used to search through a one-dimensional array to locate a specific value.

_____ 7. Nested FOR/NEXT loops provide a simple and quick way to populate a two-dimensional array.

_____ 8. A populated one-dimensional array can be changed into a populated two-dimensional array simply by reissuing the DIM statement.

_____ 9. A bubble sort is a BASIC utility to sort a one-dimensional array containing character strings in alphabetic order.

_____ 10. To restore sorted arrays back to their initial, unsorted state, simply reissue the original DIM statement.

Fill-In

1. A list or table of related data elements stored as a single variable name is known as an _____.

2. An array that stores data elements in a list format is a _____ array.

3. A two-dimensional array stores data elements in a _____ format.

4. A two-dimensional array accesses its data elements _____ by _____.

5. The integer value which indicates a specific data element in an array is known as an
_____.

6. Preallocating memory locations to store data elements in an array is known as _____ the array.

7. The most common way to search through a one-dimensional array is through a _____ loop.

8. The initial loading of data into an array is known as _____ the array.

9. A _____ is a common way to sort a one-dimensional array in BASIC.

10. An array is commonly sorted in BASIC by using a _____ FOR/NEXT loop.

Short Answer

1. What does dimensioning an array do?

2. What is the difference between a one-dimensional and a two-dimensional array?

3. What is meant by populating an array?

4. What would be the procedure for searching through a one-dimensional array to locate the highest value?

5. Explain how the bubble sort works.

Programming Problems

1. Write a program that prompts for names, sorts the names, and then displays the sorted list. The program should be flexible enough to allow the user to specify how many names are to be entered.

2. Storing information in an array rather than rereading the information over and over again allows the computer to execute commands much more quickly, therefore allowing the program to run more quickly. Rewrite the program assigned in Chapter 10, Programming Problem 2, to read all of the book information into arrays, and then use the array for any keyword look-ups. Assume that there can be no more than 100 books.

3. Change the program displayed at the end of the text in this chapter to sort by the students' final averages instead of the students' names. The student with the highest average should appear on the top of the list. The program should also display all grades for each student, along with the student name and average.

4. Write a program that prompts the user to key in a single sentence. The program should examine the sentence and calculate the number of "A"s, the number of "B"s, etc. The program should ignore spaces and punctuation, and should count the number of uppercase and lowercase letters together. After counting the number of different letters in the sentence, the program should display the statistics for the sentence, and prompt the user for another sentence, or "*" to quit.

5. It is election time, and you have been hired to write a program to help the election officials tally the results of the election. Write a program that will prompt for the number of candidates, and the name of each of those candidates. The program should allow the user to enter votes for each candidate, as well as add votes onto each candidate's running total; this part of the program should display a menu indicating all candidates for whom you can enter votes. When all votes are in, the program should sort the candidates by the total number of votes and display the election results, with the winner of the election on the top of the sorted list.

6. Change the student grading program shown on page 264 so that it uses a three-dimensional array to hold all grades for three classes, each class containing five students, each student having five grades. Also, make the STUDENT$ and AVERAGE arrays two-dimensional, so that students' names and averages can be accessed by class.

12

Input and Output Using Files

Learning Objectives

After reading this chapter you should understand:

- What files are and why they are used
- What a sequential file is
- How to open and close a sequential file

- How to write data to a sequential file
- How to read data from a sequential file
- How to print formatted reports to a sequential file

Introduction

Many business applications require a large amount of data, often provided from other sources. These data can be created on another PC by some other program, or may provide data to several programs on the same PC. Data that can be shared by several PCs or used by several programs is said to be "portable." This portability from program to program, or even from PC to PC, is accomplished by storing the data in a file. A **file** is a collection of related records. A **record** is a collection of related data items. The file structure we will be discussing is the most common, simplest type of file, the **sequential file**. A sequential file is a collection of records that are read or written in sequential order. For example, to read the tenth record in a sequential file, you must read the first nine records.

The benefits of using sequential files are:

1. Sequential files allow data created by one program to be saved to disk and then used by another program (even on another PC at a later time).
2. Sequential files can be used to hold large output files to be scanned for accuracy prior to printing or to be held until the printer is available.
3. Sequential files can be used as a central database (such as a personnel database) that contains information that can be used by several programs.

Opening a Sequential File

To use a sequential file in a BASIC program, the file must be opened. Opening a file does three things. It

1. verifies that the file exists if it is to be used for input, or creates the file if it is to be used for output;
2. allows the programmer to specify that the file is to be used for input, output, or to append to an existing file; and
3. associates a separate file number with each opened file. This allows the file to be specified in BASIC statements without having to enter the complete file name each time it is referenced.

Files are opened in BASIC with the OPEN statement (see box below).

The OPEN Statement

Purpose   Verifies the state of a file, and associates a file number with the file, to be used within the BASIC program

Format   ln OPEN <filename> FOR [INPUT] AS #<filenum>
                                      [OUTPUT]
                                      [APPEND]
where *ln* is a valid line number for a BASIC statement, *filename* is the file name of the file being opened, and *filenum* is the real number that will be used to reference the file within the BASIC program

Examples   100 OPEN "A:SALES.DAT" FOR INPUT AS #1
               500 OPEN "COST.OUT" FOR OUTPUT AS #3
               50 OPEN "PAYROLL.DAT" FOR APPEND AS #10

Notes   Valid file names for the OPEN statement are any valid DOS file names. To specify a drive other than the default, be sure to precede the file name with the drive followed by a colon. For example, if the default drive were the "A:" drive, and you wanted to open a file called NAMES.DAT on the "D:" drive, you would use a file name of "D:NAMES.DAT" in the OPEN statement. The maximum value for *filenum* is 3 unless you use the /f option when invoking BASIC, which will increase the maximum value to 15.

Files can be opened with the INPUT, OUTPUT, and APPEND modes. These file modes specify how the file can be used throughout the BASIC program and can be summarized as follows:

■ **INPUT**   Files opened with a file mode of INPUT are only used to read data into the program. At the OPEN statement, BASIC ensures that the file already exists prior to reading from it. If the file does exist, it is opened with the specified file number associated with it and the file pointer (which points to the current line of the file) is positioned at the first record. If the file does not already exist, the error message, "File not found" is printed.

■ **OUTPUT**   Files opened with a file mode of OUTPUT are used for writing data from a program. At the OPEN statement, the program checks if the file exists. *If the file does exist, it is erased and any data in this file is lost.* The file is then opened, and the file pointer is positioned at the first record of the file.

■ **APPEND**   The file mode APPEND is also used to write data from the BASIC program to a file, but unlike the OUTPUT mode, if a file already exists, the file pointer is positioned at the location following the last record in the file, and output will be appended to the original file. The original file will not be erased as it would have been if opened with OUTPUT.

Closing a Sequential File

After a file has been OPENed in a BASIC program, and all the processing to that file is complete, the file should be CLOSEd. Closing a sequential file does the following (see also box below):

1. De-allocates the file from the BASIC program, so that the file is no longer associated with the program, and is free to be reused in another section of the program or in a completely different program.
2. If the file has been opened with OUTPUT or APPEND, the last record is written to disk prior to releasing the file.
3. If a file has been opened with OUTPUT or APPEND, and the data written to the file are then to be used as input for a section of the program, the file must be closed, and then reopened for INPUT.
4. If a file has been opened for INPUT, and the programmer wishes to reuse the data, the file must be CLOSEd and then OPENed for INPUT to reset the file pointer to the first record.

The CLOSE Statement

Purpose   To close a file that has been opened by an OPEN statement

Format   ln CLOSE #<filenum> [,list of #<filenum>]
where *ln* is a valid line number for a BASIC statement and *filenum* is a file number of a file opened in a previous OPEN statement

Examples   100 CLOSE #3
500 CLOSE #1,#3,#5

Notes   Files are automatically closed at the completion of the BASIC program. However, it is considered good programming practice to close each opened file with a CLOSE statement prior to the completion of the program.

The following program is an example of the use of the OPEN and CLOSE statements.

```
100 REM Open EMPLOYEE.DAT located on the B: disk for input
110 REM Open HOURS.DAT located on the B: disk for output
```

```
120 REM Open PAYROLL.DAT for output on the D: disk
130 REM
140 OPEN "B:EMPLOYEE.DAT" FOR INPUT AS #1
150 OPEN "B:HOURS.DAT" FOR OUTPUT AS #2
160 OPEN "D:PAYROLL.DAT" FOR APPEND AS #3
            .        .        .
            .        .        .
            .        .        .
        < Processing of data >
            .        .        .
            .        .        .
            .        .        .
300 CLOSE #1, #2
310 CLOSE #3
320 END
```

This program demonstrates the opening and closing of three files. The first file open is EMPLOYEE.DAT on the B: disk. Since this file is being opened for INPUT, it must already exist. The second file being opened is HOURS.DAT, which will be located on the B: disk. If this file already exists, it will be erased since the file is being opened for OUTPUT. The third file to be opened is PAYROLL.DAT on the D: disk. This file is opened for APPEND; if the file exists, the output from the program will be written starting at the bottom of the existing data. The above files can also be opened by using variable names in the OPEN statement. For example:

```
100 INPUT "Enter filename of the Employee database";FILE1
110 INPUT "Enter filename of the weeks timecards";FILE2
120 INPUT "Enter filename of Output Payroll data";FILE3
130 REM
140 OPEN FILE1 FOR INPUT AS #1
150 OPEN FILE2 FOR OUTPUT AS #2
160 OPEN FILE3 FOR APPEND AS #3
            .        .        .
            .        .        .
            .        .        .
        < Processing of data >
            .        .        .
            .        .        .
            .        .        .
300 CLOSE #1, #2
310 CLOSE #3
320 END
```

This program performs the same opening and closing of files as the previous program; however, the user can specify where the input is to come from and where the output is to go as the program is run.

Writing to a Sequential File

When a file has been opened for OUTPUT or APPEND, you can write data records to that file using the WRITE # command. The primary function of the WRITE # statement is to write data to a file that will be read back into the same or another BASIC program. The data are written in record format, that is, data items are separated by commas, there are quotes around character variables, and there is a carriage return assumed at the end of the record, causing the file pointer to be positioned at the location following the record that was just written. The WRITE # statement is summarized in the box below.

The WRITE # Statement

Purpose   Writes a record composed of variables, constants, and character strings to a specified file

Format   ln WRITE #<filenum>, <list>
where *ln* is a valid line number for a BASIC statement, *filenum* is the file number of a opened file with a file mode of OUTPUT or APPEND, and *list* is a list of variables, constants, or character strings

Examples   100 WRITE #3, EMPLOYEE, PAY.RATE, HOURS
300 WRITE #5, "EMPLOYEE NUMBER:", EMPNUM
500 WRITE #7, "Tax Rate", .20

Notes   The format in which the data are written is the same format in which data are read in using the INPUT # statement for files discussed later in the chapter. For output to a file in a report form, the PRINT # statement, also discussed later in this chapter, is used.

The following is an example of a program that reads data from DATA statements, (name, employee number, hours worked, and pay rate), and writes the payroll data to a file called PAYROLL.DAT to be created on the B: disk. The flowchart and pseudocode used in planning the program can be seen in Figure 12.1.

Figure 12.1

Program: Weekly pay
READ employee name
Do WHILE employee name is not equal to "END"
      READ employee number, hours worked, and pay rate
      IF hours worked are greater than 40
          THEN set pay to (40 times pay rate) plus (1.5 times
               pay rate times (number of hours worked minus 40))
         ELSE set pay to hours worked times pay rate
      END-IF
      Write to output file employee name, employee number, and pay
      READ employee name
END-Do
END: Weekly pay

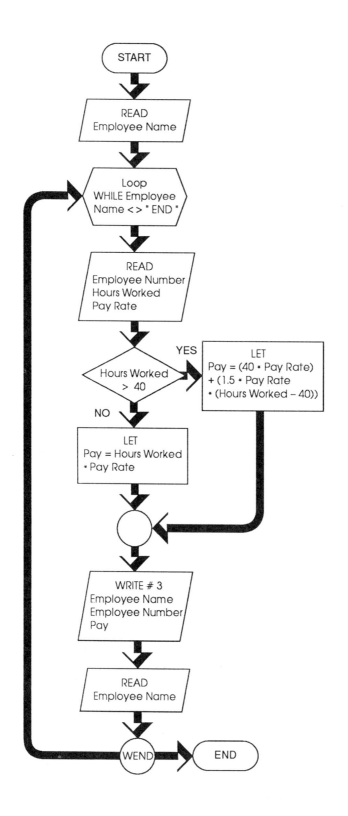

```
100 OPEN "B:PAYROLL.DAT" FOR OUTPUT AS #3
110 READ EMP.NAM$
120 WHILE EMP.NAM$ <> "END"
140    READ EMP.NUMBER, HOURS.WORKED, PAY.RATE
150    IF HOURS.WORKED > 40
          THEN PAY = (40 * PAY.RATE) + (1.5 * PAY.RATE * (HOURS.WORKED - 40)
          ELSE PAY = (HOURS.WORKED * PAY.RATE)
160    WRITE #3, EMP.NAM$, EMP.NUMBER, PAY
170    READ EMP.NAM$
180 WEND
210 DATA "JONES, M", 14323, 44, 11.65
220 DATA "SMITH, R", 23443, 39, 10.5
230 DATA "REED, L", 32423, 40.5, 9.00
240 DATA "WHITE, C", 47475, 35, 12.00
250 DATA "END"
260 CLOSE #3
270 END
```

When run, this program will create a file PAYROLL.DAT on the B: disk. If you were to TYPE the file from DOS, you would see the following:

```
TYPE B:PAYROLL.DAT

"JONES, M",14323,535.9
"SMITH, R",23443,409.5
"REED, L",32423,366.75
"WHITE, C",47475,420
```

Reading from a Sequential File

When a file has been opened for input, data can be read from that file sequentially starting from the first record until the end of the file is reached by using a modified version of the INPUT command. The INPUT # command is more similar to the READ statement described in Chapter 9 than it is to the INPUT statement described in Chapter 5. The difference between the INPUT # statement and the READ statement is that the file number of the file being read from must be specified and the data are read from a file that is external to the BASIC program rather than from a DATA statement. The data types of the input variables (either numbers or character strings) must match the data in the record being read in. A summary of the INPUT # statement is given in the box below.

The INPUT # Statement

Purpose   Reads a record composed of numeric and character strings from a specified file

Format   ln INPUT #<filenum>, <list>
where *ln* is a valid line number for a BASIC statement, *filenum* is the file number of an opened file with a file mode of INPUT, and *list* is a list of numbers, character strings, or both

Examples   100 INPUT #1, EMPLOYEE$, PAY.RATE, HOURS
300 INPUT #5, EMPLOYEE(1), RATE(1)

Note   The format in which the data are read in is the same format in which data were written using the WRITE # statement for files discussed in the previous section.

EOF Conditions

When reading data from a file using the INPUT statement, it is possible to continue reading past the end of the file, causing an error. To prevent this, you can check for an end-of-file (EOF) condition by using the BASIC EOF function. When the last record is read, BASIC sets an EOF condition for that file. It is important to test if an end-of-file condition has occurred prior to reading each record. The EOF function is summarized in the box below.

The EOF Function

Purpose   Signals when the last record in an input file has been read

Format   <testing condition> EOF(<filenum>)
where *testing condition* is a valid BASIC statement with a conditional branch based on the evaluation of the condition (in this case, EOF), and *filenum* is the file number associated with the file being read

Example   100 OPEN "NAMES.DAT" FOR INPUT AS #1
110 WHILE NOT EOF(1)
        120 INPUT #1, NAME$, STREET$, CITY$, STATE$, ZIP
        130 PRINT NAME$
        140 PRINT STREET$
        150 PRINT CITY$; ", ";STATE$;"   ";ZIP
160 WEND
170 CLOSE #1
180 END

Note   The EOF function is based on the last INPUT # command that was issued, so it is important to have the program check the EOF flag prior to reading the next record.

This is an example of a program that reads data from the PAYROLL.DAT file created in the previous example, and prints out employee paychecks. The EOF indicator determines if the program has read all of the information from the file.

```
100 OPEN "B:PAYROLL.DAT" FOR INPUT AS #1
110 CLS
120 WHILE NOT EOF(1)
130    INPUT #1, EMP.NAM$, EMP.NUMBER, PAY
140    PRINT "*********************************************"
150    PRINT "                                           ";DATE$
160    PRINT "Pay to the order of: ",EMP.NAM$
170    PRINT "Employee number: ",EMP.NUMBER
180    PRINT "The sum of ............";
190    PRINT USING "$$#,###.##";PAY
200    PRINT "*********************************************"
210    PRINT
220 WEND
230 CLOSE #1
240 END
```

When run, this program will read from the file PAYROLL.DAT on the B: disk, and print out the following:

```
***********************************************************
                                              02-12-1989
Pay to the order of:            JONES, M
Employee number:                14323
The sum of ..........  ..       $535.90
***********************************************************


***********************************************************
                                              02-12-1989
Pay to the order of:            SMITH, R
Employee number:                23443
The sum of ............         $409.50
***********************************************************


***********************************************************
                                              02-12-1989
Pay to the order of:            REED, L
Employee number:                32423
The sum of ............         $366.75
***********************************************************


***********************************************************
                                              02-12-1989
Pay to the order of:            WHITE, C
Employee number:                47475
The sum of ............         $420.00
***********************************************************
Ok
```

Printing to a Sequential File

In addition to storing data for input and output, sequential files are often used to store files that are to be printed on a printer. Since many of the reports generated in business applications are large, and the speed of most printers is slow compared to the speed of writing a file to a disk, files make a good intermediate holding place for such documents. By writing a report to a file, large reports can be produced more quickly, without having to wait for the printer. After all the print files have been generated, they can be printed together after the use has completed running the programs. This also allows these reports to be scanned with the DOS TYPE command for accuracy prior to printing, perhaps saving paper that would be wasted with a bad output listing. To be able to do this with the same versatility that the PRINT statement provides, a statement more flexible than the WRITE # statement must be used. For this type of output, we use the PRINT # statement, as outlined in the box below.

The PRINT # Statement

Purpose   Writes a record composed of variables, constants, and character strings to a specified file using the print characteristics specified

Format   ln PRINT #<filenum>, <list>
where *ln* is a valid line number for a BASIC statement, *filenum* is the file number of an opened file with a file mode of OUTPUT or APPEND, and *list* is a list of variables, constants, character strings, and print characteristics

Examples   100 PRINT #3, EMPLOYEE, PAY.RATE, HOURS
300 PRINT #5, USING "$###.##";PAY.RATE
500 PRINT #7, TAB(5), "Name: "; NAME$

Note   The format in which the data are written is the same format it would be in if a regular PRINT statement were used, except that the data would be written to the specified file rather than to the screen.

The output from the PRINT # statement looks the same as it would if it were printed to the screen, and all the same parameters and formats of regular PRINT statements are available.

Let's try an example of a program that reads data from the PAYROLL.DAT file created in a previous example, and prints out the employees' paychecks. The data are written to a file so that the blank checks may be loaded into the printer prior to printing the file, and the whole print run done in one batch.

```
100 OPEN "B:PAYROLL.DAT" FOR INPUT AS #1
110 OPEN "B:PAYCHECK.DAT" FOR OUTPUT AS #3
120 CLS
130 WHILE NOT EOF(1)
140    INPUT #1, EMP.NAM$, EMP.NUMBER, PAY
150    PRINT #3, "*********************************************
160    PRINT #3,"                              ";DATE$
```

```
170     PRINT #3,"Pay to the order of: ",EMP.NAM$
180     PRINT #3,"Employee number: ",EMP.NUMBER
190     PRINT #3,"The sum of ...........";
200     PRINT #3,USING "$$#,###.##";PAY
210     PRINT #3, "*********************************************
220     PRINT #3, ' '
230 WEND
240 CLOSE #1, #3
250 END
```

When the program has been run, a new file will have been created on the B: disk. This file is PAYCHECK.DAT, and contains the same data that were written to the screen in the program shown on page 289.

Summary

■ Sequential files are used to store large quantities of or data which are to be used in multiple programs or on different PCs

■ All files must be opened prior to being used in a BASIC program. Files can be opened in one of three ways:
   1. **INPUT** The file must exist, and data can only be read from this file, starting with the first record.
   2. **OUTPUT** If the file exists, it is erased. The file is used for output starting at the first record.
   3. **APPEND** The file is used for output only; however, data are written to the location following the last record in the file.

■ All files should be CLOSED after they are used.

■ The WRITE # statement is used to write data to a file in a format that can be read using the INPUT # statement.

■ The INPUT # statement is used to read data that have been written to the file using the WRITE # statement.

■ When using the INPUT # statement it is important to check the EOF indicator prior to reading in a record to prevent reading past the end of a file and causing an error.

■ To write data to a file in report form, the PRINT # statement is used. The PRINT # statement allows the use of the PRINT, PRINT USING, and PRINT TAB statements, and is similar to the PRINT command except that the data are written to a file rather than to the screen.

Exercises

True or False

_____ 1. Sequential files are multiple files that are stored on disk in alphabetic order.

_____ 2. Sequential files can be used as a central database that can contain information to be used by several programs.

_____   3. Before a sequential file can be used in a BASIC program, the file must be opened.

_____   4. To open a sequential file from within a BASIC program, the file must exist prior to being opened.

_____   5. A file that has been opened for OUTPUT in a BASIC program must be closed and reopened prior to using it for input.

_____   6. If you use the WRITE # statement to write data to a file that has been opened for INPUT, you will destroy all of the data that previously existed in the file.

_____   7. Subscripts can be used in an INPUT # statement to allow the program to directly read a record without having to read all of the previous records first.

_____   8. When the last record of a file that has been opened for INPUT is read, an EOF indicator is set and can be used to prevent the program from trying to read past the end of the file.

_____   9. The difference between a file that is opened for OUTPUT and a file that is opened for APPEND is that a file opened for APPEND must exist prior to being opened while the file opened for OUTPUT cannot.

_____   10. The difference between a PRINT # statement and a WRITE # statement when writing a record to a file is only the format in which the record is written.

Fill-In

1. The most common file used in a BASIC program is the _____ file to which records must be read and written in order.

2. Files allow data to be _____, and be used by several different programs and even different PCs.

3. Prior to using a sequential file in a BASIC program, the file must be _____.

4. Files that will only be used to read data into a program should be opened with a file mode of _____.

5. If you wish to add records to an already existing file but do not want to lose the data that already exists, the file must be opened with a file mode of _____.

6. To be certain that the last data element has been written to disk before releasing that file it is recommended that the file be _____.

7. Data that are to be written to a file and will eventually be read by another program should be written with the _____ statement.

8. A flag that is set after the last record in an input file is read is known as an _____ condition.

9. To use a sequential file to store data that will eventually be sent to a printer, the records should be written to the file using the _____ statement.

10. An INPUT # statement is similar to a READ statement with the exception that data items are read from a _____ rather than from DATA statements.

Short Answer

1. What is a sequential file?

2. What happens when a file is opened in a BASIC program?

3. What is the difference between opening a file for OUTPUT and opening a file for APPEND?

4. What is accomplished by closing a file?

5. How does writing a record using WRITE # differ from writing a record using PRINT #?

Programming Problems

1. Write a BASIC program that prompts for the input of a last name, a first initial, and a phone number. The program should then write these data to a file that will be read into another program. The output file is B:PHONE.DAT and should be created new each time the program is run. The program should keep prompting the user for more names, initials, and phone numbers until a last name of "QUIT" is input.

2. This program prompts the user for the name of a person from B:PHONE.DAT created in Problem 1, and looks up the phone number. The program should search the file for the name, and if the name is found, print out the last name, first initial, and phone number. If the name is not found, the program should ask the user whether the name should be added to the file. If the response is affirmative, the last name, first initial, and phone number should be added to B:PHONE.DAT in the same format as in Problem 1.

3. Write a BASIC program to use a FOR/NEXT loop to read in ten product numbers, the unit price for each product, and the number of that product sold. These ten records should be written to a file in such a way that they can be read in from another BASIC program. The filename should be B:PRODUCT.LST.

4. Write a program that will prompt the user for a product number and then search the file B:PRODUCT.LST created in Problem 3 for the product. If the product is not found, then the program should write a message to that effect. If the product is found, an invoice containing the product number, unit price, quantity, and a total cost should be printed to a file B:INVOICE.PRT, which will be printed later on.

Program Design and Development

This *Software Guide* presents a method of developing BASIC programs following structured programming techniques. When writing a well-structured program using BASIC or any high-level language, it is crucial to first develop an algorithm for that program. An **algorithm** is a step-by-step description of all the tasks that need to be done in order for the program to work correctly. Like the steps in a cookbook, these algorithms should be a list of steps designed to arrive at the result the program is to be used for. Algorithms are generally informal descriptions that are later translated into formal programming language.

The two most common ways of presenting algorithms are flowcharting and pseudocode. **Flowcharts** are graphic representations composed of a set of symbols of all the steps necessary for the algorithm. **Pseudocode** is an Englishlike description that uses several keywords to describe each step in the algorithm.

Flowcharts

Flowcharts follow the "a picture is worth a thousand words" philosophy by presenting the algorithm as a clear diagram of all the steps in the program. A set of geometric symbols are used to depict each decision, input, output, or loop, with arrows connecting each symbol to the next in the proper sequence. Consider the example in Figure A.1.

Figure A.1

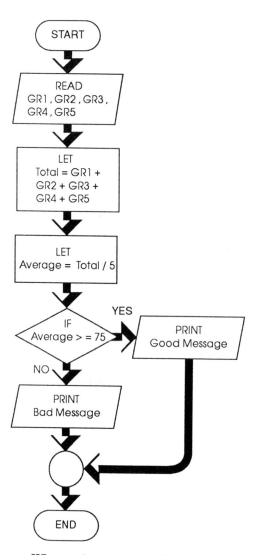

When written as a BASIC program, the flowchart would look like this:

```
10 REM Program to read in 5 grades, calculate the average,
20 REM and print a message as to whether the average is above
30 REM or below 75%.
40 REM
50 REM Input Data
60 INPUT "Enter the 5 grades:",G1, G2, G3, G4, G5
70 REM Sum the 5 grades
80 LET TOTAL = G1 + G2 + G3 + G4 + G5
90 REM Calculate the average
100 LET AVERAGE = TOTAL/5
110 REM Print messages depending on average being > or <= 75%
120 IF (AVERAGE >=75)
    THEN PRINT "Your average of ";AVERAGE;" is above average"
    ELSE PRINT "Your average of ";AVERAGE;" is below average"
130 END
```

As you can see by these examples, the flowchart presents an easy-to-follow pictorial representation of the program logic, which can then be translated easily into the actual BASIC program statements. Even a programmer unfamiliar with BASIC, can understand the logic of the flowchart, since the arrows clearly show how each step is connected to the next. By providing a common ground for programmers and non-programmers to discuss the program logic, flowcharts come in handy in the business world, where the people who understand the task the program must solve are not necessarily the programmers who will create the solution.

Although flowcharts are informal, certain rules should be followed to make them as clear and accurate as possible.

Flowcharting Rules

1. Always use the standard set of geometric symbols below to represent each step (see Table A.1).
2. Start the flowcharts at the top left corner of the page and direct the flow towards the bottom of the page.
3. Connect all flowchart symbols with flowlines, using arrowheads to show the direction of the program flow.
4. Make the descriptions within each symbol as clear and concise as possible, using standard BASIC operators, both relational and logical, whenever necessary. This allows the descriptions to be easily translated into their equivalent BASIC statement(s).
5. Never cross the flowlines.
6. Do not include statements that do not perform any actual processing such as DATA and DIM statements. Their presence is assumed.
7. Use only one START and one END.

By following these rules, it should be reasonably simple to create a well-developed flowchart that represents the algorithm necessary to create a BASIC program.

Let's take a look at a more involved flowchart to see how each of the symbols are used (see Figure A.2). In the above example, we can see the general structure of the flowchart. The terminator, *Start*, is located at the top left of the page, and an *End* is at the bottom. Notice also that there is only one start, allowing only a single entry point into the program logic. The flowchart goes from top to bottom, with the flowlines connecting each symbol in order, and no flowline crosses any other. The subroutine is separate from the main program, and has its own terminators, *Subroutine average* and *Return*, to indicate its start and end. Notice also the format of the IF statement: The flowchart will determine whether the condition in the diamond is met. If the answer is yes, the program will branch in the direction labeled *yes*, if the answer is no, the route labeled *no* will be taken. It is important to have both choices shown regardless of whether the IF statement is an IF-THEN or IF-THEN-ELSE statement. The only symbol this example doesn't show is the off-page indicator. Large flowcharts that span several pages can be difficult to follow, so the off-page indicator should be used as little as possible.

Table A.1   Flowchart Symbols

Symbol	Symbol Name	Description
	Terminator	Used to indicate the start and end of a flowchart. Also used to start and end a sub-routine.
	Input/Output	Used for all READ, INPUT and PRINT statements.
	Processing	Used for assignments and calculations.
	Subroutine Call	Used to call a subroutine.
	Decision	Used for IF-THEN or IF-THEN-Else statements.
	Loop	Used to represent FOR/NEXT and WHILE/WEND loops.
	Flowlines	Used to indicate the direction of logic flow.
	Connector	Used to connect one section of the program to another or to join multiple flow lines.
	Off Page Indicator	Used to indicate that the flowchart is continued on another page.
	Annotation	Used to provide more detail about a particular symbol.

Figure A.2

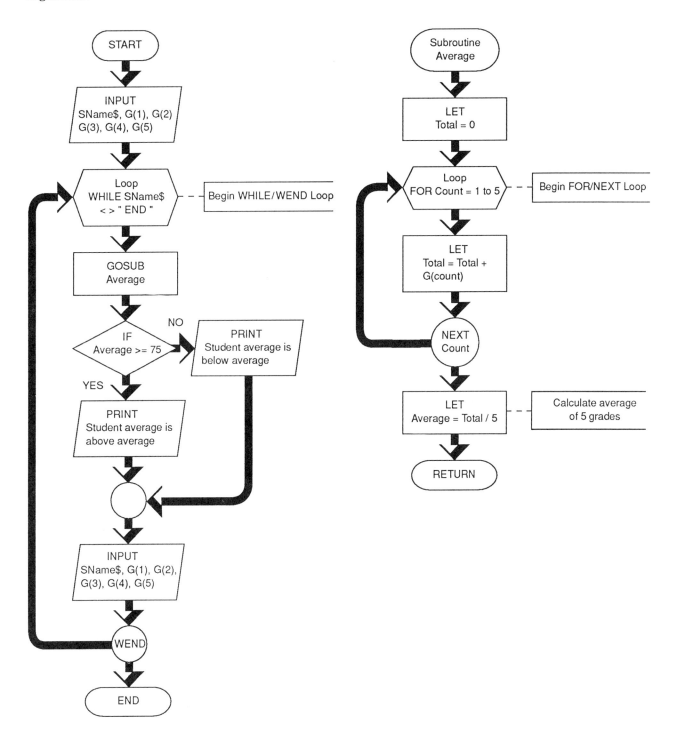

Pseudocode

Another method of representing the algorithm for a BASIC program is the pseudocode. Similar to the way flowcharts represent each step pictorially, pseudocode represents each step with an Englishlike description. While flowcharts are simpler to follow when tracing the program's logic, pseudocode is simpler to translate into a BASIC program. Pseudocode gives line-for-line descriptions that translate directly into BASIC statements. Let's take a look at the BASIC program that we flowcharted and see how it would look written in pseudocode.

```
PROGRAM: Calculate average
READ grades
SET total to sum of grades
SET average to total divided by number of grades
IF average greater than or equal to 75
    THEN DISPLAY student average is above average
    ELSE DISPLAY student average is below average
END-IF
END: Calculate average
```

Compare this to the actual BASIC program:

```
10 REM Program to read in 5 grades, calculate the average,
20 REM and print a message as to whether the average is above
30 REM or below 75%.
40 REM
50 REM Input Data
60 INPUT "Enter the 5 grades:";G1,G2,G3,G4,G5
70 REM Sum the 5 grades
80 LET TOTAL = G1 + G2 + G3 + G4 + G5
90 REM Calculate the average.
100 LET AVERAGE = TOTAL/5
110 REM Print messages depending on average being > or < than 75%
120 IF (AVERAGE >= 75)
    THEN PRINT "Your average of ";AVERAGE;" is above average"
    ELSE PRINT "Your average of ";AVERAGE;" is below average"
130 END
```

Again, pseudocode is an informal representation of an algorithm, but there are certain rules that help you to write precise, easy-to-follow pseudocode.

Rules for Writing Pseudocode

1. Start each pseudocode with a PROGRAM statement, and end it with an END statement. Each should be followed by the program's title.
2. Use short, concise phrases to describe each step.
3. Use Englishlike phrases to represent each calculation, relation, and comparison.
4. Indent loops and IF-THEN and IF-THEN-ELSE statements to make the pseudocode more readable.

In short, just make the pseudocode give short, precise, English descriptions for each step of the algorithm. Let's take a look at the algorithm flowcharted in the previous section using pseudocode.

PROGRAM: Calculate average
INPUT name
Do-While name not "END"
    INPUT grades
    EXECUTE subroutine average
    IF average is greater than or equal to 75
        THEN DISPLAY student average is above average
        ELSE DISPLAY student average is below average
    END-IF
    INPUT name and grades
END-Do
END: Calculate average

SUBROUTINE: Average
SET total to zero
Do count = 1 to 5
    Add grade (count) to total
END-Do
SET average to total divided by 5
END: Average

Most of your programming constructs would be represented in pseudocode similar to this one. It gives examples of INPUT and DISPLAY statements that input and print data. The WHILE/WEND loop is represented by the Do-While statements, the IF statement is diagrammed, and the subroutine includes a FOR/NEXT loop.

This pseudocode can be easily translated into the following BASIC program:

```
10 REM Calculate average
20 INPUT "Enter sudent name (type END to quit): ",SNAME$
30 WHILE SNAME$ <> "END"
40  INPUT "Enter 5 student grades: ",G(1), G(2), G(3), G(4), G(5)
50  GOSUB 100
60  IF AVERAGE > 75
     THEN PRINT "Student average of ";AVERAGE;" is above average"
     ELSE PRINT "Student average of ";AVERAGE;" is below average"
70  INPUT "Enter student name (type END to quit): ";SNAME$
80 WEND
90 END
100 REM Subroutine to calculate average
110 LET TOTAL = 0
120 FOR COUNT = 1 TO 5
130   LET TOTAL = TOTAL + G(COUNT)
140 NEXT COUNT
150 LET AVERAGE = TOTAL/5
160 RETURN
```

Remember that while the rules to writing pseudocode are not formal, in order to preserve the format of a well-structured program, it is necessary to follow structured programming and top-down approaches.

Debugging Hints

Introduction

As you create more powerful and complex programs using BASIC, you will undoubtedly see many different kinds of problems in your programs. Many problems,
such as syntax problems, are easy to fix since they only require correction of the
way a command or function name is spelled, or of the way that you have specified
information to a BASIC command. Other problems, such as abnormal program
ending or infinite program loops, are a little more difficult to fix. This appendix
will help you identify the problems you may be experiencing in your program, and
show you how to fix them.

Interpreting a BASIC Error Message

Anytime you attempt to run a BASIC program that is incorrectly written, BASIC
will display one or more **error messages**. An error message, as described in
Chapter 4, tells you why BASIC can no longer interpret a program. Most error
messages BASIC displays will contain the following information:

1. A description of the BASIC programming rule that was violated.
2. The line number of your program where BASIC found the error.

BASIC may also display other information describing the command name that
failed. When BASIC displays an error message while you are attempting to run a
program, perform the following steps to help identify and correct the problem.

Step 1: Did the Error Message Display a Line Number?

For instance, if you specify a variable name with invalid characters (for example,
the incorrect variable name TAX&WAGES), in an assignment statement on line
310, BASIC will display the message "Syntax error in 310," and cease interpretation of the program. In this case, the error message is telling you exactly where
the problem is. Change the line so that it follows BASIC syntax rules. You may
also want to check for other occurrences of syntax violation further along in the
program.

Step 2: Does the Error Message Contain a Command Name?

Some BASIC error messages point to a problem with the way a particular command is called in your program. For instance, if you have a FOR/NEXT loop in your program but forget to include the NEXT command, BASIC will display the error message "FOR without NEXT." If a BASIC command name is specified within the error message, check your program for all occurrences of that command, and make sure that you are using the command correctly.

Step 3: Does the Error Message Describe a Particular Error Condition?

Some BASIC error messages describe a particular "event" or "interrupt" in your program. Dividing a number by zero, for instance, generates the BASIC error message "Division by zero." Concatenation of two character strings, each of length 150, will cause BASIC to generate the error message "String too long." If the error message displayed falls into this category, check your program for commands that could generate the error condition described in the error message.

For example, if BASIC displays the message "Division by zero" when you run a program, check all statements in your program that perform division. Ensure that all information that is used in those statements would not permit division by zero. If the cause of the problem is still not clear, place IF-THEN statements in the program before statements that perform division, to verify that division by zero will not occur.

Step 4: Consult Reference Works

If you reach this step, you should consult the "Error Codes and Messages" appendix in the BASIC User's Guide. All BASIC error messages are listed in that appendix with a brief explanation of why the error message was displayed. Using this information, you should be able to understand the error message and correct the problem.

How to Trace BASIC Programs

When running a complex program, you may find errors in the information that is generated by the program, or you may find that the program is not doing exactly what you want it to do. At times, depending on the complexity of the program, you may find it difficult to follow the logic of your program. It would be useful and helpful if you could trace the interpretation of your program.

The TRON system command of BASIC allows you to monitor the interpretation of your program, on a line-by-line basis. You can use the TRON command to see exactly which lines get executed, and to see the order in which the statements are executed, showing you the flow of the program. (See the summary in the box below.)

If you want to trace your program, issue the BASIC system command TRON before issuing the RUN command. Then when you enter the RUN command, TRON instructs BASIC to display the line number of each line of your program as it is read, interpreted, and executed. After you issue the TRON command, all pro-

The TRON and TROFF Commands

Purpose   To instruct BASIC to start or end program tracing

Format   TRON
              TROFF

Examples TRON
              TROFF

Notes   Issuing TRON instructs BASIC to begin program tracing. Issuing TROFF instructs BASIC to end program tracing. When BASIC traces program execution, the line number of each executed line is displayed, enclosed in square brackets. Any BASIC commands that display output to the screen or printer actually execute. Any BASIC commands that read information for use by the program also execute.

grams that you run in a BASIC session will be traced, until you either exit BASIC, or until you issue the TROFF system command, which instructs BASIC to stop program tracing.

To better understand what TRON does, let's consider the following program:

```
100 'Sample program to READ several numbers and display average
110 '
120 SUM=0
130 COUNT=0
140 READ NUM
150 WHILE NUM<>-999
160   COUNT=COUNT+1
170   SUM=SUM+NUM
180   READ NUM
190 WEND
200 AVERAGE=SUM/COUNT
210 PRINT "Average of "COUNT" numbers is "AVERAGE
220 END
300 'Data for program
310 DATA 2,3,7,8,9,4
320 DATA 34,546,32,3,4,64,3
330 DATA -999
```

This program reads in several numbers until it reads in the number −999, which is an end-of-data marker in the program. As the program reads in each number, the variable COUNT is incremented by 1, to keep track of how many numbers are read in. After the end-of-data marker is read, the average of all numbers is calculated and displayed.

Without BASIC program tracing active, when the program is run, it will display the following:

```
Ok
run
Average of 13 numbers is 55.3077
Ok
```

If we wanted to see which lines get executed and how often they get executed, we can issue the TRON command and rerun the program. Doing so will display the following:

```
Ok
tron
Ok
run
[100] [110] [120] [130] [140] [150] [160] [170] [180] [190] [160] [170]
[180] [190] [160] [170] [180] [190] [160] [170] [180] [190] [160] [170]
[180] [190] [160] [170] [180] [190] [160] [170] [180] [190] [160] [170]
[180] [190] [160] [170] [180] [190] [160] [170] [180] [190] [160] [170]
[180] [190] [160] [170] [180] [190] [160] [170] [180] [190] [200] [210]
Average of    13 numbers is    55.3077
[220]
Ok
```

After the RUN command is issued, the line number of every line that BASIC interprets is displayed on the PC screen, inside square brackets. Notice that even though lines 100 and 110 are comments, BASIC displays those line numbers in the trace; remember that comments are read by BASIC, but are not actually executed. We can see from the trace that the FOR loop was executed thirteen times, indicated by lines 160–190 showing up in the trace repeatedly.

The TRON command can be particularly helpful when diagnosing programs with any kind of loop structure, or when a program has logic that is difficult to understand.

The STOP, PRINT, and CONT Commands

Sometimes when you are running a program, you may realize that the information the program is generating and displaying is incorrect. Unfortunately, it may be quite difficult to isolate which statement of the program is at fault. Repeated running of the program may only confound the matter, as the problem may correspond to an error in the middle of the program.

The STOP command, used in conjunction with the CONTINUE (CONT) system command, can help you check the progress of your program (see below). Specifying the STOP command in your program causes BASIC to temporarily cease interpretation of your program to allow you to check on the values of variables. This process of temporarily stopping your program is sometimes referred to as **program checkpointing**.

The STOP Statement

Purpose   To temporarily stop the interpretation of a program

Format   ln STOP
where *ln* is a valid line number

Example   100 STOP

Notes   Program execution can be restarted by issuing the CONT system command. While the program is stopped, you can display the values of variables by using the PRINT system command.

Let's change our first program to STOP after ten numbers have been read in.

```
100 'Sample program to READ several numbers and display average
110 '
120 SUM=0
130 COUNT=0
140 READ NUM
150 WHILE NUM<>-999
160   COUNT=COUNT+1
170   IF COUNT=10
        THEN STOP
180   SUM=SUM+NUM
190   READ NUM
200 WEND
210 AVERAGE=SUM/COUNT
220 PRINT "Average of "COUNT" number is "AVERAGE
230 END
300 'Data for program
310 DATA 2,3,7,8,9,4
320 DATA 34,546,32,3,4,64,3
330 DATA -999
```

We've added the IF statement in line 170 to issue the STOP command as soon as COUNT equals 10. When we run the program, the following is displayed:

```
Ok
run
Break in line 170
Ok
```

The error message "Break in line 170" is displayed because BASIC found a STOP command and ceased interpretation of the program. The "Ok" prompt is then displayed; you can now use the PRINT system command (see box below) to display the values of any variables within the program.

The PRINT System Command

Purpose   To display the values of any variables within a program

Format   PRINT variablename
where *variablename* is the name of a variable within the program

Examples   PRINT EMP.NAM$
                PRINT SALARY

Note   Multiple variables can be specified by the PRINT system command, as long as they are delimited by either commas or semicolons.

Let's assume that we thought there might be an error with the summing of the numbers. After the program is stopped, we can easily display the values of all suspect variables, without affecting the program, as shown in the following:

```
Ok
run
Break in line 170
Ok
print count
 10
Ok
print num
 3
Ok
print sum
 648
Ok
```

If you find that the values of the variables are not what you had expected, you can change the program to correct any errors you may find, and rerun the program. If you are assured that the program is running correctly, you can restart the program immediately after the STOP statement by issuing the CONT system command. You can also press function key F5 to have BASIC issue the CONT command for you. CONT tells BASIC to continue interpreting the program where it left off (see box below).

The CONT System Command

Purpose   To continue the interpretation of a program after a STOP command has been executed

Format   CONT

Example   CONT

Note   If any lines of the program are modified while the program has been stopped, the CONT command cannot be used to restart the program

---

If we issued CONT after displaying the values of COUNT, NUM, and SUM in our program, BASIC would continue interpretation of the program on line 180, and would display the average of the numbers.

```
Ok
run
Break in line 170
Ok
print count
 10
Ok
print num
 3
Ok
print sum
 648
Ok
cont
Average of 13 numbers is 55.3077
Ok
```

If you attempt to issue the CONT command when the program hasn't stopped or if you have modified the program while it was stopped, BASIC will display the error message "Can't continue."

Intercepting BASIC Errors

In some programs, you may find that you do not want BASIC to terminate a program, should some error occur. For instance, suppose you wrote a program that performed calculations on many pieces of data specified in DATA statements. It seems senseless to let BASIC cease interpretation of the program should there not be enough items in the last DATA statement to satisfy the last READ request.

When you want to allow your program to intercept common BASIC errors before BASIC ends your program, you can include the ON ERROR GOTO statement within your program. ON ERROR GOTO instructs BASIC to take an unconditional branch to the specified subroutine in the event of an error (see box below).

If you specify an ON ERROR GOTO statement in your program and an error occurs, BASIC will execute the error handling subroutine, starting at the line number you specify on the ON ERROR GOTO statement. The error handling subroutine has two distinct tasks:

1. to determine the type of error that occurred, and
2. to provide appropriate error handling code, or abort the program.

When the error handling subroutine is called in the event of an error, two system variables are assigned information; they are important when determining the severity of the error. The two system variables are ERR and ERL.

The ON ERROR GOTO Statement

Purpose   To allow a program to intercept or trap errors before BASIC terminates the program, and to specify the line number of the error handling subroutine

Format   ln ON ERROR GOTO linenum
where *ln* is a valid line number, and linenum is the line number of the error handling subroutine

Examples   200 ON ERROR GOTO 1000
550 ON ERROR GOTO 0

Note   If the line number specified after GOTO is 0, then error interception is turned off, and BASIC will display the corresponding error message and terminate the program.

The ERR system variable contains the error code of the last error that occurred in the program. When the error handling subroutine is called in the event of an error, ERR will contain a numeric code of the error that caused the error handling subroutine to be called. The ERL system variable contains the line number of the line in which BASIC detected the error.

For instance, if a division by zero were attempted on line 130, ERR would contain the value 11 (the error code for "Division by zero"), and ERL would contain 130 (the line number). If a READ statement on line 4000 was executed but there weren't enough DATA statements to satisfy it, ERR would contain the value 4 (the error code for "Out of Data"), and ERL would contain 4000. For a complete list of all BASIC error codes and their meanings, refer to the error code section in the BASIC User's Guide.

Depending on the severity of the error flagged, the error handling subroutine can take appropriate action. In instances where corrective action can take place, the error handling subroutine can display an error message describing the event and the corrective action that will take place. If the error isn't severe enough to warrant the termination of the program, the RESUME command (see box below) can be used to return control to either the command that caused the error, or to the next command.

The RESUME Command

Purpose   To continue program execution after an error handling subroutine is called

Format   ln RESUME place
where *ln* is a valid line number, and *place* is either 0, NEXT, or nothing

Examples   1540 RESUME
2020 RESUME NEXT

Notes   If 0 or nothing is specified after RESUME, then BASIC will continue interpretation at the line that caused the error. If NEXT is specified, BASIC will continue interpretation at the line immediately following the one that originally caused the error.

Let's examine the sample program below to see how an error handling subroutine works.

```
100 'Sample program to read several numbers and display average
110 '
120 'Set up error handling for program.
130 ON ERROR GOTO 300
140 SUM=0
150 COUNT=0
160 READ NUM1,NUM2,NUM3
170 WHILE NUM1<>-999
180   COUNT=COUNT+3
190   SUM=SUM+NUM1+NUM2+NUM3
200   READ NUM1,NUM2,NUM3
210 WEND
220 AVERAGE=SUM/COUNT
230 PRINT "Average of "COUNT" numbers is "AVERAGE
240 END
300 '
310 'Error handler subroutine
320 '
330 IF ERR=4
    THEN GOSUB 400: RESUME NEXT
    ELSE GOSUB 500: ON ERROR GOTO 0
340 RETURN
400 '
410 'Error handler for No more data
420 '
430 PRINT "Not enough data was specified on the DATA statements to satisfy"
440 PRINT "all read requests.  The program will continue, but you should "
450 PRINT "ensure that enough data is specified before you rerun the"
460 PRINT "program."
470 'Set NUM1 TO -999 to avoid another iteration of WHILE-WEND loop.
480 NUM1=-999
490 RETURN
500 '
510 'Error handler for all other types of errors
520 '
530 PRINT "The program cannot continue because a BASIC error occurred."
540 PRINT "The error code is "ERR" and it occurred on line "ERL"."
550 PRINT
560 PRINT "Program run aborted."
570 RETURN
600 'Data for program
610 DATA 2,3,7,8,9,4
620 DATA 34,546,32,3,4,64
630 DATA -999
```

This program shows the use of ON ERROR GOTO, RESUME, ERR, and ERL. Similar to the earlier program, this program calculates the average of numbers specified on DATA statements. The READ commands on lines 160 and 200 each read three numbers at a time; the READ command on line 200 will ultimately fail, since there aren't enough DATA items to satisfy the last READ command executed. However, since we've issued the ON ERROR GOTO command on line 130, BASIC will branch to line 300 should any error occur.

When the program attempts to READ three more numbers but there aren't enough DATA items to satisfy the request, the subroutine starting at line 300 will be called. Since we have already been accumulating all numbers in the variable SUM and keeping track of the number of numbers successfully read in the variable COUNT, if an "Out of Data" error occurs, we want to stop executing READ statements and display information about the numbers read up to the time of the error. Since we can examine the error code of the last error through the ERR system variable, the error handling subroutine at line 300 determines whether an "Out of Data" error occurred. If "Out of Data" did occur, another subroutine is called to display an informative message and to set the value of NUM1 to –999. The RESUME NEXT command on line 330 instructs BASIC to return to the next instruction after the one that caused the error.

When this program is run, BASIC will display the following:

```
Ok
run
Not enough data was specified on the DATA statements to satisfy
all read requests. The program will continue, but you should
ensure that enough data is specified before you rerun the
program.
Average of  12  numbers is   54.66667
Ok
```

If some other type of error occurs while the program is running, the error handler subroutine at 300 would be called once again, but this time the program would display a more severe error message, containing the error code and the line number of the statement in error. The ON ERROR GOTO 0 specified on line 330 prevents the error handling subroutine from being called again.

The use of an error handling subroutine, utilizing the commands described above, can help in problem determination when testing a large program. It can also make a program more user-friendly in the event of an error.

In closing, you can avoid most common types of programming errors and problems if you follow the programming techniques emphasized throughout the text and in Appendix A. The liberal use of comments throughout a program makes it much easier to read and understand; the use of constants and descriptive variables can make enhancing your programs much less prone to error. Avoid using the GOTO command to prevent errors or confusion. Using BASIC's debugging tools shown in this Appendix will help you isolate and fix any problems your programs may contain.

ASCII Character Codes

The following table shows the decimal and hexadecimal codes for ASCII characters. Special, nondisplayable codes are boldfaced. When using BASIC functions such as CHR$, be sure to specify the *decimal* code for the character that you wish to use.

Decimal	Hexadecimal	Character	Decimal	Hexadecimal	Character
000	00	**NUL**	034	22	"
001	01	**SOH**	035	23	#
002	02	**STX**	036	24	$
003	03	**ETX**	037	25	%
004	04	**EOT**	038	26	&
005	05	**ENQ**	039	27	'
006	06	**ACK**	040	28	(
007	07	**BEL**	041	29	)
008	08	**BS**	042	2A	*
009	09	**HT (Tab)**	043	2B	+
010	0A	**LF (Line Feed)**	044	2C	'
011	0B	**VT (Home)**	045	2D	-
012	0C	**FF (Form Feed)**	046	2E	.
013	0D	**CR (Carriage Return)**	047	2F	/
014	0E	**SO**	048	30	0
015	0F	**SI**	049	31	1
016	10	**DLE**	050	32	2
017	11	**DC1**	051	33	3
018	12	**DC2**	052	34	4
019	13	**DC3**	053	35	5
020	14	**DC4**	054	36	6
021	15	**NAK**	055	37	7
022	16	**SYN**	056	38	8
023	17	**ETB**	057	39	9
024	18	**CAN**	058	3A	:
025	19	**EM**	059	3B	;
026	1A	**SUB**	060	3C	<
027	1B	**ESC**	061	3D	=
028	1C	**FS**	062	3E	>
029	1D	**GS**	063	3F	?
030	1E	**RS**	064	40	@
031	1F	**US**	065	41	A
032	20	**SP**	066	42	B
033	21	!	067	43	C

Decimal	Hexadecimal	Character	Decimal	Hexadecimal	Character
068	44	D	123	7B	{
069	45	E	124	7C		
070	46	F	125	7D	}
071	47	G	126	7E	~
072	48	H	127	7F	DEL
073	49	I	128	80	Ç
074	4A	J	129	81	ü
075	4B	K	130	82	é
076	4C	L	131	83	â
077	4D	M	132	84	ä
078	4E	N	133	85	à
079	4F	O	134	86	å
080	50	P	135	87	ç
081	51	Q	136	88	ê
082	52	R	137	89	ë
083	53	S	138	8A	è
084	54	T	139	8B	ï
085	55	U	140	8C	î
086	56	V	141	8D	ì
087	57	W	142	8E	Ä
088	58	X	143	8F	Å
089	59	Y	144	90	É
090	5A	Z	145	91	æ
091	5B	[	146	92	Æ
092	5C	\	147	93	ô
093	5D	]	148	94	ö
094	5E	^	149	95	ò
095	5F	_	150	96	û
096	60	`	151	97	ù
097	61	a	152	98	ÿ
098	62	b	153	99	Ö
099	63	c	154	9A	Ü
100	64	d	155	9B	¢
101	65	e	156	9C	£
102	66	f	157	9D	¥
103	67	g	158	9E	P₁
104	68	h	159	9F	ƒ
105	69	i	160	A0	á
106	6A	j	161	A1	í
107	6B	k	162	A2	ó
108	6C	l	163	A3	ú
109	6D	m	164	A4	ñ
110	6E	n	165	A5	Ñ
111	6F	o	166	A6	ª
112	70	p	167	A7	º
113	71	q	168	A8	¿
114	72	r	169	A9	⌐
115	73	s	170	AA	¬
116	74	t	171	AB	½
117	75	u	172	AC	¼
118	76	v	173	AD	¡
119	77	w	174	AE	«
120	78	x	175	AF	»
121	79	y	176	B0	
122	7A	z	177	B1	

Decimal	Hexadecimal	Character		Decimal	Hexadecimal	Character
178	B2	▒		233	E9	θ
179	B3	│		234	EA	Ω
180	B4	┤		235	EB	δ
181	B5	╡		236	EC	∞
182	B6	╢		237	ED	ϕ
183	B7	╖		238	EE	ϵ
184	B8	╕		239	EF	$\cap$
185	B9	╣		240	F0	$\equiv$
186	BA	║		241	F1	$\pm$
187	BB	╗		242	F2	$\geq$
188	BC	╝		243	F3	$\leq$
189	BD	╜		244	F4	$\lceil$
190	BE	╛		245	F5	$\rfloor$
191	BF	┐		246	F6	$\div$
192	C0	└		247	F7	$\approx$
193	C1	┴		248	F8	$\circ$
194	C2	┬		249	F9	$\bullet$
195	C3	├		250	FA	$\cdot$
196	C4	─		251	FB	$\sqrt{}$
197	C5	┼		252	FC	^{n}
198	C6	╞		253	FD	^{2}
199	C7	╟		254	FE	■
200	C8	╚		255	FF	(blank 'FF')
201	C9	╔				
202	CA	╩				
203	CB	╦				
204	CC	╠				
205	CD	═				
206	CE	╬				
207	CF	╧				
208	D0	╨				
209	D1	╤				
210	D2	╥				
211	D3	╙				
212	D4	╘				
213	D5	╒				
214	D6	╓				
215	D7	╫				
216	D8	╪				
217	D9	┘				
218	DA	┌				
219	DB	█				
220	DC	▄				
221	DD	▌				
222	DE	▐				
223	DF	▀				
224	E0	α				
225	E1	β				
226	E2	Γ				
227	E3	π				
228	E4	Σ				
229	E5	σ				
230	E6	μ				
231	E7	τ				
232	E8	Φ				

BASIC Quick Reference Guide

The following quick reference list describes the commands, functions, and system variables that have been covered in the text. For a complete list of DOS commands, refer to the DOS Reference Guide. For a complete list of BASIC commands, functions, and system variables, refer to the DOS BASIC Reference Guide.

Table D.1 DOS Commands

Command Name	Description	Page
CD	Change current directory (Same as CHDIR)	56
CHDIR	Change current directory (Same as CD)	56
CHKDSK	Scan specified disk for errors	39
CLS	Clear the PC screen	40
COPY	Copy a file to another name or location	42
DATE	Change or display the date in the PC clock	63
DIR	Display the names of files on a DOS disk	30
DISKCOPY	Copy the contents of one diskette to another	45
ERASE	Delete the specified file or files	49
FORMAT	Format the specified disk for DOS use	40
MD	Make a directory (Same as MKDIR)	56
MKDIR	Make a directory (Same as MD)	56
PRINT	Print a DOS file on a printer	53
RD	Remove a directory (Same as RMDIR)	57
RENAME,REN	Rename a file	47
RMDIR	Remove a directory (Same as RD)	57
TIME	Change or display the time in the PC clock	63
TYPE	Display the contents of a DOS file on the screen	52

Table D.2 BASIC Program Statements

Command Name	Description	Page
CLOSE	De-allocate a file opened by an OPEN statement	283
CLS	Clear the PC screen	120
DATA	Specify numeric or string information in program	202
DEF FN(variable)	Create a user-defined function	248
DIM	Define size of an array	261
END	Terminate program execution	72
FOR/NEXT	Execute section of code a given number of times	186

Table D.2   BASIC Program Statements (Continued)

Command Name	Description	Page
GOSUB	Perform unconditional branch to subroutine	155
GOTO	Perform unconditional branch with no return	170
IF-THEN	Make a decision based on expression	126
IF-THEN-ELSE	Make an extended decision based on expression	134
INPUT	Prompt user for input and read information	110
INPUT#	Read information from sequential file	288
KEY	Turn line 25 key display on or off	120
LET	Assign a value to a variable	73
LPRINT	Print information on a line printer	225
LPRINT USING	Print formatted information on a line printer	225
ON ERROR GOTO	Enable, disable, identify error handling routine	310
ON-GOSUB	Perform conditional branch to subroutine	176
ON-GOTO	Perform conditional branch with no return	178
OPEN	Prepare a file for input/output operations	282
PRINT	Print information on the PC screen	112
PRINT #	Create output file on disk for printing	290
PRINT USING	Print formatted information on the PC screen	218
READ	Read information from a DATA statement	204
REM	Define a comment within a program (can also use ')	71
RESTORE	Reset BASIC pointer to a DATA statement	214
RESUME	Return to program after error handling routine	310
RETURN	Terminate subroutine and return to main program	156
STOP	Temporarily stop execution of program	307
SWAP	Exchange the values of two variables	274
WHILE/WEND	Execute section of code conditionally	194
WRITE #	Create output file suitable for use by INPUT #	285

Table D.3   BASIC System Commands

Command Name	Description	Page
CLS	Clear the PC screen	120
CONT	Continue execution of program after STOP statement	308
DELETE	Delete specified lines from program	96
EDIT	Edit specified line	93
FILES	Display names of files on specified DOS disk	100
KEY	Turn line 25 key display on and off	120
LIST	Display specified lines of program on PC screen	92
LLIST	Print specified lines of program on printer	93
LOAD	Read and load program into memory	101
NEW	Clear memory of any previous program	88
PRINT	Display values of variables	308
RENUM	Renumber lines within a program in memory	97
RUN	Begin execution of program in memory	90
SAVE	Save program in memory to disk	98
SYSTEM	Exit BASIC and return to DOS	103
TROFF	Turn BASIC tracing off	305
TRON	Turn BASIC tracing on	305

Table D.4   BASIC Functions

Function Name	Description	Page
ABS	Returns the positive value of the specified number	235
ASC	Returns the two-digit ASCII code of the first character of the specified string	245
CHR$	Returns the single character that corresponds in ASCII code to the specified number	225
EOF	Returns 1 if the end of the specified file has been reached	288
FIX	Returns the integer part of the specified number	236
INSTR	Returns the beginning position of one string in another string	241
INT	Returns the greatest whole number less than or equal to the number specified	235
LEFT$	Extracts characters from the left side of a string	238
LEN	Returns the length of the specified string	240
MID$	Extracts characters from anywhere within another string	239
RIGHT$	Extracts characters from the right side of a string	239
SPACE$	Returns the specified number of spaces	244
SPC	Skip a specified number of spaces in a PRINT or LPRINT statement	217
STRING$	Returns a specified number of copies of the first character of a specified string	244
STR$	Returns the string equivalent of the specified number	246
TAB	Skips to the specified column in a PRINT or LPRINT statement	216
VAL	Returns the numeric equivalent of the specified string	247

Table D.5   BASIC System Variables

Command Name	Description	Page
DATE$	Contains the current date from the PC clock	79
ERL	Contains the line number of the last line that caused an error	310
ERR	Contains the error code of the last error	310
TIME$	Contains the current time from the PC clock	79

Glossary

ABEND see *abnormal ending*.

abnormal ending the termination of a program before its execution is completed.

accumulator a variable used to store the running total when summing a list of numbers.

adapter (also called an **expansion card**) a circuit board that connects a microcomputer to some external input or output device.

address a pointer to a particular location in the computer's memory. Addresses are used to refer to values stored in memory.

algorithm a step-by-step description of how to perform a particular task.

application package a program that enables a computer to accomplish useful tasks.

archive attribute a file attribute that is turned on when the file has been changed since the last time it was backed up.

argument a value that is passed to a function. Functions use one or more arguments.

array a group of values stored in a list or table format which are referred to by a single variable name. See also *one-dimensional array, two-dimensional array*, and *three-dimensional array*.

ASCII the acronym for American National Standard Code for Information Interchange. ASCII is a set of standard character codes used for information storage on many different kinds of computers.

assignment statement a statement that assigns a value to a variable. This is often referred to as a "LET" statement.

BASIC the acronym for Beginner's All-purpose Symbolic Instruction Code. BASIC is an easy-to-use programming language that was developed by Professors John Kemeny and Thomas Kurtz of Dartmouth College.

BASIC system commands commands that allow the programmer to edit, list, or run a BASIC program, as well as many other operations.

bit the basic unit of data processing; 0 or 1, off or on.

block any section of text, from a single character to a whole document, that can be marked and treated as a single entity.

boot up to load the operating system into a computer's primary memory and begin its execution.

branch to jump from one instruction to another. See also *conditional branch* and *unconditional branch*.

browse to skim through the records of a data base.

bubble sort a technique for sorting an array of data in ascending or alphabetical order.

bug an error or problem in a computer program.

bus a set of wires and connectors that links the CPU to memory and other computer components.

byte a contiguous group of eight bits; the amount of memory it takes to store a single character.

calling a subroutine the process of branching to a subroutine from a main section of code.

character any single letter, number, punctuation mark, or symbol. It is important to note that the computer interprets spaces as characters also.

chip see *integrated circuit chip*.

code page a conversion table that tells DOS how to translate data stored as numeric values into letters, numbers, punctuation, and other symbols to be displayed or printed.

color graphics monitor a monitor that can display both text and graphics in more than one color.

command processor the program in an operating system that translates and acts on the commands entered by the user.

compiler a software program which translates a program written in a programming language into machine code. See also *source file* and *module*.

computer an electronic device that performs calculations and processes data into information.

concatenation merging two smaller character strings together to produce a larger character string.

conditional branch a statement that will sometimes cause a program to leave its normal flow and execute statements at another section, depending on whether certain conditions are met. An ON-GOSUB is an example of a conditional branch. See also *branch* and *unconditional branch*.

control panel lines at the top or bottom of the screen used to display information, messages, menu choices, and prompts.

cross loop loops that overlap, thus creating an error.

CPU central processing unit; the part of a computer that performs control operations, calculations, and logic.

cursor a small, blinking underscore or box that marks the position where characters appear on the screen when typed.

cut and paste the process of marking a block of text and moving it from one location in a document file to another location.

daisy-wheel printer a printer with solid, raised characters embossed on the ends of little arms arranged like the spokes of a wheel; for producing slow, but letter-quality output.

data numbers, text, pictures, sounds that are to be processed into information.

data base an organized collection of one or more files of related data.

data base management package software that lets you create, add to, delete from, update, rearrange, select from, print out, and otherwise administer data files such as mailing lists and inventories.

debug to remove the bugs from an imperfect computer program.

default the predefined settings for certain features (margins, line spacing, column widths, etc.) that a software package uses automatically when alternate settings have not been explicitly established.

delete to remove, erase, or destroy one or more pieces of information.

delimit to separate one item from another. On DATA statements, the comma is used to delimit one item for another.

descriptive variables a variable whose name describes the type of values that the variable can hold. The use of descriptive variables is good programming practice.

descriptor field an area in a PRINT USING template that dictates how information will be formatted. Special symbols are used within each descriptor field to specify how to format output.

desktop publishing the use of a computer and laser printer to produce near-typeset quality documents.

device controller a set of chips or a circuit board that operates a piece of computer equipment such as a disk drive, display, keyboard, mouse, or printer.

device driver a file in an operating system that contains the programming code needed to attach and use some special devices.

dimensioning defining the size of an array. In BASIC, the DIM command is used to define the size and number of dimensions of an array.

directory a list of the files stored on a disk; another term for subdirectory.

disk a medium, consisting of one or more flat surfaces on which bits are usually recorded magnetically, used by computers to store information.

disk buffer an area of memory that DOS uses to temporarily hold data being read from or written to a disk.

disk drive a computer system component that reads and writes programs and data on disks.

diskette a floppy disk.

display output screen on which the computer presents text and graphic images; monitor.

display adapter a circuit board or set of chips that controls a monitor.

document the paper output of a word processor.

documentation the user manual or technical information about a computer or software package.

document file a collection of text created by a word processing program in such a way that the text includes embedded formatting codes.

DOS disk operating system; an operating system that is stored on a disk.

DOS shell a program that enhances PC-DOS or MS-DOS.

dot-matrix printer a common type of printer that constructs character images by repeatedly striking pins against the ribbon and paper.

draft mode the fastest print mode, in which low-quality characters are formed by a single pass of the printhead.

edit to make changes to a file.

editor a software program included as part of the computer's operating system that allows you to input and change files.

element the value stored in a particular location within an array. See also *index*.

end-of-data-marker an item specified as last in a data list, thus marking the end of the data list.

endless loop see *infinite loop*.

EOF flag an indicator that determines if the last record of a file has been read. In BASIC, the EOF function is used to check for an end-of-file condition.

error message a message indicating that an error has occurred. In BASIC, an error message is usually displayed only when a program can no longer execute.

expansion board a circuit board that plugs into an expansion slot.

expansion slot an internal connector that extends a computer's bus and accepts an additional circuit board.

expert system a computer program that contains a collection of facts and a list of rules for making inferences about those facts.

export to produce a file with one software package that is ultimately to be used by some other software package.

field a group of related characters in a data base record.

file a collection of information stored on a disk and loaded into primary memory when needed by a program; in a data base, a group of related records.

file attribute a characteristic of a DOS file such as *read-only* or *archive*.

file locking a feature of DOS that allows only one person to use a file or part of a file at a time.

file sharing a feature of DOS that allows two or more people to use the same file at the same time.

filter a program that accepts data as input, processes them in some way, then outputs them in a different form.

floppy disk an inexpensive, flexible magnetic medium for storing computer programs and data.

floppy disk drive a disk drive that accepts floppy disks.

flowchart a graphic representation of an algorithm using various symbols to denote certain operations.

function a procedure designed to perform a specific task in order to return a single value to a specific location in a program or subroutine.

function keys on an IBM-compatible computer, the keys on the left side or top of the keyboard labeled F1 through F10 or F12. Such keys are usually used to perform common operations with different software packages.

global pertaining to or acting upon an entire document, spreadsheet, or data base file.

graphics any kind of graphs, plots, drawings, and other images not restricted to text characters.

hard disk a high-capacity, completely-enclosed, rigid magnetic medium for storing computer programs and data.

hard disk drive a disk drive that contains one or more hard disks.

hardware the physical components of a computer system.

high-level languages programming languages with Englishlike statements, generally used in the creation of applications software.

IBM-compatible any computer that works like a comparable IBM model and can run the same software.

import to use a file in one software package that was originally produced in another software package.

index a numeric value that indicates the position of a particular element within an array.

infinite loop a program containing a loop structure where the condition to exit the loop can never become true. As a result, the process will continue indefinitely.

information a more organized and useful form of input data.

initialize the action of assigning a value to a variable before that variable is used in other statements within a program. Before using a variable as an accumulator, it is necessary to initialize the variable to zero.

ink-jet printer a printer with a mechanism for squirting tiny droplets of ink to form text and graphics on paper.

input any data or information entered into a computer.

integrated circuit chip a thin slice of semiconductor material, such as pure silicon crystal, impregnated with carefully selected impurities; commonly used in computers and many other electronic devices.

integrated software a package that combines word processing, spreadsheet, data base management, communications, and graphics applications.

interpreter a software program that translates a program written in a programming language into machine code a line at a time. GWBASIC is an example of an interpreter.

iteration one execution of all statements defined within a loop.

K the abbreviation for kilobyte; 1K = 1024 bytes.

keyboard the device with which you type input into the computer.

laser printer a high-quality printer that uses tightly-focused beams of light to transfer images to paper.

letter-quality like the output of a good electric typewriter.

line number a whole number from 1 to 65528 that BASIC uses to determine the order in which lines in a program are executed.

list format the way in which items on DATA statements are stored in memory. The first item on the first DATA statement in a program will be the first item in the list, followed by the second item of the first DATA statement, etc.

load to copy a program or data file from disk into memory.

local area network (LAN) a system in which several microcomputers are connected together so that they can share hardware, software, and data.

logical operator a special operator that allows the evaluation or negation of multiple conditional clauses. The three logical operators available in BASIC are AND, OR, and NOT.

loop a method of repetitive processing.

low-level languages programming languages composed of machine or assembly languages. They are usually machine-specific.

M the abbreviation for megabyte; 1M = 1,048,576 bytes.

machine code the series of 1s and 0s that make up the only language that hardware can understand.

magnetic disk a semi-permanent storage medium that can be erased and written over and over again.

memory the part of the computer that stores programs and data temporarily.

menu a list of options available in a program.

microcomputer a small computer that uses a single microprocessor chip as its central processing unit.

microprocessor a central processing unit made up of a single integrated circuit chip.

modem *mo*dulator-*dem*odulator; a device that enables a computer to transmit and receive programs and data over ordinary phone lines.

module a file containing machine code, created from a source file by a compiler.

monitor a computer display screen.

monochrome graphics monitor a single-color screen that can display both text and graphics.

monochrome text monitor a single-color screen that displays sharply-defined characters, but no graphics.

motherboard the main circuit board of a computer.

mouse an input device consisting of a small box with one or more buttons that is slid across the table top and allows the user to manipulate objects on the screen and select menu options.

nested IF statements an IF-THEN or an IF-THEN-ELSE statement that has a THEN or ELSE expression that is another IF-THEN or IF-THEN-ELSE statement.

nested loop a loop defined completely within another loop.

NLQ near letter quality; a dot-matrix print mode that produces attractive output by having the printhead make two or more passes over each character.

numeric keypad on an IBM-compatible computer, the area on the right side of the keyboard arranged like the number keys on a calculator.

object file see *module*.

one-dimensional array an array defined to hold one list of elements.

on-line connected to and controlled by the computer.

operand see *operator*.

operating system the software that controls and supports a computer system's hardware.

operator a special symbol denoting an arithmetic operation between two numeric values. The "+" symbol can also denote a concatenation of two string values.

output any information produced by the computer; the computer's responses to a user's input.

partition a section of a hard disk that contains an operating system.

personal computer a microcomputer.

piping a feature of DOS, symbolized by the | (vertical bar), that allows the user to take the output of one command that would normally go to the display screen and feed it as input to another command.

pixel picture element; a tiny dot on a computer display.

pointer see *address*.

populating an array the action of initially assigning values to each element in an array.

portable programs programs that can be run by several types of computers with little or no modification.

primary memory where a computer stores the programs and data it is currently using.

printer a device for producing computer output on paper.

print zone the five equal sections of fourteen spaces each contained within the first 70 character spaces on each line of a screen.

program a sequence of step-by-step instructions that run a computer.

program checkpointing temporarily stopping a program to check the values of variables.

programmer a person who creates computer programs.

programming language a set of symbols and rules to direct the operations of a computer.

project management package software to help you formally plan and control a complex undertaking.

prompt a symbol or statement that indicates the computer is waiting for a response from the user.

pseudocode an Englishlike description of all steps in an algorithm.

RAM Random Access Memory; the portion of a computer's primary memory used to store programs and data temporarily; also known as read/write memory.

read-only attribute a file attribute that, when turned on, prevents a file from being changed or deleted.

record a collection of related data items.

recursion a subroutine that calls itself repetitively.

redirection a feature of DOS, symbolized by >, <, >>, that allows you to send the output of a command to some other program or output device.

relational data base a data base that is organized in two-dimensional tables of rows (records) and columns (fields).

relational operators special symbols used in conditional clauses that allow comparisons to be made between values. The valid relational operators are <, >, =, <=, >=, and <>.

replaceable parameter a feature of DOS that allows the user to pass information to a batch file while it is running.

resolution the sharpness of a display screen.

ROM Read Only Memory; permanent primary storage that is encoded with programs and data at the factory, and can be read and used, but never erased, changed, or augmented, by the user.

scroll to shift what is on a computer display screen so that other areas are visible.

separator a special character used to separate items on a PRINT statement. The comma and semicolon are two examples of separators.

sequential files a collection of records that are read or written in sequential order.

software a program or set of programs that tells a computer system what to do.

sort to arrange the records of a data structure in some particular order.

source code the collection of programming language instructions in a source file.

source file a file containing source code, used as input to a compiler or an interpreter.

spreadsheet a table of columns and rows of numbers, text labels, and formulas used in an electronic spreadsheet package for the manipulation of numerical, financial, and accounting data.

spreadsheet package software that lets you manipulate spreadsheets.

string a collection of characters. A string can consist of letters, numbers, punctuation, or any other characters that can be typed on a keyboard.

string variable a location in memory that can hold a collection of characters consisting of letters, numbers, punctuation, or any other characters that can be typed on a keyboard.

structured programming a programming technique that dictates modular, efficient design, *without the use of GOTO statements*. This is often referred to as top-down programming.

subroutine an independent group of statements that is located outside the main program. A subroutine performs a separate, limited task.

substring a portion or part of a string.

system board the main circuit board of a computer.

system software the software that handles the many details of managing a computer system.

system unit in IBM-compatible computers, the box that contains the central processing unit, memory, circuit boards, disk drives, and power switch for the system.

system variable a location in memory that holds a value that is assigned by the user and defined by the operating system. DATE$ is an example of a system variable.

template a string that describes where and how information will be printed on a PRINT USING statement.

three-dimensional array an array defined to hold multiple tables of elements. A three-dimensional array can be thought of as a cube.

top-down programming see *structured programming*.

trailer record see *end-of-data marker*.

truth table a table showing the results for all conditions when using a specific logical operator or set of logical operators.

two-dimensional array an array defined to hold a table of elements. A two-dimensional array can be thought of as a flat surface.

type violation the attempt to assign an incompatible variable in an assignment statement. For example, if you are attempting to assign a string to a numeric variable, the type violation message will appear.

unconditional branch a statement that will always cause a program to leave its normal flow and execute statements in another location. For example, a GOSUB statement will cause an unconditional branch. See also *branch* and *conditional branch*.

upwardly compatible an operating system or software package that adds new capabilities, yet retains all previous features.

user-defined variable a variable that the programmer creates and defines.

utility a small, specific program that adds handy features to a particular operating system or application package.

variable a name that identifies the location of a particular value in the computer's memory.

windowing environment software that allows you to divide your screen into two or more boxes and run a separate program in each one.

word processing package a software package used to create, enter, edit, format, store, and print documents.

Answers to Exercises

Chapter 1   The Microcomputer

Multiple Choice

1. c	6. c	11. a	16. c
2. a	7. c	12. b	17. d
3. d	8. b	13. a	18. c
4. b	9. a	14. b	19. b
5. a	10. d	15. d	20. c

Fill-In

1. IBM-compatible	11. dot-matrix
2. processing	12. software
3. hardware	13. languages
4. bus	14. application
5. RAM, ROM	15. graphics
6. hard disk drives	16. desktop publishing or page layout
7. pixels	17. integrated
8. VGA	18. windowing
9. mouse	19. project
10. cursor	20. expert

Chapter 2   The DOS Operating System

Multiple Choice

1. c	6. a	11. d	16. a
2. b	7. c	12. b	17. b
3. a	8. c	13. c	18. d
4. d	9. b	14. d	19. c
5. d	10. a	15. b	20. a

Fill-In

1. files	6. eight
2. PC-DOS, MS-DOS	7. classify
3. memory	8. Escape or Esc
4. date, time	9. Ctrl-Break
5. DIR	10. prompt

11. CHKDSK
12. formatted
13. COPY
14. global
15. format

16. rename
17. ERASE or DEL
18. text
19. PRINT
20. MD or MKDIR, CD or CHDIR, RD or RMDIR

Chapter 3   Introduction to BASIC

True or False

1. False
2. True
3. False
4. True
5. True

6. False
7. False
8. True
9. True
10. False

Fill-In

1. Low-level
2. portable
3. compiler, interpreter
4. variable
5. Single precision

6. reserved keywords
7. parentheses
8. concatenated
9. DATE$, TIME$
10. Comments

Short Answer

1. Programs written in high-level languages are easier to read and write, as well as debug, due to the readability of the code. They also tend to be more portable than programs written in low-level languages.

2. A compiler takes an entire source file and creates a text deck or load module of machine code that can then be executed. An interpreter converts each line of the source code and then executes that line of code before proceeding to the next line of code, and continues doing this until the entire program is executed.

3. Comment statements are used to describe the purpose of the program, identify the author, environment, and creation date of a program, as well as describe each step of the program so that it can be easily understood.

4. A variable is a name that is assigned to represent a location in memory where a value is stored.

5. The order of operation for numerical expressions is:
   (a) Any expressions within parentheses are evaluated first.
   (b) Exponentiation and negation are evaluated next, from left to right.
   (c) Multiplication and division are evaluated next, from left to right.
   (d) Addition and subtraction are evaluated last, from left to right.

Programming Problems

1. (a) Valid
   (b) Invalid (spaces are not allowed)
   (c) Valid
   (d) Valid
   (e) Invalid (cannot start with a number)
   (f) Invalid (cannot use a dash)
   (g) Invalid (cannot start with a $)
   (h) Valid

2. (a) −9
   (b) 11
   (c) 6
   (d) 5
   (e) 15

Chapter 4   Introducing Microsoft's BASIC

True or False

1. True
2. False
3. False
4. True
5. False
6. False
7. False
8. False
9. False
10. False

Fill-In

1. System commands
2. NEW
3. LIST, LLIST
4. RENUM
5. floppy disk, hard disk
6. .BAS
7. DIR
8. memory
9. CLS
10. SYSTEM

Short Answer

1. If you make several changes to a program, including the addition of several lines, your program may contain sections of code where the lines are numbered consecutively, in increments of 1. If you need to add more lines to your program, you may not be able to as there might not be "free" line numbers in certain places of your program. In this case, you would use the RENUM command to allow the insertion of lines.

2. If the line to be duplicated appears on the screen, you can move the cursor up to the line, change the line number by typing over the existing line number, and change anything else on the line. After making all required changes, you must press the Enter key while the cursor is on that line. You can also issue the EDIT system command for the line to be duplicated, and follow the same procedure as described above, of changing the line number and anything else on the line, and then pressing the Enter key.

3. You can key in the line number of the line to be deleted, and then press the Enter key, or you can use the DELETE system command to delete a line or group of lines from a program.

4. When you issue the CLS command, any text on the PC screen would be erased except for the 25th (key display) line of the screen, and the cursor would be displayed on the upper left-hand corner of the

screen, beneath the "OK" prompt. If you then issued the SYSTEM command, you would end your BASIC session, your program would be lost, and you would return to DOS.

5. When you issue the FILES command, the names of files on the current disk drive would be displayed on the PC screen. When you issue the LOAD command, a BASIC program would be loaded into memory, overwriting the program that you keyed in. The program that you keyed in would be lost.

6. One way is to issue the LIST command once again. When you see line 400 on the screen, press the CONTROL and NUMLOCK keys at the same time. Another way is to issue the LIST command, specifying the range of lines you want to see, in this case 200–400. Another way is to use the LLIST command, to print a copy of your program to a printer.

Programming Problems

1. (a) Invalid (spaces in line number)
   (b) Valid
   (c) Invalid (must enter a command after a line number)
   (d) Invalid (space needed after line number and before single quote)

Chapter 5   Input and Output Using BASIC

True or False

1. False
2. True
3. True
4. True
5. False

6. False
7. False
8. False
9. True
10. True

Fill-In

1. INPUT
2. ?
3. PRINT
4. blank line
5. double quotes

6. zones or columns
7. 5, 14
8. semicolon, comma
9. CLS
10. KEY

Short Answer

1. By using the INPUT statement in a BASIC program, greater flexibility is added since a user can run the same program for a variety of data values without having to change the source code.

2. A "Redo from start" message would be issued if an incorrect data type were provided as data to be assigned to an INPUT variable. For example, if an INPUT statement, such as 250 INPUT SIZE, SHAPE$, COLOR$ were executed, and data *big*, *round*, *green* were entered, the error would occur because a character string "BIG" was given where the INPUT statement was expecting a number.

3. Yes. You could use the PRINT command to display the prompt message immediately before the INPUT command. The cursor could remain on the same line as the prompt message text if you put a semicolon after the message text in the PRINT command.

4. You should use a comma as a separator between items if you want to display output in tabular format and you are not printing more than 5 columns of data and each column no wider than 14 characters. You should use a semicolon as a separator between items if you are printing more than 5 columns of data; though using a semicolon does not necessarily generate tabular reports. If a program were to display information pertaining to a customer's account at a bank, such as the customer's last name, social security number, bank account number, and total amount invested at the bank, you would want to use commas as separators. If the program were to also display the customer's first name, mother's maiden name, and phone number, you would want to use semicolons as separators.

Chapter 6   Decision Making

True or False

1. True
2. False
3. False
4. True
5. True

6. False
7. False
8. False
9. True
10. False

Fill-In

1. IF-THEN
2. CONTROL, Enter
3. relational operators
4. ASCII code
5. Logical operators

6. OR
7. false
8. truth table
9. NOT, AND, OR
10. indent

Short Answer

1. The six relational operators are the equal to (=), less than (<), greater than (>), less than or equal to (<=), greater than or equal to (>=), and not equal to (<>) signs. The purpose of relational operators is to give a means of comparing to values, and returning a value of true or false depending on whether the condition is true or false.

2. Character strings are compared one character at a time, going from left to right, based on the numeric value of the ASCII code for each given character being compared.

3. The logical operator AND allows for the evaluation of two conditions; if both those conditions are true, then the expression consisting of the two conditions separated with the AND is true. If either or both conditions are false, the expression is false. The logical operator OR does basically the same thing, except that if either or both of the two conditions are true, the expression is true. If both conditions are false, the expression is false. The NOT operator returns the opposite value of the condition evaluated, so if the condition is true, then NOT condition is false, and vice versa.

4. In an IF-THEN statement, an expression is executed only if a condition proves to be true. If the condition is false, then the program continues executing at the next line in sequence after the IF-THEN. For an IF-THEN-ELSE, in addition to being able to execute an expression if a condition is true, there is also an expression that will be executed if the condition is false.

5. When writing IF statements of any complexity, it would be difficult to fit the entire statement on a single line. This is especially true for nested IF statements. Since the statement is going to span multiple lines, and there can be several THENs and ELSEs if the statement is a nested IF, it can become very difficult to match which IF goes with which THEN and/or ELSE. Indentation is used to line up the THENs and ELSEs, to show that they are continuations of that statement.

Programming Problems

1. (a) True
   (b) False
   (c) True
   (d) False
   (e) True
   (f) False
   (g) True

2. (a) False
   (b) True
   (c) True
   (d) False
   (e) True
   (f) True
   (g) False

3. (a) False
   (b) True
   (c) True
   (d) False
   (e) True

Chapter 7   Unconditional Branching

True or False

1. False
2. True
3. True
4. False
5. False
6. False
7. True
8. True
9. False
10. False

Fill-In

1. unconditional branch
2. GOSUB
3. calling
4. recursion
5. GOTO
6. menu
7. ON-GOSUB
8. RETURN
9. ON-GOTO
10. top-down

Short Answer

1. When GOSUB is used in conjunction with the RETURN statement, BASIC remembers the line number of the next statement after the GOSUB statement. While GOSUB causes an unconditional branch, the use of the RETURN statement forces control to return to the line after the GOSUB. If you used the GOTO statement, the programmer would be forced to return execution to the line following the GOTO.

2. In addition to providing greater readability, subroutines should be placed at the end of the program, following an END statement, to prevent them from being executed as part of the main program rather than being called via a GOSUB statement.

3. Yes, a subroutine can call itself. This is known as recursion. This, however, is not necessarily good programming style, as a subroutine that indiscriminately calls itself may lead to an infinite loop, resulting in a message: "Out of memory in <ln>."

4. By the very nature of the ON-GOSUB statement, it lends itself very nicely to the development of menus. The ON-GOSUB statement branches to a designated subroutine based on the numeric value of a variable. This allows for a list of all possible options to be displayed, with a number representing each possible choice. When an option is selected, the ON-GOSUB branches to the appropriate subroutine.

5. A well-structured program is easy to modify in comparison to a poorly structured one because of the top-down approach with which a structured program is written. This approach means that if a change is going to be made, none of the lines of code above the modification are affected, and only the lines of code immediately following the changes are directly affected. This is different from an unstructured program where unconditional branching using GOTOs could lead to statements in other sections of the program being affected by a change.

Chapter 8   Looping

True or False

1. False	6. True
2. True	7. False
3. False	8. True
4. False	9. True
5. True	10. False

Fill-In

1. accumulator	6. relational, logical
2. WHILE/WEND	7. endless, infinite
3. NEXT	8. ABEND
4. nested	9. TO
5. STEP	10. cross

Short Answer

1. A loop is used when a certain section of code should be repeated for a specified number of times or until a given condition is no longer met. The loop prevents the need to code the same section of code multiple times.

2. The fundamental difference between a FOR/NEXT loop and a WHILE/WEND loop is in how to specify when the loop stops looping. When using the FOR/NEXT loop, the loop stops after a certain number of iterations are complete. The WHILE/WEND loop keeps looping until a designated condition is no longer true.

3. To prevent WHILE/WEND loops from becoming infinite loops, there must exist a condition within the loop that will eventually become false. To accomplish this, it is important to ensure that some event will change a variable which is in the WHILE conditional expression and that condition will become false.

4. A nested loop is a FOR/NEXT loop or a WHILE/WEND loop that resides inside another FOR/NEXT or WHILE/WEND loop. This allows the inside loop to be executed multiple times for each iteration of the outside loop.

5. The START, MAXIMUM, or STEP values should not be changed within the FOR/NEXT loop primarily because this could produce unpredictable results. This may create an endless loop, terminate the program, or complete successfully with incorrect results.

Chapter 9   Advanced I/O

True or False

1. False
2. True
3. False
4. True
5. True
6. False
7. False
8. True
9. False
10. True

Fill-In

1. list format
2. separator, delimiter
3. pointer, address
4. end-of-data
5. RESTORE
6. TAB function
7. templates
8. $$
9. !
10. LPRINT CHR$(12)

Short Answer

1. You could have the first data item in the list set to the number of data items that follow. The program would then have to have a READ statement that would assign this value to a variable, which could then be used within a FOR/NEXT clause. This method is not better than using end-of-data markers as it still forces the programmer to have to count the number of data items; this is time consuming for large lists of data, and is prone to error.

2. If end-of-data markers weren't unique, the program would cease to read in new data as soon as a marker was read in. This would potentially prevent the program from reading in all data, should an end-of-data marker be located in the middle of the data.

3. If the DATA statements contain odd numbers of sets of data, using RESTORE with a line number may indiscriminately cause READ statements to read data out of sequence. This could cause a program to fail, particularly if different types of data are specified in the DATA statements.

4. (a) The statement must have commas separating the data items 89, 55, and 43.
   (b) Each character string specified on a DATA statement must have double quotes at the beginning and end of the string.
   (c) You cannot use the semicolon as a delimiter on a DATA statement; the comma is always used as a delimiter.
   (d) Each character string specified on a DATA statement must have double quotes at the beginning and end of the string. Each of the strings has single quotes, which are invalid.
   (e) You cannot use the semicolon as a delimiter of items on a READ command; you can only use a comma.
   (f) The RESTORE command takes either no item or a line number. F above shows an invalid example of specifying a string.
   (g) The PRINT command does not have a closing double quote for the string "Total amount in checks is $".
   (h) The TAB function only allows numbers 1 through 255 to be specified. TAB(300) is therefore invalid.

5. (a) PRINT USING "!_. & phone number is &"; FIRSTNAM$,LASTNAM$,PHONE$
   (b) PRINT USING "& lives in & on &"; FIRSTNAM$,TOWN$,STREETAD$
   (c) PRINT USING "& lives in & on \   \";FIRSTNAM$,TOWN$,STREETAD$
   (d) PRINT USING "& lives somewhere in &";FIRSTNAM$,TOWN$
   (e) PRINT USING "!_. & made $$##,###.## in commission last year_.";
       FIRSTNAM$,LASTNAM$, COMMISSION

6. (a) Pay to the order of John H. Smith   ****7,342.45
   (b) Smith, J   765-43-2100   Entertainer $55,673.99
   (c) Left-handed widget   456   6.39 $2,913.84
   (d) Profit for Acme Inc. was $23432.00+
   (e) Profit for ZZ Co. was $3423.93–
   (f) John H. Smith,   1515 Chest   33030 $7342.45
   (g) J. H. Smith
   (h) Pay to the order of John H. Smith   %$55673.99

Chapter 10   Functions

True or False

1. False
2. True
3. False
4. False
5. True

6. True
7. False
8. True
9. False
10. True

Fill-In

1. returns	6. LEN
2. arguments	7. first character
3. FIX, INT	8. STR$, VAL
4. ABS	9. DEF FN
5. MID$	10. $

Short Answer

1. (a) The INT function returns a numeric result, which can not be assigned to a string variable.
   (b) The MID$ function requires a first argument of the string type.
   (c) The length argument of the RIGHT$ function cannot be a negative number.
   (d) A user-defined function name must begin with the characters "FN".
   (e) The MID$ function requires a first argument of the string type.
   (f) The INSTR function returns a number; the LEFT$ function requires a first argument of the string type, which is not being returned by the INSTR function.
   (g) The INSTR function returns a number; the conditional expression is invalid as it is testing the equality of a number to a string.

2. (a) "Vi"
   (b) "perations"
   (c) "Vice-President of Operations"
   (d) "of"
   (e) "President"
   (f) "President of Operations"
   (g) 28
   (h) 6

3. (a) 355.42
   (b) "$199,355.4211"
   (c) ",,,,,,,,,,,"
   (d) "Bravo!"
   (e) "   "

4. A function returns a value, while a subroutine does not. A function must be called with arguments, while a subroutine does not take any arguments. A function call can be used anywhere within any numeric or string expression, while a subroutine call is a BASIC statement (GOSUB).

5. The use of functions makes a program much easier to read. Functions provide a convenient means of performing operations that would otherwise be difficult or impossible. The use of user-defined functions allows formulas to be defined in only one place in the program, making programs smaller and easier to maintain (using a function, you only need to change one line in the program).

Chapter 11   Arrays

True or False

1. True	6. True
2. True	7. True
3. False	8. False
4. True	9. False
5. False	10. False

Fill-In

1. array	6. dimensioning
2. one-dimensional	7. FOR/NEXT
3. table	8. populating
4. row, column	9. bubble sort
5. index	10. nested

Short Answer

1. Dimensioning an array preallocates enough contiguous memory locations to hold all of the possible data elements that are going to be stored in that array. This allows for an array to be processed quicker, since all of the elements are stored together in memory.

2. A one-dimensional array is a list of data elements. This list is stored and accessed as if it were a single column with multiple rows of data. A two-dimensional array is stored as a table. The two-dimensional array holds multiple rows and columns of data elements.

3. Populating an array is when data values are entered and stored in their designated memory locations. Populating normally implies the initial loading of data into the array when it is first created. A one-dimensional array is usually populated using a single FOR/NEXT loop, while a two-dimensional array would normally be populated using nested FOR/NEXT loops.

4. The first step to locate the highest value in a one-dimensional array would be to assume that the first value is the highest. A loop would then be used to go from the second value to the last value. If anywhere throughout the loop the current value is higher than the value of the one currently stored as the highest, the highest value is replaced by the current value. This continues until the entire array is exhausted, leaving the current value in the variable which was initially given the value of the first element.

5. What the bubble sort does is compare the first two values in an array. If the first value is greater than the second, then the two values are swapped. If not, the values remain where they are. Then the second and third values are compared. If the second value is greater than the third, then the two values are swapped. This continues until the second to last and the last are compared, swapping the greater value into the last position. At this point the last location holds the greatest value. The sort then begins again from the first element to the second to the last. This will leave the second greatest value in the second-to-last location upon completion of this loop. This continues, moving the higher values to the end, until the entire array is sorted.

Chapter 12   Input and Output Using Files

True or False

1. False	6. False
2. True	7. False
3. True	8. True
4. False	9. False
5. True	10. True

Fill-In

1. sequential	6. closed
2. portable	7. WRITE #
3. opened	8. EOF
4. INPUT	9. PRINT #
5. APPEND	10. file

Short Answer

1. A sequential file is a collection of records that are stored on disk, outside of a program. These records can be accessed from DOS or other programs, and can even be moved from PC to PC.

2. When a file is opened, the file is verified for its existence if the file is opened for INPUT, or created if the file is opened for OUTPUT. The OPEN statement allows the program to specify whether the file will be used for INPUT, OUTPUT, or APPEND, and assigns a file number by which the file can be addressed throughout the program.

3. If a file is opened for OUTPUT, if the file already exists it is erased and the data are lost. If a file is opened for APPEND and that file already exists, when data are written to the file, they are written at the end of the file following the existing records.

4. When a file is closed, it is no longer associated with the program and its file number is available to access another file. If the file had been opened for OUTPUT or APPEND, the last record is written to disk prior to the file being de-allocated from the program. If the file had been opened for OUTPUT or APPEND, or if the file had been opened for INPUT and needs to be reused from the beginning, the CLOSE statement is used to free up the file so that it may be reopened for INPUT with the file pointer pointing to the first record in the file.

5. When a record is written using WRITE #, it is written in a format that would allow it to be read in again using INPUT #. The individual data elements are separated by commas, and character strings are enclosed in quotes. When PRINT # is used to write a record, the record can be formatted as if it were printed to the screen or a printer using a regular PRINT statement, and the file can be directly printed from DOS in the same format.